Trading Beyond
the Matrix

Trading Beyond the Matrix

THE RED PILL FOR TRADERS AND INVESTORS

Van K. Tharp, PhD

WILEY

John Wiley & Sons, Inc.

Library of Congress Cataloging-in-Publication Data:

Tharp, Van K.
    Trading beyond the matrix : the red pill for traders and investors /
Van K. Tharp, Ph.D.
        p.   cm.
    Includes bibliographical references and index.
    ISBN 978-1-118-52566-1 (cloth); ISBN 978-1-118-54201-9 (ebk);
    ISBN 978-1-118-54202-6 (ebk); ISBN 978-1-118-54211-8 (ebk)
        1. Speculation.   2. Stocks.   3. Investments.   4. Investments—Psychological
aspects.   I. Title.
    HG6041.T44 2013
    332.64—dc23

                                                                2012046817

This book is dedicated to
She who constantly whispers,
"Remember Who You Are!"
and displays a universe filled with light.

Contents

Acknowledgments

I've been working with traders and investors for about 30 years. Over that time, numerous people have helped shape the thinking that has gone into this book. Tharp Think, as I call it, is a product of the knowledge of my modeling work with many, many successful traders and investors. I can acknowledge only a few of those people by name. However, everyone who contributed in any way has my deepest thanks and appreciation.

I'd like to thank Jack Schwager for allowing me to be part of the original *Market Wizards* book and helping me meet some great people. I'd like to acknowledge Ed Seykota, Bill Eckhardt, and Tom Basso for helping me understand position sizing strategies and their overall importance to meeting your objectives.

I'd like to thank all of the people with whom I've done one-on-one consulting and those who have been part of my Super Trader program. You've shaped the thinking in this book far more than you know. You're an incredible group of people, and I hope I've transformed your lives as much as you have mine.

I've personally taken many transformational journeys over the past 30 years, and I'd like to acknowledge my teachers. Some of you were great teachers simply because you pushed my buttons and helped me look at issues that needed work. Thank you all.

Others were teachers because you were a model or you showed me how to look at the issues. Some of those people include: Sri Amma-Bhagavan, Mother Meera, Narasimha Kumarji, Doug Bentley, my guides at Oneness University and in Fiji, Emile Webb, Vijay Thakur, Leo Fishbeck, Wendell Will, John Grinder and his team of NLP trainers, Robert Dilts, Wyatt Woodsmall, Lee Coit, Rajinder Loomba, Enid Vien, Bruce DuVe, Harry Palmer, Byron Katie, David Hawkins, Frank Kinslow, Tad James, Eckhard Tolle, Libby Adams, Diadra Price, Michael Milner, Stuart Mooney, Matthew Ottenberg, and many, many others.

Next, I'd like to mention those who made contributions to this book. The techniques in this book wouldn't mean much without the stories of those whose lives have been transformed by them. To that end, I'd like to acknowledge David Witkin, Laurens Bensdorp, Rick Freeman, Ken Long, Martin Horsey, Peter Wechter, Kim Andersson, Curtis Wee, Thanh Nguyen, and the three people who made anonymous contributions. Sharing your insights and your breakthroughs with the world takes great courage, and I salute you for it.

I'd like to thank my staff at the Van Tharp Institute for their support while completing this book. Becky McKay and Shannon Mante have been invaluable with proofing and edits. Cathy Hasty, R. J. Hixson, Frank Eaves, and Revathi Ramaswami continually support me in the day-to-day operation of the company; without you, this book wouldn't have been possible. Last, but not least, I'd like to acknowledge Jillian Ellis. Jillian has not only been a great source of support, she also drew all the cartoons, which brighten up the book and bring humor to a serious subject.

I'd also like to acknowledge all of the great traders I've had the privilege of working with over the years. Many of you have made millions of dollars in profits in your trading career by following the concepts contained in this book. Whether you helped me understand the concepts better or helped me prove to others that these concepts work, I extend to you my deepest gratitude.

I'd like to acknowledge my attorney and agent for this book, Lloyd Jassin. Lloyd has been a source of support who encouraged me to do the right thing with this book. Without Lloyd, I probably wouldn't have found the great support team I now have at John Wiley & Sons.

I'd like to thank Debra Englander, my editor at John Wiley & Sons, for seeing the potential in this book. It's not an "average" trading book, but she was able to see beyond its uniqueness to the potential impact it could have, and I hope, will have. She was able to get me everything I wanted through my new arrangement with Wiley. In addition, I'd like to thank my entire support staff at Wiley.

Last, I'd like to thank the three people to whom I feel closest— my wife Kalavathi, my son Robert, and my niece/daughter Nanthini. I love you. You are my inspiration. Thank you for being there.

My deepest thanks go to all of you and to the many other people who also contributed but were too numerous to mention or that I may have inadvertently forgotten.

V.T.

Foreword

Doug Bentley
Oneness Guide for North America

To become financially prosperous and successful is a real accomplishment in one's life. It's worth the time and effort to achieve for anyone living in our modern society. We study hard in schools and work hard in our jobs and careers just to make the advances necessary to grow in our financial success. Our western world offers countless ways to grow and prosper. However, throughout all of this, why is it that some people seem to have luck and ease on their side where as others seem to struggle in any direction they head in? What is that missing piece that lies beyond one's own physical effort that is the difference between success and failure?

As humanity grows, we are becoming more and more aware of the correlation between one's external life and one's internal state of being. We are seeing how a person's body becomes unhealthy when suffering from stress, fear, sadness, or hurt. Furthermore, as we look closer we see that the external world is a reflection of our internal world. It seems to be mirroring and playing out our beliefs on how life should unfold for us. Do we deserve success? Do we deserve love? Will it work out for us? Will it fail? We actually take a stand on these things, and so all these ideas that we have about ourselves will impact what happens in our everyday lives. They impact our relationships. They impact our prosperity. They impact our happiness. Indeed, they impact every sphere of our lives.

Take two people, with the same passion, drive, and intelligence. One person feels that everything she does will be successful because she deserves it, while the other believes that he will always fail because he doesn't deserve it. What happens is that they get what they believe about themselves. One will succeed, while the other will fail. And yet they are unaware of what they are doing to themselves.

So what is the solution to this? What can help us become aware of this internal world so we can start seeing our unconscious belief patterns? What can heal all of this? It's simple—Awakening! And it starts with a simple awareness of what is going on inside of you.

There is a journey as ancient as humanity itself. It is a process of flowering in consciousness that brings a person into alignment with who she really is. It gifts the experience of deep inner awareness and knowingness into one's truth. And from this place of internal seeing and experience, one flowers naturally into becoming authentic and starts operating from a place of inner integrity.

So, you might be asking, how does this help me in making money and in becoming successful? It's simple. When you are clear and aware of your own self each moment, you are in tune with others and the situations you find yourself in. This place of being gives you access to a type of intelligence that arises beyond the mind and is spontaneous. You can call it your gut feeling. Dr. Tharp calls it the ability to trade in the now. Others call it being in the zone. But it is so much more. This inner wisdom is the genius of all the great beings who have been on our planet, from Lord Buddha to Steve Jobs.

People with access to this deep inner world were creative and intelligent. What they put their focus on was achieved with success. Each day was a discovery of growing beyond their limiting beliefs, as they would become aware of them in each new situation they encountered. This process was automatic and effortless; it was just a happening for them. They could achieve great things because of this internal flowering and grace surrounded them in their efforts.

Are you sold yet? Do you want this? And if so, where do you sign up?

Try as you may, what is being spoken of isn't something you can do on your own easily. It isn't a simple practice that you perform each day and you are there. It is something that has to be given to you.

The ancients all understood the secret to true success lies within the consciousness of all persons. If they are a flowered human being, they will have great success; if they are not, then they struggle. The flowering of a human being is a neurobiological change that needs to take place. There is a dormant spiritual energy in your body that must awaken. Once it is awakened, however, it starts flowing naturally, pushing you into higher states of awareness and consciousness.

In the ancient times, when people were passionate about awakening, they would have to travel long distances to seek out an Awakened Being who could then transfer the Awakened state into the seeker.

This transference was historically called Deeksha, and was considered the rarest and most priceless blessing a person could receive. Often the initiate must study for a long time under the guidance of the master before it was offered.

Deeksha is not something that you could just go and find in the past, and hasn't been publicly known in our modern world until very recently. However, the good news is that Deeksha is back. It is accessible to anyone who has a passion to grow and awaken.

Deeksha is grace, nevertheless outside of any religious framework. It is a very sacred and divine energy transfer that awakens the spiritual energies within you and causes changes to your brain by balancing it out and activating the less active regions, in turn making a person more aware and intelligent. It activates the automatic process of awakening, which is an endless journey of growth and expansion throughout your daily life.

Yes, you can start looking at yourself and finding your own limitations. But without assistance in starting this journey, it is very slow and full of obstacles that can stop you in your tracks. However, once grace starts flowing the journey really starts, and a really deep healing naturally happens within one's self. This healing is a natural releasing of all of the stored hurts and charges that lock our hindering belief systems in place and stop us from having the success we work so hard towards. The process is beautifully described in Section II of *Trading Beyond the Matrix*.

As people flower in awakening they grow deeply and naturally in touch with their divine. They begin to experience whatever they ask for or intend to happen in their life. It all unfolds with tremendous ease and grace. They feel that life is now working with them. You are going with the flow or trading in the now. Suddenly, achievement becomes a fun journey as opposed to a struggle.

Life is to be enjoyed, and life should be an abundant experience for each person. However, for one to have this kind of reality, one would need to flower and grow in consciousness. There are millions of people who are becoming awakened across the planet right now because of Deeksha, and they are moving into a reality where life is an amazing and empowering experience of growth and joy.

One such person is Van Tharp, who is not only in an awakened state but also helping others awaken as well. He is an amazing person who is helping business people discover greater success in their external lives by helping them grow in their internal lives.

Within these pages you will read some amazing journeys, Super Trader Journeys. You'll receive many great insights and teachings to help you achieve the success you are after. I hope you accomplish what you are passionate about in life and that the journey to your goals is joyful and filled with grace and ease.

Preface

UNDERSTANDING TRANSFORMATION

Van K. Tharp, PhD

I've been coaching traders for nearly three decades. Occasionally, someone asks, "If Van Tharp is such a good trading coach, why doesn't he just trade?" That statement makes a big presupposition: namely, that the money one gets from trading or even trading success is the be-all and end-all of life, which certainly is not the case for me. My mission has always been to help people transform for the better; I just happen to do it through a trading metaphor. I thrive on the comments I get about how I've changed peoples' lives. For example, here are a few of the comments I've gotten recently:

> Your program is not only helping me in my trading, but also in my business. I've been much more peaceful and open ever since I starting working with you. It's helped me with everything I do in my daily life.
>
> — *H.T., Atlanta, GA*

> Before taking your workshop, my life was filled with wants. After the class, I am more in line with my inner Self, and I just want to be. In addition, prior to the workshop, I scored 20 on the Happiness Test. After taking two classes, my score increased by 63 points to a nearly perfect 83. Thank you.
>
> — *T.H., Franklin, VA*

> It's difficult to say how big an impact you've had on my life because you made the change so deep that everything has changed. This is a beautiful gift, and I want to thank you very much for everything you have done for me! . . . I'm not alone

anymore, and I've found the path of true happiness. I know what my life's mission is and what I have to do to follow my bliss. I feel like I'm starting a new life again.

—*D.M., Quebec City, Canada*

After attending your workshop, I came back feeling like any dream was possible. When I started applying the techniques to my sales job, I had my biggest commission month in my 27-year sales career. I made $200,000 for a month's work—more than triple my prior career high. Now I can't wait to start manifesting in my new trading career.

—*E.M., Washington, DC*

To make a long story short, my life changed from a chance meeting with a soft-spoken teddy bear named Van Tharp. I jumped from the life path of financial fear to a life path of fun and adventure. The changes I have gone through have improved both my marriage and my ability to think.

—*J.G., VA*

Such comments about transformation are the engine that makes The Van Tharp Institute (VTI) run, because, as I've said, our mission is one of *transformation through a trading metaphor.* I thrive on it and my staff thrives on it.

Recently, I realized that we actually take people through three levels of transformation: (1) transformation of the trading game; (2) psychological transformation around beliefs, stuck feelings and conflicting parts; and (3) what I call Level III transformations, which occur when you make enough transformations that you actually produce a major change in your consciousness.

After the three levels of transformation became clear to me, I better understood what people need most to succeed. This book is designed to convey that information, with a number of chapters written about each level of transformation.

But let's talk about the title of this book, *Trading Beyond the Matrix: The Red Pill for Traders and Investors.* When I first saw the movie, *The Matrix,* I loved it, not for the action but for the metaphor. In fact, I recently watched it again and discovered that I didn't remember a lot of the details, just the metaphor.

The metaphor suggests that we are all programmed. We live in a world of illusion shaped by our programming. And at some level, we seem to know that, and we seem to know that there is something better. At this point, you have a choice. You can take the blue pill and go back into a comfortable sleep where nothing changes. In this case, it means put the book back on the shelf and do nothing. Or you take the red pill and, as Morpheus says in the movie, "see how deep the rabbit hole goes." Read this book, do what it suggests, and your life will change forever.

We really are so programmed by our beliefs, which we get from our parents, our churches, our schooling, our friends, and the media. We believe what we believe, and that tends to shape our reality. We'll explore that extensively in Chapter 7 of this book. However, once you take the red pill (hopefully this book, for you), you can begin to explore whether or not those beliefs are useful for functioning at a high level within the Matrix.

In the *Matrix* movie, Neo actually gets reprogrammed like a computer, but you can do the same thing by becoming aware of how your beliefs program you and whether or not that programming suits you. And as you start to do so, you begin to function as at a very high level within the Matrix.

So now, let's look a little more closely at the three levels of transformation.

Level I: Transformation of the Trading Game

The first level we offer is transformation of the trading game—from rules that assure big money wins to rules that give the astute trader a huge edge. These new rules consist of the Tharp Think concepts I require everyone in my Super Trader program to know and understand as the cornerstone of their training. These rules are given in Chapter 6, the summary of Section I of this book. Most of them are not my rules; they come from my modeling work with great traders. But I don't know of anyone else with a program that emphasizes all of them.

In one of my advanced workshops, I teach the concept that we all play "games" in life. A game can be defined as any interaction consisting of two or more players with a set of rules that generally define how the game is won or lost. I'm using the concept of the "trading game" to symbolize a big-picture description of all aspects of trading.

I believe the financial markets are part of a huge game, and at the top level—where the rules get set, made and changed—there is Big Money. Big Money makes its own rules and profits no

We all play games in life.

matter what you or any individual trader does; they are much bigger than that. Big Money controls the U.S. government. You might have noticed, for example, where U.S. Treasury leaders so often come from and where they go afterwards. The last six secretaries of the treasury have included two people with strong ties to Goldman Sachs, a former president of the New York Federal Reserve, and a chief economist at the World Bank. The other two were both former company CEOs. Much controversy has been associated with these men, but it is generally ignored by the public.

In addition, the Federal Reserve, which prints dollars, is not government owned or controlled. Instead, it is privately owned by some of the richest people in the world.[1] It's interesting to note that the U.S. income tax and the Federal Reserve were created almost simultaneously. And right now the Federal Reserve is stimulating the economy by giving money to the very people who own it—the big banks.

Big Money has also created a two-party political system in which people argue over everything except what is really going on and what is really important to the future of the United States—something that might be true of almost every country in the world.

The real issue today, for example, is government spending. But the political parties tend to argue over whether or not it is fair for the rich to pay hefty taxes.

This game is a little like the programming in the *Matrix* movie. We're all programmed by our beliefs and our beliefs all say that we should play this game. And that means that you need to fight the crowd in order to function at a super human level within the Matrix. Everyone is a part of the system because they adopt the beliefs of the system and thus support it even if those beliefs do not support them.

As Morpheus says, "most people are so inured, so hopelessly dependent on the system that they will fight to protect it." Does that sound familiar?

Trading is not easy to do, but becoming a trader is easy. There are no obstacles whatsoever to anyone opening a trading account. My wife, for example, currently has a trading account with less than $100 in it.

I've said for a long time that if trading were easy, Big Money would monopolize it. They'd do so by making the entry requirements so steep that it would be impossible for an average person to trade, perhaps through an education and exam system that would weed out most people. Today, for example, brokers have to take a Series 7 exam even though passing this exam has absolutely nothing to do with success in the market.

If you want to know Big Money's rule, just watch the financial media for a week or so. They'll imply that:

- Selecting the right investment (i.e., picking the right stock) is everything.
- When you find the right investment, buy it and hold it for the long term.
- You must spend a lot of time analyzing the market to find the right investment.
- You should listen to experts for advice, including newsletter writers, brokers, and investment gurus on television.

My experience indicates that those old rules are what cause most people to be net losers in the markets. Through my modeling work with top traders and investors, looking at what they do and how they think, I've come up with a new set of rules. We call these rules Tharp Think. Let me repeat: they are called Tharp Think, not because I invented them, but because we are the only organization I know of that emphasizes all of them collectively.

The new rules consist of four primary rules, but we've broken them down into numerous technical and psychological rules. Level I transformation is probably the most basic transformation you must make as a trader/investor. We will be exploring many of the new rules and concepts in Section I of this book.

Level II: Understanding the Matrix and Reprogramming Yourself

I love the premise for the movie *The Matrix* because "the Matrix" is much more real than most people realize. When you name something and assign adjectives and phrases to that name, you give meaning to the world (e.g., dog, small dog, hyperactive dog, dog that would be a good pet, dog that needs discipline-training classes). We shape our entire world by our words, thoughts, and beliefs. This is the Matrix.

And to change it, you have to take the red pill.

> You take the blue pill, the story ends; you wake up in your bed
> and believe whatever you want to believe. You take the red pill,
> you stay in Wonderland, and I show you how deep the rabbit
> hole goes.

When you take the metaphorical red pill, you learn that the whole world is shaped by your beliefs and open up to an amazing world of possibility. You're free to transform yourself by releasing nonuseful beliefs and adopting useful ones.

My intention for this book is that it be a red pill for traders and investors. You can put it on the shelf, go back to sleep, and believe whatever you want to believe about what it takes to be successful in the market, or you can read it and find out just how deep the rabbit hole goes for you. It's your choice.

There are several things you must do as you go down the rabbit hole. First, you must examine your beliefs. You don't trade the markets, you trade your beliefs about the markets; and if your beliefs are not useful, you're in big trouble. Everyone has beliefs about the market, including nontraders and noninvestors, and if you really examine them, you'll find that most are not that useful.

Examine your own beliefs. What does each belief get you into? What does it get you out of? What happens, for example, when you believe that the secret to market success is to be a good stock picker? Who would you be if you didn't have your beliefs? Are your beliefs useful? Do they serve you?

If one of your beliefs is not useful, you can always replace it with another, more useful belief. This is easy to do—unless the old belief is charged with emotion. Emotional charge will hold a belief in place, and you cannot release it until you release the charge. Consequently, another part of the journey down the rabbit hole is examining the charge stored inside you that holds many of your nonuseful beliefs in place and releasing it.

As you travel down the rabbit hole, you meet a lot of parts or different aspects of who you think you are. For example, you might have the following parts:

- A *perfectionist* part that won't let you do anything until you're sure things are perfect. This part's definition of *perfect* might be making money on every trade. Not very useful, but people do have parts like this.
- The *risk manager* who cannot stand to lose money and who is always afraid to do anything that might cause him to lose money.
- The *researcher* who is always trying something new. This can be useful to a trader, but it can also be distracting.
- The *excitement-seeking part* that wants to do things in the market that provide you with big thrills. Good trading is usually boring, so a part like this is probably not helpful at all.
- You could have *a part like your dad* that criticizes you whenever you do anything wrong. If that sort of dad is in there, you probably feel put down and often criticize yourself in order to protect yourself from your dad's criticism.
- Perhaps *your mom* is in there, and she's always saying, "Please get a real job."

You probably have thousands of parts like these. Each part has its own set of beliefs. Each part has a positive intention for you. But you can probably see that parts could become very conflicted and lead you to the point where you cannot do anything. Thus, one of your jobs as a potential Super Trader is to clear out the crowd and bring your mind toward oneness and serenity.

Much of our education for traders involves this sort of work. Imagine looking at all of your trading beliefs and eliminating those that don't help you win. On top of that, imagine eliminating all the beliefs that limit you. Now imagine eliminating all the beliefs about the universe that seem to indicate that you can't win because the universe (or God) is against you. Lastly, imagine getting all of your parts unified so there is no conflict inside. This is how powerful personal transformation can be. In Section II of this book, you'll see the impact of various types of transformation at Level II.

Level III: Trading Beyond the Matrix

There is one other aspect of *The Matrix* that is really fascinating. Toward the end of the movie, Neo is able to step beyond his programming. He is able to do things that you shouldn't be able to do within the Matrix. And that brings us to the final level of transformation: trading beyond the Matrix by changing your level of consciousness. Here consciousness refers to your level of awareness. And you might raise it if you actually transform or eliminate 1,000 beliefs. It might happen if you transform 50 to 100 parts of yourself to move toward unity.

However, for some people it might be even easier than that. Transform five significant issues that have dominated your life, and you understand the process and can go on to accomplish anything. But let's look a little deeper into what raising your level of consciousness might mean.

The late David Hawkins was one of the most successful psychiatrists in the world. He had a very high level of consciousness and performed miracle cures on his patients. He eventually closed his practice to pursue a Ph.D. in psychology, his thesis on measuring the levels of human consciousness. Much of his thesis was then turned into a popular book entitled *Power vs. Force*.

In *Power vs. Force*, Hawkins describes human consciousness using a log scale from 1 to 1,000, with 1,000 being the highest level of consciousness achievable by a human being. Hawkins postulated that only a few (e.g., Jesus, Buddha, Krishna, etc.) ever achieved the 1,000 level. He goes on to say that, for much of the past 5,000 years, human consciousness as a whole has been just below 200—the level that separates the positive from the negative. According to Hawkins, Gandhi[2] had a consciousness of 700 and was able to defeat the British Army, whose collective consciousness was 175. That's the power of the log scale difference between power (high consciousness) and force.

Raising your level of consciousness doesn't just help Gandhi, it can help you as a trader. If you are trading at a low level of consciousness, you are probably trading out of fear, greed, or desperation. Now imagine how that would change if you were to trade from a level of acceptance or peacefulness. The difference would be enormous.

One of our goals at the Van Tharp Institute is to help traders take large leaps forward in consciousness. Imagine again the impact of getting rid of around 1,000 to 5,000 nonuseful beliefs in a year. That probably would raise your consciousness several hundred points. A number of my Super Trader candidates have had such increases in their consciousness, and in Section III of this book, I'll share some of their stories.

Your Personal Application of This Material

Some people might read this book with the idea that it constantly talks about our various workshops and programs. That's inevitable, because these Super Trader journeys were all taken by people I've worked closely with during the past five years. They are mostly Super Trader candidates (meaning they are still in the Super Trader program at the Van Tharp Institute) or graduates of the program, which means they're going to talk a lot about what they've done.

However, this book is mostly about psychological transformation, and every technique we use is clearly described in this book. Consequently, there is nothing we do, at least in the Super Trader program, that you couldn't do on your own.

You might have beliefs that suggest that key information is missing, or that it isn't for you, or that it doesn't fit you. This book will probably stimulate a lot of other beliefs for some of you. As you read, you may say to yourself, *I don't believe that,* in which case you'll be right—because that particular belief actually shapes your reality. However, you should make sure you at least run such beliefs through the belief examination paradigm given in this book before deciding to hold onto them. You'll probably find that most of them limit you, stop you from action, and block you from true happiness.

First, you will learn the technical basis of Tharp Think. Those principles are clearly listed in the introduction to Section I. In fact, the principles in Section I are clear enough that you should be able to design a great system that fits you for one particular market type with no problem at all, unless you have psychological issues blocking you. For those of you who don't think you can do it, the psychological principles are given in the introduction to Section II.

Second, you'll learn how to determine what parts you have in Chapter 9. Exercises are given for doing that in the chapter. Once you understand which parts of you control your trading, it's a fairly simple exercise to get each part to give you 20 beliefs that you can run through the Belief Examination Paradigm. See Chapter 7 for a description of the Belief Examination Paradigm.

When you've run 200+ beliefs through that paradigm, it should be easy for you to determine which ones are useful and should be kept and which ones are not useful and should be eliminated. And you'll be able to easily change any nonuseful beliefs—unless they have a lot of charge stored in them.

If you have a lot of beliefs with charge in them, the feeling release methods in Chapter 8 are very clear. You should be able to apply them immediately to your charged beliefs.

My chapter about following Internal Guidance also has step-by-step instructions. To develop a strong Internal Guidance, you need to eliminate any parts that do not trust your Internal Guidance—something you can do using the Transformational Meditation Technique illustrated in Chapter 11. In addition, steps are given for deepening the bond you have with your Internal Guidance in Chapter 10.

Section III contains a number of chapters in which some of my students describe their transformational journeys. These should help you understand how important it is to take this kind of journey and what could happen to you after you take the journey.

Finally, each section ends with a practical application chapter. You will get specific Tharp Think concepts that apply to that section, specific steps you can follow, and even a question-and-answer section pertaining to the material in that section. These checklists are the same checklists I give my Super Traders, and I seriously debated whether or not to include them. However, my mission is about transformation, and my expectation is that it will have some sort of transformational effect on the reader. If it does, then I've accomplished a lot.

SECTION I

TRANSFORMATION OF THE TRADING GAME

UNDERSTANDING THE BASICS

Van K. Tharp, PhD

The first level we offer is transformation of the trading game—from rules that assure big money wins to rules that give the astute trader a huge edge. These new rules consist of the Tharp Think concepts I require everyone in my Super Trader program to know and understand as the cornerstone of their training.

Two Sets of Rules

So what happens if you read a few books on how to trade/invest and watch the financial media talk about investing for a significant period of time? What happens is that you would come to believe certain rules.

- Selecting the right investment (i.e., picking the right stock) is everything, and when you find the right investment, you should buy and hold if for a long time.

1

- There is some Holy Grail method out there for selecting the right investment, and that might involve spending a lot of time analyzing the market to find the right investment. Warren Buffett, for example, is quoted as saying "you should know every detail of every listed stock," as if that were the key. If it seems like a lot of work, it is. But don't worry; that's not the key to success in the markets.

Other rules might include:

- The market will determine whether you make money. You are at the mercy of the market in the short term, but if you hold on, you will prevail. The market eventually goes up.
- If you do lose money, it's not your fault. Find someone to blame and a good lawyer to help you sue them.
- The market is efficient.
- Asset allocation is very important (even though most people aren't even sure of what that really means).

My experience indicates that these rules are what cause most people to be net losers in the markets. Through my modeling work with top traders and investors—looking at what they do and how they think—I've come up with a new set of rules. We call these rules Tharp Think.

Let's look at these rules. First, you must understand that trading profitably and consistently is not easy. Sure, you can go into a brokerage company and open an account; that part is certainly pretty easy. As the e-trade baby says, "See, I just bought stock." And the industry wants you to think it really *is* that easy—that even a baby can do it with the right trading platform.

Can you imagine being allowed to perform open-heart surgery simply by strolling into an operating room and declaring that you want to do so? Of course not. It doesn't work that way. Similarly, can you imagine building a bridge just by reading a book and then being put in charge of a construction team? Or, worse yet, giving a few orders to the construction team and then going along on your merry way? Again, it doesn't work that way.

Big Money wants you to think otherwise. They want you to believe that you need only turn on some financial program and listen to the stock picks. But trading with no preparation can be as fatal to your account as an untrained surgeon would be to a patient or a bridge built by someone with no understanding of engineering would be to anyone with plans of crossing it.

Thus, the first new rule is that trading is as much a profession as any other. It takes significant time (several years) and a deep commitment to become a successful trader. I hold a similar belief to author Malcolm Gladwell, who says that the best people in every field usually excel because they have successfully practiced their craft for well over 10,000 hours. And when it comes to trading, it's not just 10,000 hours of practice, because I've definitely seen people who have put in 10,000 and learned very little. I think that it's probably 10,000 hours of practice at doing it well.

The first new rule is that trading is as much a profession as any other.

The second new rule is that trading reflects human performance just as much as any top athletic endeavor. You must understand that you are responsible for the results you get. Thus, you should devote significant time to working on yourself in order to be successful.

The second new rule is that trading reflects human performance just as much as any top athletic endeavor. You must understand that you are responsible for the results you get.

The third new rule is that objectives are important. Furthermore, you achieve your objectives through position sizing™ strategies. The quality of your system just tells you how easy it will be to use position sizing strategies to achieve your objectives. Most people don't even think about objectives, except that they'd like to make a lot of money and avoid losing, and they don't have a clue about position sizing strategies. They learn that asset allocation is important, but they never understand that what makes it so important is the "how much" factor, which is what position sizing strategies are all about.

The third new rule is that objectives are important. Furthermore, you achieve your objectives through position sizing strategies.

The fourth new rule is that trading/investing is all about probability and reward-to-risk ratios under specific market conditions. When you understand these rules and the market conditions at any given time, you can use statistics to predict some boundaries for your performance. While you cannot predict the future, you can get a good idea what your performance will be through statistics and proper sampling under the different possible market conditions. As you begin to understand this, you'll be amazed at the changes that occur.

The fourth new rule is that trading/investing is all about probability and reward-to-risk ratios under specific market conditions. When you understand these rules and the market conditions, you can use statistics to predict what your performance will be under similar market conditions in the future.

The four primary rules above have many parts and other rules that are required to implement them. Together, they form what I've been calling Tharp Think. When traders join my Super Trader program, the first thing I require is that they thoroughly understand all of the Tharp Think rules. That checklist is given in Chapters 6 and 12.

How much should I risk?

What the rules seem to have in common is (1) a statistical approach to markets that (2) relies on thinking about reward-to-risk rather than being right. They also emphasize that great performance is a function of what the market gives you, your system, and you, as shown in the diagram below where the three circles intersect.

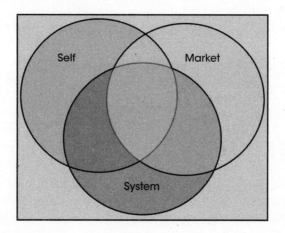

Stay Aligned

Can you see how the "old rules" that everyone seems to learn can lead to disaster, while the second set of rules is a major transformation of the trading game and can lead to success?

Section I Contents

In Section I of this book, I present three chapters written by my Super Trader candidates to show the effect of a Level I transformation on their trading.

Chapter 1 is by a new candidate who talks about his growth as a result of adopting Tharp Think and how, at one point, he was able to make 130 percent on his capital as a result of doing so. He also discovered that he was very inefficient in his trading, which is why he joined the Super Trader program in the first place. While he was up 130 percent, his mistakes probably cost him another 50 percent. In other words, without mistakes, he would have been up about 180 percent instead of 130 percent. Now he's in the Super Trader program working on making Level II transformations.

Chapter 2 is by someone who did an amazing job of applying the Tharp Think rules. First, he figured out how important Tharp Think was. Then he found someone to help him program various systems he'd developed in an automated trading platform. Finally, he hired someone else to trade the system. Because this other person had no psychological investment in the trades and was being paid for mistake-free performance, they could trade it with nearly 100 percent efficiency.

My first Super Trader graduate wrote Chapter 3. In it, he talks about his personal journey to success. He started out as a bank loan officer who wanted to trade and, as a result of going through the Super Trader program, he found some unique ways of applying Tharp Think to alternative forms of investment, such as real estate. Within a year of joining the program, he was able to give up his well-paid job as a bank loan officer and become a full-time investor/trader. And because his passive income far exceeded his expenses, he was financially free—something he'd never been able to accomplish back when he was still "working" for a living.

In Chapter 4, one of our instructors, Ken Long, shares his journey. Ken has a master's degree in systems design and a doctorate in decision making under uncertain conditions. He's constantly developing great systems and teaches them in our courses. Ken regularly publishes the monthly performance of these systems as well as the performance of his students when he conducts live trading classes at the Van Tharp Institute.

Finally, Chapter 5 is by a former institutional broker who used to make huge six-figure salaries executing the orders of institutional traders. He knew many of the London-based institutional traders and says that there were very few who really knew what they were doing. Of course, after 20 years of watching the behavior of most traders, he thought *he* knew what *he* was doing. It took a journey into Tharp Think for him to start making the kind of progress that transformed his trading.

I Just Made 130 Percent—and That Was Just the Beginning

David Witkin

Dave Witkin is a part-time management and information technology (IT) consultant who has been trading on and off for 15 years. His passion for trading blossomed in the mid-1990s when he read the 1994 edition of Hagstrom's *The Warren Buffett Way*. After exploring fundamental analysis, his trading interests broadened to technical analysis and options. He was primarily trading options in 2000 when the market changed course and he saw his account value drop to near zero. This wake-up call gave him a much-needed respect for risk and initiated his journey to understand the methods of the best traders in the world so that he could eventually become one of them. In 2010, he had a breakout trading year using many of the methods recommended by Dr. Tharp, and finally decided to commit to making trading a full-time career. He is currently working to complete Dr. Tharp's Super Trader program. He's finished with the psychological portion and he expects to begin trading full-time in 2013.

 Before: Inconsistent trader with no real risk management approach other than gut feel. Most trading years were losing years.

 After: Developed a well-defined position-sizing approach with controlled risk. Made 130 percent with no more than a 20 percent drawdown in the first year he applied the Tharp Think principles.

"That's another 1R* loser," Van announced to the class as he drew the final marble from the bag. There was an audible groan from most students—but not from me. "Okay," I thought, "maintain your composure. No matter what, *do not* smile. Smiling would be bad. Just think about dead cats or something."

The 25 or so guys in the class were just like me—reasonably smart, decent people trying to transform themselves into world-class traders, and each was sacrificing the Saturday before Super Bowl Sunday as proof of dedication to the craft. I certainly didn't want to alienate any of them, but Van's announcement meant I'd just won the pot in a game designed to illustrate a critical trading concept. The pot was small, but the win proved I had made a major change in how I thought about trading. To me, the win meant that, in a class of smart, driven traders and in front of one of the top trading coaches in the world, I was the top dog that day.

"No matter what, *do not* smile. Just think about dead cats or something."

It was February 2011 and I was attending a "Tharp Think" seminar in Cary, North Carolina, a small town just outside of Raleigh. For me, the seminar was an opportunity to celebrate the end of my

---

*It means that you have lost what you risked. 1R means one unit of risk.

best trading year ever—over a 130 percent gain—and to reinforce the concepts most responsible for getting me there.

Learning to Trade

My path to trading was anything but direct. After working briefly in information technology (IT) after high school, I went to college and received a liberal arts degree. When I graduated, I worked a couple of IT jobs until I found a home as an IT and management consultant at a Big Five accounting and consulting firm.

By this time it was 1998, and I had become fascinated with making money in the markets. It seemed incredible to me that millions of people could come together to find the "right" price for a company, and the people who were great at it could become as rich as Warren Buffett. The company I worked for gave me the opportunity to spend seven months in Germany. That was a great opportunity to lock myself in my small apartment and read everything on trading I could get my hands on, and maybe do a bit of trading myself.

Germany was a perfect place for me to focus on learning to trade. I didn't speak the language and didn't know anyone except the people I worked with, so I read in my spare time. First, I focused on fundamental analysis, reading books about how people like Warren Buffett, William O'Neil, James O'Shaughnessy, and David Dreman invested and identified companies worth buying. Next, I learned about technical analysis from Martin Pring, Stan Weinstein, and Trader Vic. Then I found options, reading the whole 800-page *Options as a Strategic Investment,* by Lawrence McMillan, as well as books by George Fontanills and others. I became fascinated with limited risk and the incredible complexity of trades I could create using options. *Wow,* I thought, *these things are amazing. There is an option strategy for every possible situation, and look at the leverage! Woo-hoo!*

I liked saving money and had managed to put away $20,000, so I started trading. Sometimes I'd do some fundamental screening and then decide to buy a few stocks. Other times I'd find momentum stocks and buy options that were expiring in a few months. I also subscribed to some newsletters and would pick and choose investments that sounded good to me, primarily looking for those I thought had the best chance of a significant return. In hindsight,

I really didn't have much of a trading strategy. There were no real entry criteria other than the caveman approach: me see, me like, me buy. There was no predefined exit point where I'd admit I was wrong and get out, and I decided how much money to allocate to each position by gut feeling.

Unfortunately, I lost on more trades than I won, which confused me. After all, I'd done my homework and learned tons about how great traders won in the market. I had good reasons for entering every trade. *I should be winning much more money,* I thought. When I talked to people at work, it sounded like *they* were making money—a lot of it. But why? I knew I'd studied more than they had. When I talked to them, they didn't know anything about the fundamentals, or Warren Buffett, or technical analysis, or cool option terms like "delta," "theta," and "gamma." I understood *gamma,* for heaven's sake! How cool was that? I thought I was destined to make money.

Even though I lacked a trading system, the markets were excellent, and even though I was losing more money than I thought I should, I was still making money. By 2000, I'd managed to build my starting capital into about $75,000 by saving a bit more from my day job and benefiting from what, in hindsight, was a fantastic market. My family never had much money—my clothes always seemed bargain-basement compared to my friends and the highlight of many family "vacations" consisted of visiting relatives—so $75,000 seemed like a small fortune to someone like me who was still in his twenties. I still felt I should be making more though, so I continued to read and learn, but, overall, I was proud of the little pile of money I'd made. I'd done it on my own, after all, which made it even more meaningful.

"Danger, Will Robinson, Danger!"

In late 2000, I read something on the Internet suggesting that to win in trading you needed to have the right psychology. This was an angle I hadn't thought of—you needed the right psychology to be a good trader? Could this be true? I was skeptical. The guys at the office didn't seem to give a hoot about psychology, and they were making money. I made money, and I was sure my psychology wasn't special. Even so, I decided I would explore it before ruling it out.

My introduction to trading psychology would come in the form of a book called *Trade Your Way to Financial Freedom* by Dr. Van K. Tharp. I didn't know it at the time, but the date I ordered Dr. Tharp's book, in 2000, was within weeks of the end of one of the longest, most profitable bull markets in U.S. history. I was 30 years old and about to lose most of my net worth. I put the book on a shelf rather than read it so I could continue to focus on making money.

When the bear market began, I continued trading as I had the prior few years—I didn't follow any real strategy, but I'd read a ton and thought I understood enough to make money. I traded some on the short side, but my primary focus was long. The market had been going up for most of the last 20 years and the downturn in late 2000 seemed like just the buying opportunity I'd read about, with "blood in the streets." Some great stocks were now real bargains: Worldcom! Global Crossing! Earthlink! Puma Technologies! I bought them all.

I soon discovered the importance of applying the appropriate metaphor to the current market situation. Yes, there was "blood in the streets," but the proper metaphor for the moment was

Don't try to catch a falling knife!

something like "don't try to catch a falling knife" or "low stocks can always go lower" or "don't fight the tape." Funny thing about trading metaphors: most of the "market experts" who quote them don't give you any truly helpful advice on when to apply one versus another. The metaphors always sound wise when someone says them, though, don't they?

Over the next two years, the S&P 500 plunged more than 40 percent and, in a show of solidarity, the vast majority of my money went down the drain with it. I was angry and disgusted with my failure and determined not to lose all my marbles again.

But how should I move forward? Clearly eeded to change what I was doing, but what was the best way to do that? I thought I'd already read the right books, so what experts could I trust to help me? Was there a different way of doing things—a different trading metaphor—I should be using? My trust in the traditional "experts" had diminished in lockstep with my account value. Maybe that book by Dr. Tharp was worth a read now.

Tharp Think 101

I love to learn. Any time an author can add some knowledge to my repertoire, I'm always excited. Consequently, I devoured *Trade Your Way to Financial Freedom*, a book that seemed to be about more than just psychology. The psychological parts struck me (at the time) as being a little too intangible to be relevant to trading. I wanted to make money, after all, and still wasn't convinced that psychology was the key to making money in the markets.

Dr. Tharp clearly understood how I thought about trading, and as a result, the book grabbed me immediately. I read about "Holy Grail" systems, as Dr. Tharp refers to them—"perfect" systems that focus on picking the right stocks* and on when to enter the market, and that work whether the market is bullish, bearish, or neutral—and realized that I'd been spending my time looking for one myself. I didn't want to think about having different systems to enter the market—one when the market was bullish, one when the market was neutral, and one when the market was bearish. What a pain that would be! Wouldn't it just be easier to use one system for

---

*This is actually other people's definition. My definition of a Holy Grail system is one that produces an SQN score over 7 for a particular market type.

all markets rather than a different one for each type? Not only that, but also having one system per market type would mean I'd need a way to determine the market type. In other words, this approach would require me to do more work.

Unfortunately, Dr. Tharp said that expecting a system to work in all types of markets was insanity. *Ugh*, I thought, *implementing this guy's ideas is going to take time and effort.* My brain was already trying to find a way out of putting in the work his suggestions required. In hindsight, I see that I had no concept of the amount of work required to implement all his ideas. *Double-ugh.*

He also said that making a lot of money in the markets would not be fast or easy. *I don't like this guy*, I thought. Although many of his ideas made sense, I really didn't want anyone telling me how hard trading would be. After all, I'd read tons of books and done more work than most people. The work should be hard for *them*, those people who hadn't done as much work as I had, but not for me. I wasn't done with the first chapter yet, and this guy was already frustrating me. Just give me the bullet-point list of how to make money!

Still, I kept reading, and Dr. Tharp kept pressing my psychological buttons. He said there was very little chance anyone could give me a system I could use to make a lot of money in the market. He didn't say the system couldn't be built, only that if someone gave it to me it probably wouldn't work for me. I started thinking Dr. Tharp was off his rocker. He seemed to be saying that if someone gave me a perfectly good system I'd screw it up somehow. How could he make such a broad statement? I'm smart, disciplined, and successful in my nontrading career, so he must have been talking about other people, not me (it would take me nearly a decade to realize he was right, and my inability to find a system that consistently worked well for me was a direct result of continuing to look to others for the *perfect* system).

So, why did I keep reading? I guess because many of the ideas did resonate with me. For example, Dr. Tharp said that winning traders often lose on more trades than they win—maybe winning only 35 percent of the time. Making money while winning less than 50 percent of my trades was exactly what I experienced in the late 1990s, and Dr. Tharp clearly understood the phenomenon. He discussed having a positive expectancy, or mathematical expectation of profits, and provided a simple formula to calculate it. Because losing is a part of the game, he discussed the importance of learning how to accept losses as part of trading and not making them worse by failing to admit when you are wrong on a trade. All of these ideas resonated with me.

Dr. Tharp also talked about the importance of taking responsibility for your results. In other words, if you decide to trade based on newsletter recommendations, as I did, and lose money, it is your fault, not the newsletter's fault. You chose the newsletter, and you chose to invest based on its recommendations. You decided to trust the newsletter's published results, showing they won 75 percent of the time. You decided not to paper-trade the recommendations for six months to confirm the results before starting to trade real money. You didn't stop to find at least one independent source who had confirmed the newsletter's track record before trading. You, you, you!

While it was frustrating to take full responsibility for my losses, I knew it was the right way to view the situation. Have you ever blamed someone else for your poor trading results? If so, go ahead and try the taking responsibility exercise above with any external sources you counted on for trading advice, and see if you can figure out how you might have caused the disaster you blamed on them. Your broker told you to buy that stock, and you trusted him? It was your choice. Your money manager vanished with $1 million, your entire net worth? You didn't do enough background checks on him because you didn't consider the possibility that he might steal your money. You also chose not to split your money into three equal parts and give each part to a different money manager. Try the *it wasn't my fault* game yourself next time you lose money. If you can't trace the results back to you, ask other people to help you, and tell them to be relentless.

Yes, it is, of course, true that many events are unlikely and that none of us has the time to explore every option for every decision. If we did, nothing would get done. But what about the big decisions, like where to invest your entire net worth, or whether to start trading with real money with a system you haven't paper traded? Aren't these decisions big enough to warrant some contingency planning?

When you stop and really think about it, how could I fix something if I didn't think that allowing it to happen was my responsibility? Is it possible I didn't do all the checking I should have on that newsletter because I didn't know whom to talk to? Or maybe I didn't independently validate the results because I didn't know how and didn't think about paying some college kid $500 to do it for me because that would be too expensive? Maybe I didn't want to wait to make money and thought about all the money I *wouldn't* be making if I paper-traded the system for six months?

Chances are you're at least somewhat like me and avoided (yes, avoided!) taking a few prudent actions that could have saved you a pile of money. Test yourself; if you aren't able to come up with 5 to 10 things you could have done differently, you're not trying hard enough. More importantly, you're likely to continue struggling with trading in the future.

As I continued reading, the book talked about a number of psychological biases that cause most people to do exactly the wrong things in the market. For example, we don't have the mental capacity to take in all the information the market makes available, so we generalize, delete, or distort the information. Consequently, if you believe that trend-following systems don't work, you probably feel content to ignore information about how to trade them. Ala-kazam! You've just seen a judgmental bias in action. You generalized (trend-following systems don't work), and as a result you were able to massively cut down the amount of trading-related information you have to pay attention to. But was your generalization correct?

Another bias is the so-called lotto bias, which describes the confidence people develop about their chances of success when they have some control over the information necessary to win. For example, many traders become irrationally confident they will win because they are using a group of indicators—moving averages and oscillators, for example—to tell them when to enter the market. Other people, like me, feel the same irrational sense of control and chances for success because they get to choose which of the newsletter's recommendations to buy. Ugh.

As I read on about the other biases and how they affect traders, I was hooked. Dr. Tharp gave compelling examples, and I could see my own actions in many of the behaviors he discussed. The book said that most people think of a trading system as the answer to the question: When do I enter the trade? At the time, I couldn't have agreed more; I was totally focused on market entry. Unfortunately, when to enter is the least important part of a trading system. I've heard Dr. Tharp and Linda Raschke, another market wizard, say they have tested random-entry trading systems that make money, albeit not enough to be easily tradable. These systems enter the market on a coin toss and use good exits to accept losses and take profits, and they seem to confirm the relative importance traders should ascribe to exits, not entries.

Even with all of the things that resonated with me, though, there were plenty of things that didn't, at least not immediately. For example, Dr. Tharp argued that a good trading system would have 10 parts, the most important of which is objectives. Objectives? Seriously? I want to make as much money as humanly possible, that's my objective! Anything less would limit my potential, wouldn't it? What crazy person would want to limit how much money he could make in any year? Unfortunately for my ego, I discovered as I continued reading that the book made a good case for determining your objectives before designing or trading a system. *Darn*, I thought. *This Tharp guy is really starting to annoy me.*

Not All Lessons Are Equal

I found a number of the book's concepts provocative, but by far the most potent for me was the power of position sizing strategies. A position sizing strategy is simply the part of the trading system that answers the question, "How much will I risk on this trade?" Sounds simple, doesn't it? It is, and it isn't.

What if I told you I would put you into a fully automated trading system with the following characteristics: It wins 35 percent of its trades, and when it wins, the winning trades are, on average, three times the size of the losers? What if I also told you I had been trading the system for 25 people, each in a separate account, for the past 10 years? While some years were better than others and the system was in negative territory for at least a portion of every year, all of the last 10 years were profitable for *every* account. All of the accounts were with the same broker, started with $100,000 and had exactly the same commission structure, and the system only traded liquid markets. Sound interesting?

Here's the twist: While the system made money every year, the percent-gain realized was very different for each of the 25 accounts. The gains ranged from 4 to 95 percent gain last year and from 2 to 72 percent the prior year. The previous eight years showed similarly diverse performance across accounts. The performance was independently validated by a credible accounting firm and found to be completely accurate.

But how could this be? Remember, this is a fully automated system—the trades were entered and exited automatically, everyone started with the same equity, took exactly the same trades, and exited at the same time. Small differences in percentage gains across accounts could be accounted for based on slippage, but slippage couldn't come close to causing this range of differences. What was going on here, you ask?

The answer is *position sizing strategies*. Each trade was exactly the same for each account—with the exception of *how much* money was risked on each trade. The owner of account one risked 0.5 percent of account equity per trade, had the smallest drawdowns and the smallest gains every year; the account owner's objective was to minimize drawdowns. The owner of account 25 used a more complex position sizing strategy, which risked more and more money as the account equity moved further into positive territory. Account 25 also experienced significant drawdowns, the largest being 65 percent. This account owner's objective was to make at least 50 percent per year, even if it meant a maximum drawdown of up to 75 percent. And because he was willing to suffer the drawdowns, most years he made at least 50 percent.

These sample accounts show just two possible methods of using position sizing strategies[1] to achieve objectives. There are a number of other position sizing methodologies that could be combined to build thousands of strategies. For example, most traders recognize the importance of volatility in markets, and, while not universally the case, many traders feel that more volatility equals more risk. So what if you took smaller position sizes when the market displayed significantly higher-than-normal volatility (e.g., double the average true range measured over the past 90 days)? Or what if you combined position sizing strategies by risking 1 percent of account equity except when the volatility goes above some predetermined threshold? Each of thousands of position sizing possibilities could result in a different ending equity level despite taking *exactly* the same trades.

The variability in results sounds too incredible to be true, you say? I'm right there with you—or at least I was until I did some independent research, which seemed to support the case that position sizing was capable of making this kind of difference in returns. I also used some software to test the impact of position sizing strategies on my own, which cemented the case for me.

But don't take my word for it—there's an easy way for you to test it yourself, and it won't cost you more than $20. Remember the marble game I mentioned at the start of this chapter? The marble game is nothing more than an example of using position sizing to achieve your objectives (e.g., one objective being to win the game at all costs, even if it means going bankrupt). Here is how you play:

- Put the 100 marbles described in the last bullet below in a black bag.
- A person randomly pulls out one marble each turn, and the game ends after 60 marble pulls.
- All players (why not invite the family to play? Trust me, it's fun!) start with $100,000 and choose the amount to bet *before* each marble pull.
- The minimum bet is 0.5 percent (½ of 1 percent), and the maximum bet is 100 percent of your equity as it stands prior to each marble pull.
- After each marble pull, the result is recorded (i.e., the marble chosen), and the marble is returned to the bag.
- There are different colored marbles in the bag, each with a distinct outcome:
  - 65 black marbles, where you lose whatever you bet
  - 15 blue marbles, where you win whatever you bet
  - 7 green marbles, where you win 2 × your bet
  - 6 yellow marbles, where you win 3 × your bet
  - 3 silver marbles, where you win 5 × your bet
  - 2 gold marbles, where you win 10 × your bet
  - 2 pink marbles, where you win 20 × your bet*

---

*If you do the math, this system produces 65R in losing trades and 122R in winning trades. However, there are 65 losing marbles and only 35 winning marbles. Thus, you have a 65 percent chance of losing on a given draw compared with a 35 percent chance of winning. But if you add up all the wins and losses, it totals (122R – 65R = 57R) + 57R. Expectancy is the average R-value, which in this case is 57R/100, or 0.57R. Thus, on average, you'll make 0.57R per trade in this system.

Remember—the point of the game is to help you understand the importance of position sizing strategies. Every player gets exactly the same trades (i.e., marbles); the only difference is the size of each bet. That being said, the marble distribution above is actually similar to the trade distribution of many good trend-following systems (i.e., you lose 65 percent of the time, but, if you use an appropriate position sizing strategy, the size of your winners makes the system very profitable).

Yes, Dr. Tharp's book was an eye-opener for me, so you might think I started using what I learned from the book to my advantage right away, and to some degree I did. Over the following years, I continued to trade lightly, still somewhat shell-shocked from my earlier losses. I continued to learn and test systems, but never to the point where I was comfortable enough to trade them with real money. I kept reading books by Dr. Tharp and began accepting some concepts I rejected earlier, like the importance of objectives. I continued to take some newsletter trades; some won, some lost. On balance, I probably broke even. Regardless, my trades were too small to make a significant impact on my bottom line.

Too small, that is, until 2004. Late that year I decided I would be comfortable risking some money on a "proven" mechanical system. I searched the Internet and found a system designer who sold me two complementary black-box systems—that is, systems whose underlying logic is hidden, so that you can only see the trades it spits out—for about $3,000. The back-tested results were excellent. Collectively, with a position size of 1.5 percent of equity on each trade, the two systems returned better than 50 percent per year with a worst-case drawdown under 35 percent over a 25-year period, and the results were reasonably consistent across years. I removed myself completely from the trading equation by finding a Commodity Trading Advisor (CTA) to trade the systems on my behalf and waited for the money to roll in.

About two years later, I closed the account after losing 50 percent of my money. Ugh. Again, I thought I'd made good decisions, carefully researching the systems before buying them, and allowing someone else to trade them mechanically on my behalf. Unfortunately, it appears the system designer curve-fitted the results. Curve-fitting means you optimize the system on historical data until you get results that look fantastic. The problem with curve-fitted systems is that they tend not to do so well in the future. This was another lesson learned the hard way: if you don't know how the system was tested, there is a good chance it wasn't confirmed effectively and the results aren't worth the paper they're printed on.

For the next few years, I did very little trading, choosing instead to watch the markets and continue reading and learning on my own again.

Finally, Some Winning Marbles

In early 2010—almost 10 years after buying *Trade Your Way to Financial Freedom*—I thought I might be ready to try trading again on my own. I was still scared of losing, but believed that if I kept my position sizes relatively small, I could stop trading and limit my losses. To promote discipline, I created a few simple rules for myself:

1. Never risk more than two percent of total account equity on any trade.
2. Always enter a stop-loss order along with an entry order (my broker allowed both to be entered at the same time as linked orders—very helpful).
3. Reduce my position size or just get out if I start to feel uncomfortable.
4. Use trailing stops to exit the market.
5. Focus on trading two low-risk ideas: (a) channel breakouts and (b) bounces off support.
6. Enter trades only when I believe there is a good risk-reward ratio of at least three to one.
7. Get out of the market completely for at least two weeks if I experience an account equity drawdown of 35 percent.
8. If a position is going against me or taking too long to move in the direction I thought it would move, exit before the trade hits the stop loss if I no longer feel good about it.[2]

This set of rules was not even close to what Van would consider a comprehensive trading plan, but it helped me do enough things right to capitalize on some big, very profitable trends.

I waited until May to take my first trade of the year, a natural gas bounce-off-support trade. The trend was strong, and I added to my position as natural gas moved up, while locking in profit by moving up my stops as the trade went in my favor. The trade ended up being a 5R winner—in other words, I made about five times what I risked on the trade. If I'd lost on this trade, I'm not sure I would have been confident enough to keep trading, which is very significant when you consider my results for the year.

While I still lost more trades than I won—I think I only won about 30 percent of my trades—the winners were big, and I did well. As of December 31, my account value was up more than 130 percent, and I never experienced a drawdown greater than 20 percent. I was excited—so much so that I took screen shots of my account equity each time I reached a new equity high, almost as if I needed visual evidence that my results were real. As much as I wanted to have a year where I made 100 percent+, I wasn't sure I could really do it.

Despite the success, I made tons of mistakes that cost me some very significant money. My guess is that I probably would have made at least 180 percent, probably more, without the errors. For example, in December, my wife gave birth to our first child, and I didn't follow my positions as closely as I should have while I was with her in the hospital. I had my stops in place, but I wasn't able to exit on intuition as I did at other times when I saw the market wasn't moving quickly in my direction.

Also, I held too many positions—sometimes as many as 15 at once—and it turned out that some of them were correlated. After experiencing a drawdown as a result of correlations, I subscribed to a correlation service. The service provided a matrix of correlations, and I was more careful only to take positions with little to no correlation over the most recent 1-, 5- and 10-year periods. Unfortunately, I learned the hard way that correlations on any given day don't really care about historical correlations over 1-, 5-, and 10-year periods—another lesson with a high price tag. Big ouch!

Also, as I continued to trade, I noticed that my criteria for taking trades became more lax. Sure, I still looked for breakouts and bounces off support, but I seemed to get less picky about only taking the trades that looked the strongest. I became more impulsive. I found I really wanted to be in trades because I was afraid I might miss a big move if I wasn't in the market, and missing a big move would be painful. As a result, I had far more losing trades later in the year and forfeited profits as a result.

I also wasn't very methodical about keeping a trading log and reviewing it to find and address my mistakes. I looked over my trades and noted some of my mistakes, but I didn't set aside the time I needed to do a good job of it. If I had, I have little doubt I would have avoided at least some losses.

I also risked way too much per position early in the year. After a couple of months risking about 2 percent of account equity per trade, the account fluctuations told me I was risking too much. I cut back to 1.5 percent and later to 1.25 percent. These reduced-risk levels still allowed me to have significant gains, but, more importantly, they reduced my daily account fluctuations and improved my peace of mind. I find it funny now, but before 2010, I remember thinking, "How will I ever make any real money if I only risk 2 percent of equity per trade?" If this statement rings true to you, play the marble game risking 2 percent of equity per trade, and then do it again risking 10 percent of equity per trade, and prepare to be enlightened.[3]

I firmly believe that looking for good reward-to-risk trades and using a reasonable position sizing method were the most important

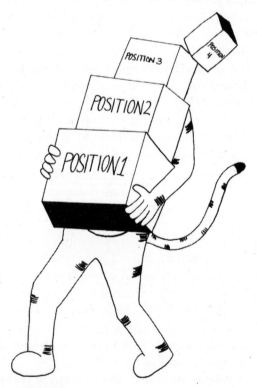

I held too many positions.

factors in my results. The scientist in me is the first to admit that there was some luck involved on individual trades—but it would be hard to make the case that luck was a major factor on the 100+ trades I made over seven months. Even with all of my mistakes, I used enough of Dr. Tharp's principles to knock the cover off the ball.

So, what now? I've stopped trading and am going to take some time—at least a year—to focus on becoming a more efficient trader. As Dr. Tharp defines the term, *efficiency* means reducing the number of mistakes you make to the point where they have little impact on your results.

I've mentioned a number of things I plan on improving, but I haven't talked about my psychology. You may recall my views about the value of "trading psychology"; at the start, I was doubtful that psychology was important, let alone a key to trading success. Dr. Tharp wrote about the importance of a trader's psychology in *Trade Your Way to Financial Freedom* and other books, but it didn't completely resonate with me. After all, why would psychology matter if I had a good plan and stuck to it? Wouldn't that take psychology out of play?

It took about 10 years, but I've come to realize the answer is probably "no." Psychology was the reason I made those mistakes in 2010. Psychology is the reason I haven't invested more time in pursuing my dream of becoming a full-time trader; I was scared of walking away from a lucrative day job and of what my family would think. And psychology was responsible for the mental chatter, uncertainty, and discomfort I felt as I traded, and I'm sure it cost me in terms of returns. So, as with other Tharp Think concepts I initially resisted, I've come to believe that psychology is a big factor in becoming a consistently successful trader, and I'm planning on spending the next few years getting mine where it needs to be.

2

The Automation of Tharp Think

Laurens Bensdorp

Laurens Bensdorp is a 40-year-old Dutch businessman, and former whitewater-rafting guide. He made his transition to trading in 2000 at the top of the tech bubble—a difficult and treacherous environment that taught him valuable lessons in discipline and risk management. Since 2008, Laurens has made double-digit returns trading his family's money through his proprietary automated trading systems. Laurens has a passion for helping people get the most out of their trading. Having himself felt the pain of consistently losing during his early years of trading, he likes to share the path to becoming profitable as a trader. His mission in life is to be happy and help others grow. Consequently, he now provides trading education and coaching through his new business, "The Trading Mastery School," and through his website, www.tradingmasteryschool.com. Laurens lives with his lovely wife and three children in Argentina.

 Before: Invested with brokers and lost a good deal of money following their advice.

 After: Developed an automated system based on Tharp Think and has made an average of 50 percent per year with no drawdown bigger than 17 percent.

When I first started trading in the year 2000, I had no specific trading goals because I didn't even know the importance of goals. At the time, the media was basically saying, "Everyone makes money in stocks. It's easy." So I just wanted to make money.

I had the privilege of helping my parents trade their retirement accounts. Their money was invested at one of the high-profile investment banks in The Netherlands. Such banks are quite impressive—huge luxury buildings filled with employees in fancy suits who provide very special and friendly treatment. And they seem so knowledgeable. They must be very rich, intelligent, and smart, I thought, to afford this wonderful office building and expensive decorations. I was so naïve back then. I didn't know yet that the customers pay for it all through the huge commissions the banks charge.

The bank employees seemed to have an incredible knowledge about any and every kind of investment. I was totally overwhelmed by all the terms they used. To get up to speed, I studied each evening for hours, watched all the financial channels, and read every financial magazine I could get my hands on. It was 2000, and everyone was telling me how easy it was to make money in the stock market.

At the beginning of 2000, my family's portfolio had some incredible profits, so it all seemed true. The bank's strategy seemed sound and easy to follow. It was basically buy and hold. But when a stock started going down, they simply told us to buy more because the actual buying price would be lower by averaging down. This sounded very logical and smart to me because, at that time, I was told that stocks in the long term would make an average return of at least 12 percent per year. It also made perfect mathematical sense to me that averaging down would be a good thing as you lower your buying price and just need a small move upwards to be back at break-even.

Suddenly it was April of 2000 and stocks started to fall. Some stocks were falling very quickly. I was shocked to see that within a few months, the whole portfolio had lost about 30 percent. We had long discussions with all kinds of fancy advisors. They all said the same: "No worries; in the long run, they'll come back."

Remember, though, that I was educating myself, and not all of what I was reading was useless. I was finding evidence that stocks were highly overvalued and that there was enough room for even more loss in the portfolio. I had a discussion with the portfolio advisor, and he said, "This is not a good time to sell. You will be selling with a loss, so just wait until you break even." Unfortunately, we had "Worldcom" in our portfolio, which, as you all know, ended up going to zero.

My personal style has always been to do things on my own. I tend to be someone who goes against the crowd. This characteristic of my personality has turned out to be very important for the decisions I've made as an investor/trader. My belief that the stock market was due for an even further correction was so pronounced that I convinced my father that it was best to liquidate the whole portfolio. Yes, we'd take a loss, but at least we'd prevent much bigger losses from happening. I am very fortunate to be able to say that my father always had a lot of confidence in my judgment, so he agreed with me.

I called the bank to liquidate the portfolio, and they had 1,001 excuses for not selling, like:

- It's just a paper loss; don't make it a real loss.
- You're selling everything? Why don't you wait until it comes back—it always does!
- You should be buying *more*, not selling.
- If you buy and double up now, your initial purchase price will be lower, and it will be easier to get back to break-even.

These excuses were just ridiculous to me. A loss is a loss, paper or not.

Consequently, I lost all faith in the so-called top advisors. We liquidated the whole portfolio, a move that turned out to be a very wise decision. The total loss of the portfolio was limited to 30 percent, which taught us a valuable lesson. If we'd held on until we reached the bottom, the portfolio would have suffered a total loss greater than 75 percent.

My Journey into Doing the Trading Myself

After this lesson, it was clear to me that if I wanted to create excellent trading results, I had to educate myself further. I read all sorts of trading books, including a lot about trading systems. *Market Wizards* by Jack Schwager was probably the book that influenced me the most, but, of course, I skipped the last chapter on trading psychology. Jack interviews the world's top traders, and it's incredible to see the similarities that exist among all of them, regardless of their strategy.

- Their focus on money management or what we now call position sizing strategies.
- Their understanding of the importance of reward-to-risk.
- Their emphasis on personal psychology.

During the next few years, I didn't make any money, but I didn't lose a lot, either. I wasn't happy with the results, but I was still in the trading game. One day, I was speaking to a fellow trader and he mentioned Van Tharp's name. Intrigued by this discussion, I went ahead and read the last chapter in *Market Wizards* and was really excited by what it had to say, so I also bought *Trade Your Way to Financial Freedom* and read it in two days. It blew me away. In addition, I bought two courses from the Van Tharp Institute and went to a couple of system workshops.

As a result of this journey, I was beginning to understand what trading successfully was all about. I also came across a free article by Curtis Faith that detailed the Turtles'[1] actual trading rules. Curtis illustrated a statistical approach to trading that perfectly meshed with what I was learning from the Van Tharp Institute. A light bulb turned on inside my head.

Suddenly, I understood low-risk ideas and how I could make money following a statistical approach to the markets. Here are a few things I learned.

A light bulb turned on inside my head.

First, I always needed to predefine where I was wrong about a position before I entered the market. This would define my initial risk, which was called R for short. My goal was to keep my losses at 1R or less and to have profits that were much bigger than 1R. This is the golden rule of trading. For example, if I have seven 1R losses, a 3R loss and two 10R winners, I will have a net profit of 10R. My average profit over the 10 trades would be 1R per trade (which Dr. Tharp calls expectancy), and I would have made this despite being right on only 20 percent of my trades. This started to make sense.

Second, I can look at the profit and losses produced by my trading in terms of the initial risk. Thus, my trading system will produce a distribution of R-multiples. If I have enough trades, my sample of R-multiples will be big enough to give me an idea of what the system's performance will be like.

When pollsters predict elections, they do exit polls of how people say they voted. If they poll enough people from different areas representing people of different political persuasions, they can generally predict how the election will turn out. It suddenly dawned on me that I could do the same with a trading system. Get enough R-multiples, and I could predict how I will generally perform in the future.

But what about sampling people of different political persuasions? Well, Dr. Tharp says that this is like seeing how the system will perform in different market types. If I collect enough samples from a quiet bull market, pretty soon I'll know how the system will perform in quiet bull markets. But I won't know anything about volatile bear markets. When I have enough samples from volatile bear markets, I'll also know how the system will perform under those conditions. And if I collect enough samples from all the different market types—quiet bull, volatile bull, quiet sideways, volatile sideways, quiet bear, and volatile bear—then I'll eventually know how the system will perform under every condition, so that if we're in a volatile bear market, I'll know what to expect. I'll have a large sample of R-multiples that will give me a pretty good idea.

Doing this brought up another idea that Dr. Tharp frequently brings up. He says that it's easy to design a system that works well in any one particular market type, but insane to expect that it will perform well in all market types. Buy-and-hold growth stocks worked well in 1999, but were terrible in 2000 and 2001. If I know when my system works well, I can stop trading it when the conditions are not right, and I can design other systems that *do* work well in the new climate. Wow, what an insight!

I also understood that I need to have very specific objectives. Through Dr. Tharp's teachings, especially the games he plays in the workshops and his great book, *The Definitive Guide to Position Sizing*™ *Strategies,* I learned that it is through position sizing strategies that you actually meet (or fail to meet) your objectives.

Finally, I began to understand that I could only trade a system that fit me. Even if I discovered a great system, I probably couldn't trade it if it didn't fit my personality, my beliefs, and my needs.

But if I could find something that was close and then adopt it to fit my beliefs, I could probably trade it well. To me, the system needed to meet the following criteria:

- Having a setup and trading style that fits my personality. I'll talk about how I discovered that later.
- A 1R exit strategy, which took me more than a year to find. Doing so required lots of backtesting on as many stocks as possible.
- The strategy had to work on all U.S. stocks. My belief was that, if I was right conceptually, the same strategy should be profitable in the stock markets of other countries as well. That turned out to be true.
- Having the right position sizing strategy to meet my objectives, which turned out to be a lot of work.
  - First, I had to thoroughly understand the potential drawdowns of the system in terms of R. What are my chances of a 10R drawdown? A 20R drawdown? A 40R drawdown?
  - What was the risk tolerance of the people I was trading for (in this case, my family)? My experience is that people greatly overestimate their risk tolerance. They might think they can tolerate a 30 percent drawdown but find that they get very nervous when they experience a 15 percent drawdown. Through position sizing strategies, I could make sure that the maximum drawdown my family could tolerate would be very unlikely to occur. For example, if my position sizing strategy was to risk one percent of the portfolio per position with a one percent chance of a 20R drawdown, then, by risking 0.75 percent per trade, I would know there's only a one percent chance of a 15 percent drawdown in their account.

So, how did I discover the type of setup that fit me? One day, I stumbled upon the work of Larry Connors. Larry is a big believer in mean reversion, meaning that if something strays too far away from the average, it is likely to come back. Connors has developed many trade setups around the concept of mean reversion. If you understand the principle, you have a trading edge.

Armed with this concept and a number of other beliefs I'd developed from my study, I came up with a system. Now, I have a variety of systems that all operate according to the same beliefs:

- Only trade in the direction of the stock's long-term trend.
- Wait for a pullback if going down or an up move if going short.
- Then, intraday, you enter on a buy order even lower than yesterday's low, when the stock is completely exhausted and there are no sellers left (this is the hardest part, because you have to go against the herd and buy stocks that are declining in panic).
- Sell when the stock reverts back to its mean.

Lastly, I learned something that blew me away. A trading "mistake" is defined as not following your rules. Trading mistake-free allows me to achieve the expectancy of my system, while making lots of mistakes will cause my system to perform below its expectancy. The more I thought about it, the more it redefined my concept of what it means to be right. Most people think of being right as making money on every trade. But what if being right simply means *following your rules* on every trade? Making money on every trade is probably impossible to do, but trading mistake-free is quite doable. That got me to think, "How can I trade mistake-free?"

Curtis Faith's presentation of the Turtles Rules resonated with me, and I discovered that he was involved with software called Trading Blox. I bought the software, thinking that if I could automate my ideas need™, I'd be less likely to make mistakes.

I found a programmer who was very good at programming in Trading Blox. I hired him to program my system. I told him what I wanted and soon I had my system fully automated. The results were absolutely in line with what I expected, and the system's testing results were very good. I now had statistical evidence that the strategy I was about to trade had a real edge.

At one of the workshops I attended at the Van Tharp Institute, I met two very good programmers. I decided to share my exact rules with both of them under a gentlemen's agreement not to reveal it to anyone else. Their job was to help me verify if the code was correct and to improve it. This resulted in a very pleasant cooperation through which we combined my ideas with their programming. They both worked on different platforms, but the results were quite similar, and that gave me more confirmation.

I backtested every market type I could imagine, and it gave me confidence that the system would work. I tested a large stock portfolio (i.e., more than 7,000 U.S. stocks and 2,500 Canadian stocks) under all sorts of market conditions and market types.

I did everything we could think of to try to disprove the system's edge. This was a tough task; it goes against human nature to try to destroy a great-looking system on paper through testing, but doing so helped me gain more confidence in the robustness of the system. When all this worked out as I had expected, I had the confidence to trade the system at the maximum possible position size I could use to meet my objectives.

Lastly, I did everything I could so that I would understand every single component of my system under every conceivable market condition. I'm certain that I know the worst possible outcome. This comes from backtesting and from using common sense to imagine different scenarios. For example, what would happen if the market closed down 50 percent in a single day? Would that break my system?

Training Someone Else

At this point, I had a complete system that suited me. Actually, I had several systems that worked under different market conditions. Those systems fit my beliefs. I thoroughly understood them. And I knew they would make money in the long term if I could just follow them. But that still presented one problem.

First, I had another business. I often had to travel, and although my systems did well historically, they still needed my daily attention. They were short-term systems that required active order management. To enter the market, they required a lot of work before the market opened, and they required active monitoring.

Another secret to trading success I learned from Dr. Tharp is that you need to know your strengths and weaknesses. Order management and short-term monitoring of systems was not my strong point. But I had a solution—hiring someone to trade for me, somebody with different characteristics. I found someone who was extremely focused on details and liked to work on his own the whole day, and it ended up being the perfect solution for me.

It took me 10 days of training to teach him all the software and how to do the work. I actually discovered that doing the trading the way I wanted was quite labor intensive, so I developed some great ideas that fit me and my beliefs. I hired a programmer to test it thoroughly and see if I had a consistent edge. Then I hired an employee to trade it by strict rules; he gets paid a bonus each month if he makes no mistakes. I also made it clear that if he deviated from his daily tasks, he was out of a job, regardless of what the daily results were in dollars; doing this emphasized for him the importance of following the rules no matter what. Through this procedure, my trading is nearly 100 percent efficient—mistake-free.

The process of teaching others the system was great because it increased my knowledge as well. What's more, I could replicate it if necessary because the process was well-documented. The initial training took about ten days. I built spreadsheets that reported all R-multiples, all trades, and all kinds of reporting protocols to me on a daily basis. Consequently, I would know exactly what was going on at any time of the day. At the end of the trading day, I would get all of the important trading statistics from my employee, who took care of all the details.

This process has worked perfectly for me. Indirectly, through my automation and my employee, I've been trading full time since 2009. I can still have another job, because the whole trading process takes me (after the training) about 15 minutes a day, during which I review the three daily reports my employee sends me.

Why This Is Possible

Until I began to master Tharp Think, I was having big issues with who I was as a person and what my purpose was. I lacked conviction and direction. It was a big issue for me because I knew that I had tremendous potential, but I wasn't using any of it. I felt useless, and it affected my self-esteem.

I now know what my weaknesses are. As I already mentioned, I'm not a detail person, but I can hire people who *are* good at details.

I'm also aware of my strengths, and having confidence in them has led me to use them to their maximum potential. For example, I'm good at creating things, especially trading strategies. My mind is always full of ideas. That's a great thing, because it gives me opportunities and flexibility.

My mind is always full of ideas.

My big issue, though, has always been that I never follow through on most of those ideas. Why? Because I don't want to do the work. I don't want to program. I don't want to log trades or look at all the R-multiples and trading statistics. That's why the best strategy for me is to write down my conceptual trading ideas and hire a programmer to write code to see if the ideas really have an edge. By doing this, I double my leverage. We trade the systems at more than 99 percent efficiency—less than one mistake per 100 trades. Few traders can say that.

Since I put all of this together, I've made an average of about 50 percent a year—and that's been during some very nasty markets. We have never had a drawdown higher than 17 percent and never longer than three months. Thank you, Dr. Tharp.

Addendum

While doing this interview, I was noticing a lack of commitment from my employee. This didn't result in any mistakes, but reports were coming in late and protocols weren't being followed as agreed upon. Consequently, a lot of alarm bells started to ring in my head.

Whenever I start seeing things like that, mistakes soon follow, so I had to take action. I addressed the issue by suggesting that he work closely with me for two weeks from my home. I'd monitor him, work on his issues, and get him focused again. But, once we started, he seemed to completely lack motivation. The dedication he'd shown over the past two years was gone, and he quit his job. Immediately, I took the following steps:

- I suspended trading.
- I paid my programmer friend to build an automation interface between my backtesting software, Trading Blox, and the broker software. What was once labor-intensive work could now be done with three clicks in less than a minute.
- I decided not to recruit a new employee immediately, because at the time I was in the process of moving with my family from Columbia to Argentina.
- Because part of the labor is automated already with the new software, the new training process only took a couple of days.
- When settled in Argentina I started trading again and hired a new employee. Because of the enhanced automation it is even easier to trade the system. Furthermore, the margin for error is even lower.
- During the time that I was not trading I used my time to develop different systems for different market types. Now I trade five different systems simultaneously, which individually work in bull, bear, and sideways markets. This is exactly the power of Van Tharp's teaching of using market types for different systems. The conclusion was stunning because combining five average systems, all designed for different market types, plus the appropriate triggers for when to trade them, gives a huge increase in performance.

3

From Commercial Loan Officer to Financially Free Trader Investor

Rick Freeman

Rick Freeman is the president of Wealth Management Solutions, LLC, a money management firm. After graduating from the University of Iowa with a bachelor's degree in finance in 1982, he embarked on a 24-year career in commercial banking, ending as a regional commercial banking manager for Wells Fargo in 2006 with responsibility for a $1 billion loan portfolio in the San Francisco Bay area. He began active trading in 1997 and later took a number of trading courses through the Van Tharp Institute that ultimately led him to enroll in the Super Trader program in 2005 with the goal of becoming a full-time trader. That goal was realized in 2006 when he ended his commercial banking career and moved from California to Florida to pursue his dream of trading and proprietary investment management. He is the first graduate of the Van Tharp Institute Super Trader program. He now lives with his wife and children in Palm Harbor, where he manages a proprietary portfolio of longer-term investments for passive income and asset protection consisting of oil and gas, real estate, and precious metals. His active trading is centered tactically in currency and futures markets to capitalize on high-probability swing moves with maximum capital efficiency in both trending and countertrend market conditions. Rick is also a licensed Certified Financial Planner, having earned his certification through the University of California at Berkeley in 1998.

 Before: Bank loan officer who worked long hours and struggled to make money in the markets.

 After: Financially free trader who doubled his net worth in five years and had his best year ever when the markets collapsed in 2008.

When I first got involved with trading, I was at a turning point. I'd spent more than a decade as a commercial lender for a large U.S. bank, and now my career was beginning to plateau. After so many years in the industry, I really wasn't learning anything new anymore. I no longer felt challenged or stimulated. My compensation was starting to oscillate in a band that didn't seem to change much, no matter how well I performed. Something wasn't right with what I was doing. I needed to make a change. This was during the late 1990s, when the markets were all the rage, so I decided to pursue my interest in trading.

It seemed like the perfect fit for me. Trading offered everything my current job lacked: it challenged my creativity, it fed my constant desire to learn and grow, and it put me in control of my earning potential. I didn't have much experience with trading at the time, but I was confident that if I kept my current job while I learned the ropes, I could transition to a life of full-time trading later on.

Then, a few years later, my employer offered me a position in middle management, and I decided to take it. I was still pursuing trading, but at that point I didn't yet have the confidence to take it on as a full-time enterprise and quit my day job. Since starting my trading journey, I'd discovered both through training I'd received at the Van Tharp Institute and through my own trading results that I was a long way from having the skills necessary to trade full time. I didn't have the correct psychological mind-set, any viable trading systems, or a solid business plan. Meanwhile, the management position represented a step up in responsibility and compensation that I believed might revitalize my stationary career in commercial banking.

It wasn't to be. Though the job was certainly challenging and paid much better than my lending position had, I quickly realized that I'd underestimated the scope and nature of management. My new position exposed me to frustrating organizational politics, and the nature of the job itself often left me feeling ineffective and unproductive. I was not enjoying myself at all.

Even worse, after finally settling into the position, the same types of things that had affected me as a lender began to creep into my life as a manager. I no longer felt challenged, and I'd reached a level of advancement above which it would be difficult for me to rise in anything but limited degrees, given the fairly flat management structure of the company. Moreover, I noticed that, even though I was now a manager, my compensation was still quite banded. What I earned had little to do with how much effort I put into the job. This created a lot of internal conflict for me, because one of my core beliefs has always been that the harder you work, the more you should be rewarded. You should be fairly compensated for your efforts and suffer the consequences when you aren't performing. I began to seriously consider whether staying in commercial banking was a viable option for me anymore, and whether making the commitment to become a full-time trader and money manager was truly my calling.

My new position left me feeling ineffective and unproductive.

But now I was back in the predicament I'd been in before I took the management position. I wasn't happy at all with my banking career, but I also wasn't ready to jump off the corporate ship either. Even on a part-time basis, trading was fairly demanding; in fact, I was losing money fairly consistently. I'd kept telling myself that I still had plenty of time to develop my skills and that I could financially absorb whatever losses I suffered in the meantime because I had a full-time job, but now it was clear that I'd simply been hedging my bets, living timidly. I wasn't being honest with myself about what I needed to do.

Finally, in February of 2005, I decided to apply to the Van Tharp Super Trader program. For me, that was the decisive act; it was the moment when I finally decided to take charge of my life and become a full-time professional trader and independent private money manager. In other words, I was ready to live my dream. My transformational journey had begun.

My Initial Psychological Changes

Once I decided to take control of my life and become a full-time trader, I had to *make a wholehearted public commitment* to doing it. Once you make and declare a commitment, positive things begin to happen; the world moves to help you because you have put your intentions out to the universe so that it can respond. Making and declaring my commitments has helped me achieve the results I want in my life as well as in trading. It's probably the most important lesson the Super Trader program has taught me.

The next thing the program taught me was that *my beliefs filter my reality*; when I change my beliefs, I change my reality. The impact of this realization was nothing short of miraculous for me. Once I believed without a doubt that I could become a trader, I could go forward and actually do it.

When I understood beliefs in this way, my whole approach to dealing with them changed. I started looking at them, not in terms of whether or not they are inherently "right," but in terms of whether or not they are *useful to me*. If they aren't, then discarding them and adopting new beliefs that *are* useful is the logical decision to make. What I don't think many people realize is just how easy it can be to do this once you step back from your beliefs and analyze them objectively. Accomplish that, and change is only a thought away!

> Change Is Only a Thought Away!

Once you accept this concept, it became self-evident that *I could only trade my beliefs*. That idea may sound simple enough, but because I didn't really know what my trading beliefs were in the first place, it was initially one of the hardest concepts for me to grasp. It wasn't until I spent some time thinking through what I thought I believed about trading, considered what others I respected thought, and then decided whether I could adopt those beliefs that I began to develop an active belief framework for my trading.

Trading is probably 100 percent psychological. Even systems and position sizing strategies are psychological in nature. In the first edition of *Trade Your Way to Financial Freedom,* Dr. Tharp said that trading was probably 60 percent psychological, 30 percent position sizing, and 10 percent systems. Later, he determined that it was more useful to say that all trading success is based on psychological factors. This belief has had a huge impact on how I view trading because it forces me to look at what really moves the markets—namely, people making decisions every day based on fear and greed, which in turn generates the supply and demand that creates tradable moves. If you don't have a handle on your own psychology, you are guaranteed to lose in the markets because the market is designed to take advantage of your psychological weaknesses.

I think this is most easily seen in traders who don't use stops when initiating or managing a position. If they are exposed to a serious gap-and-run move against them, they are immediately confronted by a fear-generating situation rather than an unemotional one in which you close out the position immediately. The fear ends up trapping them until they can't take it any longer, but by then, they may have already lost a very large amount of money. It's best to avoid that psychological trap and never trade without a stop.

The marble game that Van has students play at many of his workshops also illustrates the dominant role that psychology plays in trading. Van designed the game to clearly expose numerous psychological biases and show how much they influence trader decision processes. In the game, different colored marbles get pulled from a bag for 40 to 60 "trades." The different colors represent the different R-multiple results that a trading system can generate. Even though everyone in the room receives the same R-multiple result for every trade, there are as many different equity amounts at the end of the game as there are players in the room. The only explanation for this vast difference in results is position sizing, which is influenced by a psychological decision. If you still need convincing, I encourage you to read *When Genius Failed* by Roger

Lowenstein, which details the position sizing decisions, and the psychology behind them, made at Long-Term Capital Management before its epic failure.

If trading success is largely psychological, then *you should always be working on yourself.* This belief speaks directly to the issue of remaining psychologically clear and balanced so that you can maintain discipline and focus on your trading. For me, this means identifying when I might have a psychological issue showing up in my trading—such as when I find myself wanting to tweak an exit rule or move a stop unnecessarily—and then drilling down to find out where it's coming from. If I am constantly working on myself, I'm probably minimizing these types of situations. If I'm not working on myself and not staying aware of my weaknesses, it's virtually guaranteed that those weaknesses will impact my trading.

It's hard for people to confront their demons, but if you do so, you'll be richly rewarded both financially and emotionally. Remember how the same issues seemed to plague me no matter what job I had at the bank? The Super Trader program gave me the tools* I needed to identify the negative patterns that created those issues and to finally eliminate them from my daily life once and for all.

As you begin to learn all of this, it really becomes obvious that *you are responsible for everything in your life.* You control your thoughts and, by extension, your actions. Through your actions, you create your life.

After I started the Super Trader program, it became clear to me that I hadn't been taking responsibility for my own life. After that realization, my life did a complete 180-degree turn. Things started changing a lot, and definitely for the better.[1]

I'd given up power over my own career to external circumstances and convinced myself that there wasn't much I could do about it. When I finally understood that I am entirely responsible for my outcomes, I stopped misdiagnosing what was wrong with my trading. If you spend your time blaming the market makers, brokers, your tip-giving friends and their spouses, the government, and just about anything and everything else you can come up with for your poor performance, you're allowing the real

---

*The tools are described in detail in Section II of this book.

problem—you—to go untreated. Accept responsibility for your trading mistakes and you'll learn something productive for the next trade every time. I find that much more useful than remaining in a state of denial.

Another concept I learned is that *we all have emotional "parts" that play a role in our lives*. These parts all have positive intentions, whether they seem like negative parts or not. You'll learn a lot more about parts in Chapter 9, "You Are a Crowd of Conflicting Parts Inside." Suffice it to say that identifying your parts so that you can negotiate with them effectively to produce a positive result is critical, especially in trading.

For example, fear is a common part for most people and one that can be especially damaging for a trader. I realized that whenever I was feeling fear, the positive intention of that feeling was to protect me and remind me that I didn't have enough confidence or understanding in the system I was trading and that I needed to delve deeper into the reasons why that was so before trading it. Even though fear can feel uncomfortable, it is a useful emotion if you know what it's trying to do for you.

Fear is a common part for everyone.

But perhaps my most important realization was that *I am connected to a Higher Power and that I should always stay connected to that*

Source for guidance. For a long time, I'd been disconnected from my Higher Power, and it explained why a lot of things weren't working for me. We each need to define what our Higher Power is and stay connected to it to understand where we are, where we're going, and where we want to be.

Later in this book, you'll read about a process called Transformational Meditation, or TfM for short. The Super Trader program includes a 28-Day Transformational Meditation course, and it really opened the practice up for me. For the first time, I was able to define my purpose in life. I understood what I was here for and what lay before me: limitless opportunity.

What I've Learned about the Trading Game

As I continued my training under Van Tharp, I started to see daily activities and interactions in a completely different way. Given that our beliefs shape our reality and that trading is entirely psychological, I started to see trading as a kind of game. Like all games, trading has rules that were designed by people. Once you understand and fully accept this, you realize that nothing is stopping you from creating your own game, with your own rules—rules designed so you can win! I was exposed to this concept in the Van Tharp Institute's Peak Performance 202 workshop, and it blew me away. The more I thought about it, the more examples I came up with that confirmed its truth. You are completely free to design your own trading systems—and your life, for that matter—around the game you want to play, with yourself as the house that always wins.*

In order to understand the trading game, you have to understand the overall arena in which that game takes place—the larger context that represents the money game. Our monetary system and government sit at the top of the financial food chain, working together to control our money—even going so far as to amend the Constitution in 1913 to obtain the power to extract income taxes. We don't have much power over the rules at that level, but we do have the power to make those rules work for us. Dr. Tharp includes the words "Financial Freedom" in the title of his first three books,

---

*Early in this book, you were presented with the notion of the trading game, invested in by big money with rules so that they would always win. What you are learning in this section of the book are ways to change the rules so that *you* can win.

and for good reason—it's an important concept. Essentially, financial freedom is just a different way of playing the money game. Instead of working for money the way most people do, you make your money work for you. When your passive income exceeds your expenses, you win.

Learning this was big for me because I had literally never thought about financial freedom in those terms. I thought that those who made the most money or had the most toys won. The "system" had been deeply ingrained into my way of thinking. I'd been taught that success meant going to school, getting a good job, going into debt for cars and houses, working with my nose to the grindstone for 40 years, and retiring with a gold watch and a retirement fund I wasn't entirely sure would support me through my golden years.

That was the situation I'd been in as a commercial banking lender and manager. The income I earned was limited to salary and bonuses that were taxed at the highest marginal rate at both state and federal levels. Any stock option grants I may have received were not readily exercisable until they vested in several years, and because I didn't have the power to manage them myself, they were vulnerable to market prices.

Once I understood the concept of passive income, though, I knew what I needed to do to win my own money game. I knew that investing and trading gave me a much better opportunity to generate passive income and gain financial freedom than playing by the old rules, and that realization filled me with confidence and a new sense of focus.

The Financial Freedom version of the money game plays a big part in my trading business. Today, I constantly look for new sources of passive income. For instance, after taking advantage of a significant municipal bond trading opportunity from late 2008 to 2010, I reinvested a portion of the profits into investments in passive real estate and oil and gas. These provide me with income diversification while still fitting into my Big Picture economic view. The passive income smoothes out my trading profits over time, reduces volatility in my overall portfolio curve, and reduces my trading risk. Infinite wealth is the ultimate financial goal, and it's available to all people who can simply change their own beliefs and take the necessary steps toward financial freedom.

Shortly after I quit my job to pursue full-time trading, I became financially free through a low-risk, highly profitable real estate trade I'd identified while in the Super Trader program. I hadn't even finished the Super Trader program yet, but already my plan to become financially free was playing out right in front of me. That plan was tested when I had an unexpected split with my real estate partner during the course of the deal that caused me to reexamine and reformulate my overall business plan. In the end, though, it proved to be nothing more than a small diversion that ultimately led me down the path I'm currently on. I simply respected the process and used it as a guide for taking responsibility and staying on track toward consistent, successful results.

Understanding the Trading Game

Any form of passive income requires some work. It's nothing compared to the 40 to 60 hours a week you put in at a conventional job, but you still have to do some things to keep it going. If you collect rent, you have to work to find a good deal so that the rental income is a positive cash flow, and then you have to maintain that flow. If you collect royalties, you have to do something to obtain those royalties in the first place. I could now work 10 to 12 hours a week to maintain my passive income. And wouldn't any trading activity that requires only a few hours a week, once the system is in place and operating, be another example of such "passive" income? Of course it would! That's where Tharp Think came into play.

According to Tharp Think, *trading isn't about "picking the right stock,"* as so many book titles would lead you to believe; it's about *creating a low-risk idea* that can be traded to withstand the worst-case scenario in the short run so that the long-term expectancy of the idea can be realized. This belief was especially eye-opening to me when I read about it in *Trade Your Way to Financial Freedom*. It got me to focus more on probabilities than on being "right" about the stocks I picked.

I'd been part of the crowd that thinks picking the right stocks is the be-all and end-all of trading, so when I first encountered this new way of seeing the trading game, I had to prove it to myself. Having majored in finance and worked in the banking industry, my first instinct was to get out my calculator and run scenarios with varying reliability, expectancy, and position sizing models. When I did, the results confirmed what Van was saying. I got even deeper confirmation of the belief after taking several of the technical courses taught at the Van Tharp Institute, where good, high-quality systems are presented. I even did some of the work for the instructor, doing calculations on the systems to see how good they really were. And they were good.

An extension of this belief is that *your trade entry isn't that important.* You really don't have to know where the market is going in order to be successful. In fact, you could probably make money with a random entry system; you'd basically have a 50/50 chance of success. This concept blew me away because it directly contradicted the value most of us are ingrained with from an early age—that you must be "right" at least 70 percent of the time or so to be considered successful.

At first, I wasn't sure if I could adopt this Tharp Think principle; I'd always believed that I had to be in control of everything to succeed. But after reading that Tom Basso had proved in a research project that he could make money in real-life trading a random entry system, I became a believer in the unimportance of entries. Reading about the success of the Turtles in the 1980s further convinced me. Although they traded a defined system, their reliability was notably below 50 percent. Now, when I evaluate trading results, I focus less on reliability and more on expectancy, opportunity, variance, and whether an idea will work for me.

The important thing to remember here is that trading a system without first understanding the Big Picture is putting the cart before the horse. *You need to analyze the Big Picture first and then develop a system that aligns with your understanding of it.* You'd think that, because I'd been a commercial banking analyst, I would have already known this, but I have to admit that I didn't. I was generally a microanalyst, and at first I struggled with how to understand the Big Picture—how to assemble what I knew on a micro level into a larger context that would somehow illuminate my understanding of the markets and my own trading strategies. It's taken a lot of study and research for me to finally gain confidence in my ability to size up what's happening on a Big-Picture scale, but it's transformed my trading.

Once you gain the ability to see the Big Picture, knowing where to focus your trading efforts becomes fairly straightforward. It makes structuring your trading strategies much easier and takes some of the mystery out of system design. But that design must not only align with your Big-Picture understanding of the markets, it must also fit you and your psychology, and must align with your understanding of yourself. This seems like yet another simple concept, but it was much harder for me to define, at least in practice. After I made my transition to full-time trading and money management, I had to learn largely by trial and error what was going to work for me. And with practice and experience, I've discovered my own trading approach.

In order to create an effective system that fits your psychology, you must *first set objectives*. There are probably as many objectives as there are traders. Once you understand your objectives, you begin to realize that a Holy Grail system won't help you meet them. Instead, *it is through position sizing strategies that you really meet your objectives.* Position sizing strategies tell you "how much" throughout the course of a trade.

For me, this is the really fun part of trading. It's where I get to figure out how I will reach my objectives through position sizing algorithms that are based on my goals and my system's trading characteristics. It gives my analytical mind a maximum workout because there is virtually no limit to what you can do with position sizing strategies. They give you the creative license to design anything you want based on your objectives and risk tolerance.

When I learned about position sizing strategies and their importance in meeting my goals, I became convinced that they were *the* key to success. I gravitated away from using a lot of indicators, focusing instead on simplicity in the system design so that I could spend more time on what really counts—a good position sizing strategy. In one workshop I attended, the exact same system was applied to a number of trades using three different position sizing algorithms, and the results were all completely different from one another. There can be no better proof in my mind that position sizing strategies are the key to profitable trading.

People tend to believe that there is one Holy Grail system. That is, that there is one system that will make them a lot of money in any market. But that's not true. When the market changes, your system should change with it; a one-size-fits-all approach simply will not work. This is precisely why you need to understand the Big Picture first. Of course, this means that you must have a way of tracking market conditions so that you know when things are changing.

Your system's results will likely let you know anyway, but having an early-warning system is a better strategy. It's pretty easy to find a great system for any one market type—such as the go-go years of the late 1990s—but it's a mistake to assume that that same system will work for all market types. You should have systems for each of the various market conditions, so that when markets change, you can change with them.

Whatever the market type, *your system must have a positive expectancy to be tradable.* This was one of the early ideas I picked up from reading *Trade Your Way to Financial Freedom.* There are many, many ways to make money through trading, but *all* of them *must* have a positive expectancy; on average, they must make money on each dollar risked over a large number of trades, or they will be losing ideas.

Expectancy is one of the core principles of successful trading. I believe that if you don't understand and pay attention to it, you will be trading blindly. Your account will blow up.

And since your psychology is so important to successful trading, it should be obvious that you should only trade systems that "fit" you. This was yet another simple concept, it seemed, but much harder to define for me in practice. It took me quite a while to figure out what was going to fit me. In addition, what I thought would fit me initially, wouldn't fit me now. I learned somewhat by trial and error what was going to work after I made my transition to full-time trading and money management. I feel that I have defined it well and am very comfortable with how I've designed my trading and money management business.

Trading in a way that fits you is very important. As I eventually found out, what I initially thought would work when I was still employed actually didn't end up working that well. Even after I made the transition to full-time trading, things still weren't quite working out. It wasn't until I really decided who I wanted to be as a trader/money manager and determined what kind of trading systems I wanted to employ to meet my Big Picture analysis that what would "fit" me became apparent. Of course, everyone has to start somewhere to define his "fit." You really have to think through it—otherwise, you're simply asking for a lot of unnecessary frustration and headache.

Another obvious key point that most people don't think about is that you must set objectives. There are probably as many objectives as there are traders. Once you understand your objectives, you begin to realize that a Holy Grail system won't meet them. It might help, but you really meet your objectives through position sizing strategies. Position sizing strategies tell you "how much" throughout the course of a trade. When I learned about position sizing strategies and their importance in meeting my goals, I became convinced that they are *the* key to success. Develop a system with a positive expectancy, and you'll meet your goals through the appropriate use of position sizing strategies.

So How Do You Get a Positive Expectancy System?

A positive-expectancy system usually comes from the Golden Rule of Trading, which is to cut losses short and let profits run. The first key is to *always know your initial risk, defined as 1R.* Your average loss should be smaller than 1R, and your profits should be much larger. That's the key to a positive expectancy system. It's all about reward-to-risk ratios.

You must define your initial risk in terms of R or your dollars risked in terms of the distance between entry and stop multiplied by your position size. If you don't, then you'll have no way of knowing how well your system is going to perform, because you won't have a reference point for calculating your trade performance once the position is closed.

The second key to creating a positive expectancy system is to *make trades only when you think the potential reward is at least two times the size of the initial risk.* Once you commit to that standard, you start thinking about the reward-to-risk ratio of every trade. In fact, you start looking at your profits and losses as a function of your initial risk, which Dr. Tharp calls your R-multiple.

The third key is to understand that *exits are much more important than entries,* because it is through exits that you control your reward-to-risk ratio. I think a lot of traders avoid exits because they're too focused on the issue of "control" and "being right" with entries. Again, once I realized how important it was to cut losses short and let profits run, I had no problem adopting this belief. In fact, it underscored just how important it is to be able to take a planned loss when your stop is hit because the concept of exits applies to losing positions as much as it does to winning ones, if not more so.

The other paradigm shift that came out of this belief for me was how difficult it is to structure good exits. Setting a stop loss for capital preservation is very easy to do, but defining profit-taking exits is an entirely different matter.

The fourth key is to *understand a system as a distribution of R-multiples with a mean expectancy and a standard deviation.* If you aren't able to quantify a statistically relevant sample size of trades expressed in R-multiples, you have no way of knowing what to expect from your system. I don't accept any trading idea without first considering its R-multiple trade distribution; I really can't form an opinion on its merits without doing so.

The fifth key is to *favor simple systems with a few logical, robust variables over highly optimized systems.* As I mentioned before, I had a lot of success with municipal bond trading, and that wasn't based on anything fancy—just the basic forces of supply and demand. If you want complexity, focusing on position sizing strategies is the best place to spend your time and effort. For me, the fact that I don't have to get overly complicated with my trading approach—that doing so can even be detrimental to it—is incredibly refreshing.

Getting a System That Works

As my trading has evolved, I've drifted away from indicator-based approaches and toward a simplified approach that doesn't allow or require any indicator settings—that focuses mostly on pure price and volume-based methods. That way, I know I won't be tempted to optimize, which essentially guarantees failure. It also increases the odds that a system will remain robust in the future, because there are no settings that I can change. Keeping things simple is always a good idea, especially when it comes to trading.

When Tom Basso used to help Van teach workshops, he said that *extensive backtesting is not required if you really understand your system.* I had a hard time accepting that idea at first, but I soon began to notice that whenever I felt the need to test a system, it was because I either didn't understand the system or didn't have the confidence to trade it even if I did understand it. By relying on backtesting, I was really saying that I didn't trust my system and that I needed some kind of proof that it had worked in the past. But knowing what it did in the past is not the same thing as knowing what it will do in the future.

It also became clear that I must harbor some conflicts with my own beliefs about the underlying system if I had to backtest it extensively. Today, the first things I check in a system are the underlying beliefs that guide its logic.

I think your time would be better spent on live-trading very small sizes until you have a sample of at least 30 trades, but preferably 50 to 100. Once you have a sufficiently large sample, you can calculate your R-multiple distribution and then run Monte Carlo simulation on that distribution to give you an idea of what you might expect in the future. By doing testing in this fashion, you introduce your psychology into the system, giving you a more realistic idea of whether you can even trade the idea in the first place. You also get a glimpse into possible future results upon which reasonable objectives can be built. I know that Monte Carlo simulation has its limitations, but even a small window to the future is better than a rearview mirror to the past.

A good way to measure the *quality of a trading system and its results is to use the System Quality Number® rating, or SQN® rating.* I thought the SQN concept, first introduced in the *Definitive Guide to Position Sizing™ Strategies,* was a big breakthrough for traders. The SQN rating essentially measures how easy it will be to use position sizing strategies to meet your objectives. The higher the SQN score, the easier it will be. The beauty of the SQN rating is that it allows you, in one number, to measure any type of system and determine whether it's worth pursuing or not.

Moreover, once you understand how the SQN score works, it is very helpful with system design and management. Understanding the various ways you can get a high SQN has provided me with good guidance about the type of systems I may want to pursue.

Trading Psychology

Now that I had the concepts of systems down and how to use them to meet my objectives, trading psychology again entered into the picture. A lot of traders equate trading "mistakes" with trading losses, but they're not the same thing. *A trading mistake is defined as not following your trading rules.*

Understanding the importance of being disciplined in following the rule set of a trading system was a big help to me in getting over the need to be "right." That's where I think a lot of traders can stay stuck. They never really accept that taking losses is part of the trading game. Instead, they violate their rules for the sake of being "right" and end up losing even more than they would have if they'd simply followed the rules.

If you follow your rules, you can focus your efforts on the process of trading and let go of the tension created by always trying to be right. Concentrating on my rules helped me eliminate emotional responses to price activity—helped me find peace amid market chaos. I have found that after you have a significantly large sample size of trades, the issue of losses really gets diluted anyway. You can see your system performance in the bigger analytical picture of expectancy, SQN, and whether or not your system works in the current market type.

The logical conclusion from all of this is that trader "efficiency," not "rightness," is the key to keeping performance high. The first chapter in this section focuses on a trader who made 130 percent following Tharp Think principles, but who left 59R on the table because of mistakes. And that probably translates to another 59 percent in profits.

I understand that all Super Traders must now trade at a 95 percent efficiency level or better to graduate from the program. I didn't have that as a specific performance metric when I was in the Super Trader program, but it's certainly a worthwhile objective, so I've since adopted it as a performance metric for my own trading. Efficiency, as I understand it, measures how many mistakes are made over the course of a system's results. The score is calculated as the total number of trades without mistakes divided by the total number of trades. Thus, you can only make five mistakes in 100 trades if you want to trade at 95 percent efficiency.

I find this measure especially helpful in keeping me focused on my rules because I know that not following them will count against my efficiency. If you are honest with yourself about your mistakes, the efficiency metric can be very effective in helping you avoid errors and achieve better overall performance. The great thing about trading is that you can't avoid your errors; they will show up in your trading results. Being right becomes not making any mistakes, so I can actually be right 100 percent of the time.

Finally, the trading tasks that Van has researched to duplicate what successful traders do is a key to consistent trading results. These 12 Tasks of Trading, described in the first volume of Dr. Tharp's *Peak Performance Course,* include:

1. Self-analysis to determine if you are okay to trade
2. Mental rehearsal to prevent mistakes
3. Daily focus to point you toward your goals

4. Developing a low-risk idea (which is done way before the trading starts)
5. Stalking, moving down to a shorter time frame to lower the risk even more
6. Action that requires commitment and no thought
7. Monitoring to keep the risk low
8. Aborting if the trade goes against you
9. Taking profits when the reason for the trade ends
10. A daily debriefing to monitor and prevent future mistakes
11. Being grateful for whatever went right
12. Doing a periodic review to make sure everything is working

What I liked about learning the 12 Tasks of Trading was that they provided a consistent framework around which I could manage myself and my trading results. They enforce personal responsibility and accountability while also providing the structure to properly design, execute, and manage trading systems. Whenever I make a mistake in my trading, I first ask myself, *Was I following the 12 Tasks of Trading?* Invariably, I find that I've left out one or more of the tasks and that my mistake can be traced back to having done so. I believe the 12 Tasks of Trading are an excellent set of general rules to introduce and maintain discipline in any trading endeavor, whether you are an individual trader or part of a trading firm.

How My Life Has Changed

I'm very happy to say that I have finally realized my dream of becoming a professional trader and money manager. My wife and I left the corporate world in June 2006, packed up our family and moved from California to Florida. I've formed two companies from which I proprietarily trade and manage our investments.

It doesn't feel like work anymore because I am now following my bliss. I love what I do every day. Whenever I hit a bump in the road and imagine what it might be like to return to the corporate world, I immediately remember all the limits that were engulfing me there, and it reminds me that I can't imagine living any other way than I am right now. There is nothing like the satisfaction of knowing that you've done it—that you've made your dreams come true and now get to live them every day.

The net worth I spent 24 years building has more than doubled in the five years since I left corporate America. In fact, in 2008, when the financial world was on the brink of collapsing, I experienced my best year ever, doing better in that one year than I had in the previous 10 combined. I truly believe that this success was due to the paradigm shifts and new beliefs I gained through Tharp Think principles.

I don't fear the unknown the way I did before we made our move. I can still be fearful at times, but it doesn't have nearly the same power over me, and I find that I can quickly diminish it by digging down and trying to uncover its positive intention. I also believe that a Higher Power is at work in my life and has a plan for me, and this gives me great peace and comfort. I am a Type-A person, so it's easy for me to get caught up in things that simply aren't important to the grand scheme of my life, but I have learned to interrupt myself and plug back into my Source connection to regain my sense of perspective.

I don't fear the unknown.

I also find that I'm much more open to new ideas now because I don't have to think inside the box the way I always did in the commercial banking world. Not having any limits on your thinking is truly liberating and exciting, especially when it comes to trading. My biggest frustration now is not having enough time in the day to act on everything I want to accomplish! What a great problem to have!

I have become a better independent thinker than I've ever been—primarily as a result of the introspection exercises I've done in the Super Trader program, but also because I'm not managing anyone else's agenda now but my own. When I think back on being a commercial banker, I can't believe how detached I was working for someone else and spending somebody else's money. Now I feel much more focused on everything I do because I am *it*. My decisions about how our capital is managed determine our success or failure. Before, I never would have believed that I could actually enjoy this kind of ultimate accountability, but I can say now that I wouldn't have it any other way.

The interesting thing about Tharp Think principles is that, even though they're taught through the financial metaphor of trading, they absolutely can apply to anyone's life, regardless of whether they're a trader or not. I feel as though I paid for an education in professional trading and got a brand-new life thrown in for free.

> I feel as though I paid for an education in professional trading and got a brand-new life thrown in for free.

For instance, I'm now much more grateful for everything in my life. The practice of gratitude is humbling. Not only does it keep me grounded as a trader, it keeps me grounded as a human being. Instead of demanding that the market perform for me, I'm grateful for any success it might give me.

In addition, I've gained a much greater appreciation for living in the present and not worrying too much about everything else. For much of my life, I missed what was going on right in front of me; I was either too caught up in the pain of the past or too busy trying to anticipate the future. But the future isn't even here yet, so I can't control it, and the past has come and gone. It's done, so nothing will be gained by wallowing in it. The only thing I can control is my awareness of my thoughts. Why not just be in the moment all the time? It is definitely productive for trading.

I've also accepted that I am totally responsible for everything that happens to me. I am the captain of my own experience. I am the one who creates my results. When things go wrong in my life, I am the one who, willfully or not, wasn't paying attention. Blaming others for your failures can give you temporary relief from having to look at your own faults, but it creates a lot of emotional baggage that weighs you down and keeps you from moving forward. Not carrying around that baggage anymore has been enormously freeing, but I was only able to let it go after I admitted to myself that I was responsible for my life. It's a difficult thing to do, but when you finally get to the point where you ask yourself, *How did I create what just happened to me?* It's amazing what you can discover.

Finally, I've found great success by simply asking for what I want out of life and then letting the universe respond. The Law of Attraction is alive and well, and I definitely believe in it. One of my favorite lessons in the Transformational Meditation portion of the Super Trader program was the idea that "you get what you focus on, so focus on what you want." I have often applied that principle with great results, and I believe it can be a foundational principle for your success, too.

From Army Major to Systems Expert

Kenneth Long, DM

Dr. Ken Long is a retired army officer and combat veteran who teaches strategy, tactics, and logistics at the U.S. Army Command & General Staff College. He completed his doctorate in management (organizational development) in 2011, having researched the use of action learning to improve decision making under uncertainty. Ken began trading in 1982, and lately has been researching statistically based market indicators for use in adaptive trading systems. He is director of research for Tortoise Capital Management (www.tortoise-capital.com), a financial research firm with international and institutional clients. He is a regular workshop presenter for the Van Tharp Institute, where he presents most of their technical workshops. Ken is the proud father of three great kids and has been married to Linda for 26 years. He has a black belt in Judo and Jiu-Jitsu and coaches competitive youth soccer year-round.

 Before: Highly stressed trader who was continually frustrated by his lack of success.

 After: Statistically oriented trader who develops systems. His long-term systems consistently outperform the markets, and his short-term systems easily allow him to make 5R per day.

I first started saving and investing many years ago, when I was still a private in the army. I was a Holy Grail seeker, dabbling in a variety of methods for trading on a shorter-term basis, including the CANSLIM method of William O'Neil, the price-range level of Darvas boxes, various techniques using Point and Figure charting,

Vector Vest software, and recommendations given in various news-letters and methods promoted in popular investing books. From about 1980 to 1993, I jumped from one idea to the next, spending less and less time with each idea as my impatience and frustration with the lackluster results they produced grew. I had developed a fairly successful technique for rotating my money in and around various mutual funds, and I was wise enough to protect myself from life-changing losses by keeping my speculations in a very small por-tion of my portfolio, but I never really studied my performance because I was too preoccupied with my search for the Holy Grail.

I jumped from one idea to the next.

I seemed to have the right knowledge, habits, and experi-ence to be a successful trader. I'd been trained in the principles and practices of modern management and leadership thanks to a career in the military. I'd been an excellent student, and I was a successful professional. My education even included a master's degree in systems management.

And yet, the kind of success I was looking for as an investor continued to elude me. Some of the qualities and habits that made me successful in other parts of my life weren't helping me with my trading, and trying to separate what worked from what didn't was a challenge, one that left me frustrated at times. Just as I thought I'd learned something valuable, "the truth" would change and I would be back at square one. The net result was that I was becoming very haphazard and uncertain about my trading. I was convinced that there was something knowable about the markets, something I could apply to my trading to improve my results, but I didn't know how to discover it, and worrying that it was becoming too large a part of my life.

In the late 1990s, I was fortunate enough to come across Dr. Tharp's book, *Trade Your Way to Financial Freedom*. That book introduced me to Tharp Think and started me on a lifelong journey of research and application—of developing trading and investing strategies that fit me and my objectives. Since then I have studied and applied Van's principles, and, as a result, I am achieving my personal and financial objectives using low-risk ideas, positive expectancy systems, position sizing, and risk management.

I am grateful for the chance to share what I've learned. As I already mentioned, I began as a reader from a distance, but my involvement quickly deepened after attending a systems workshop in 1999 and participating in various VTI workshops thereafter. Van always says that I was the only person he'd ever met with a degree in "systems," and in 2000 I was invited to be a guest speaker at one of the workshops. Pretty soon I became a supportive teacher, and now I get to design and deliver my own seminars to share the things I've learned along the way. I'd like to share a few of those things here—strategies and principles that have had the greatest effect on my trading.

While playing the fascinating game of life, I've actually gotten a DM in another area that Dr. Tharp calls strange—decision making under uncertain conditions. It would have proved difficult without doing this work with Tharp Think. Tharp Think has been an important guide in my inner search for beliefs, feelings, values, and truth, and has encouraged me to achieve the goal of improving and aligning my actions and results with what I value.

What I Have Learned and How I Have Changed

The Power of Beliefs

When I first heard Van assert that everything about trading is psychological, and that I can only trade my beliefs, I took it with a grain of salt. Nothing in my experience suggested that these assertions were true. How could my internal beliefs be so important to overall results? I was certain that there had to be a number of external variables that contributed to trading performance. Still, I was intrigued enough by Van's ideas and impressed enough by his reputation that I was willing to try his suggestions under low-risk conditions. It wasn't long before my results started confirming what I heard Van saying. Once I started digging deeper into trading systems, I began to see how everything is connected at a deep level to my psychology, especially when it comes to putting my money on the line.

Here's an example of what I mean. Let's say I receive a recommendation from an expert to trade a particular market a certain way. How might my psychology influence what I do with the advice?

1. *The expert might remind me of my father (in a good way):* This might lead me to give his recommendations the benefit of the doubt, even after an objective analysis of the results suggests that his recommendations are no longer meeting the expected returns of the system.

2. *The expert might remind me of my father (in a bad way):* I might be looking for ways to criticize his recommendations and take the other side of the trade, even though it might be the wrong side.

3. *I might be stubborn:* This psychological state could drive me to persist in certain behaviors that are measurably bad for me. It could cause me to reject evidence that would lead me to a better set of rules. It could cause me to stay with a bad system too long, or trade a good system at a risk level that is too low, or reject a good system that doesn't conform to my beliefs.

4. *I might value comfort more than measuring reward-to-risk ratios:* I might reject signals taken in extreme market conditions or trade a lower level of risk than is warranted by the measured results of a system. I might reduce my risk in overnight positions, when the system relies on advantageous overnight moves after the trade has started off well. This could lead me to miss the most lucrative signals in a system that relies on taking contrarian positions.

5. *I might over-weight my own experience (overconfidence):* This might lead me to start making changes to one kind of system that are based on my experience with a different kind of system, causing it to underperform.

6. *I might under-weight my own experience (underconfidence):* This might lead me to ignore opportunities to improve a good system because I don't believe I have the skills, perceptions, or analytical experience to develop my own expertise.

7. *I might be impatient:* This could lead me to try to front-run a developing signal before the system confirms the opportunity. I might abandon a system after a streak of losing trades that, given the system's win rate percentage, was perfectly normal. I might increase the size of my risk per trade beyond my stated limits based on a normal winning streak that makes me feel overconfident.

8. *I might be overly aggressive:* This could motivate me to make risky trades, which could lead me to second-guess my entry and exit criteria because of fear of losses.

9. *I might have a persecution complex (inherited from a time when people really were trying to get me):* I might adjust the rules of a system to meet my own psychological needs and then, after experiencing results that are different from the system's published results, attribute the difference to an intent within the system, or by the system's developer, to deceive me.

10. *I might have a need for certainty about why specific trades won or lost:* This could motivate me to look for answers that offer complete explanations and overly complex models of how the market really works, which in turn could lead to further modifications that end up transforming what may have been a simple three-rule system into 40 pages of conditional rules that cannot be computed in real time.

Even the fundamental decision to grant expert status to an author or a system designer is connected to my psychological state—to my beliefs about what constitutes expert status and how much deference I should pay to expertise in a certain area.

The previous 10 examples only scratch the surface of how our individual psychology can affect the way we choose, implement, modify, and analyze a system. And, as if our personal biases weren't enough, studies of cognitive neuroscience show that the human mind comes pre-equipped with hundreds of biases that have developed over millions of years to help us adapt to life in the Stone Age, but that, in today's world of high-speed digital markets, cause us to behave in seemingly irrational ways. In other words, we're born with brains that are actually hardwired to fail in modern markets.

That might sound daunting, but there's good news: We are far from helpless. If we understand the connection between our assumptions and our actions, our beliefs and our behaviors, we suddenly have the power to change those behaviors. Since I discovered Tharp Think, I've explored my own trading decisions to see how my beliefs influence my behavior. I try to track them back to their source and examine the evidence for each one. Those that are useful, I keep; those that are not, I monitor. The goal is to collect just enough validated beliefs to develop simple, robust trading systems. Lately, I've been trying to reduce my own beliefs about the market to the bare minimum. I see them as lenses that limit my vision and distort my understanding of the world.

This way of thinking has me asking the following kinds of questions:

1. Do I have to believe in a system in order to trade it?
2. What is the purpose of the belief? Is it just to give me enough confidence to act?
3. Does a belief have to be true to be useful?
4. Where do my beliefs really come from, and how much choice do I have in them?
5. What's the difference between a belief and a value?
6. Can I choose my beliefs and my values?
7. What beliefs and values would I choose if I could?
8. What stops me from choosing and then acting on my beliefs and values?
9. What is more important than living in accordance with my chosen beliefs and values, and why?
10. What purpose do I serve?
11. How can I align my daily actions with my life's purpose and live intentionally to the best of my ability?

Statistics-Based Trading

Tharp Think tends to be statistics based. Why? I think it's because statistics help us understand the behavior patterns found in complex situations. Some things are so complex that they cannot be reduced to a set of precise rules or solved like arithmetic. However, even complex things can be thought of in terms of probabilities and a range of possible results. That's where statistics come into play.

A simple example is rolling two six-sided dice. Under normal conditions, I cannot predict what the result of the next roll will be, no matter how many times I've recorded the previous results. No amount of study will improve my ability to predict the next roll. However, given enough opportunities, I look at probabilities. By doing so, I can frame trades (bets) that will favor some two-combination numbers over others. For example, I could bet that seven will come up more often than any other combination of two numbers. In fact, the dice game of craps is actually a system designed to assure that the house will always make money over the long run—just as your system should ensure for you. This requires a belief that the system generating the results will be stable and consistent with what you've seen so far, but that's a reasonable belief, given a system that involves fair rolling of two dice.

Statistics are a way to provide insights into complex situations where individual outcomes cannot be predicted, but where broad sets of events can be described effectively. Because many markets behave in a certain way for extended periods of time, a statistics-based approach to trading can help identify favorable conditions to the degree that I can expect the system to remain stable. In a way, the use of statistics helps me trade certainty for probability with confidence. Here are a few examples:

- What is normal volatility and what's extreme (either extremely quiet or extremely volatile)?
- How big is the average move that a stock makes daily, and what's its standard deviation?
- How often does a stock gap in the morning, and what's the size of the average gap?
- How many trading opportunities will a system give me under different market conditions, and what's the expectancy under those conditions? In other words, when should I trade the system, and when should I avoid it?
- How far away from its 200-day moving average can the S&P 500 stretch? Can I use that to describe market conditions?
- How many major stocks fit a certain condition (i.e., they're below their 200-day moving average, they're overbought according to some indicator, etc.)?

To go further, statistics not only give me a way to evaluate potential opportunities, they allow me to analyze my results and determine if the system and the market are still in sync, given the kinds of results my backtesting entitles me to expect. If I understand sampling and the conditions under which I take my samples, I can determine the potential for positive future results.

Some of my best trading systems come from using statistics to analyze result patterns. Typically, I first look at the market and, using small position sizes, try to trade how I feel about it. I then examine the results and the behaviors that influenced those results, which allows me to develop rules that can be defined, measured, and implemented. I call this style of trading "Ready, Fire, Aim." To make the process work, I have to turn feelings into measurable facts. Statistics are an excellent way for me to achieve this, because they describe the market conditions that cause me to feel the way I feel about the opportunities I see. Once I describe the conditions, I can test them with rules to see if they harbor any trading opportunities. So the steps would be:

- Notice when I have an intuition about trading the market.
- Determine the market conditions using statistics. I already keep these on an ongoing basis, so all I have to do is see what they are when I get that urge.
- Look at the condition in the past (and the future) to see if it really does give me good opportunities.

There is a deep connection between a statistics-based view of the market and a decision-making process that strikes a healthy balance between thinking and feeling. Short-term trading systems provide me with many opportunities that can be described statistically, but that also give me plenty of exercise in decision making. I believe (a belief!) that I need both orientations in order to perform well in short-term trading.

I have found that my *useful feelings* seem to come from years of experience trading certain markets and symbols in a consistent, satisfying way, while *the feelings that aren't useful* seem to be connected to my all-too-human cognitive biases. However, even these feelings can be useful. In trading, my only really useless feelings are the ones that don't give me a trading edge either way. I try to remember that it's always good to feel my feelings and let them simply be what they are: an important part of my life, but one that doesn't get to command all of my decisions.

If I try to suppress my feelings or shape what I feel with my rational mind, I'm implying that I believe my feelings are something I can actually command. Instead, my feelings seem to be part of my preconscious mental processing. By the time I recognize them as feelings, they are already happening and running through my heart and mind. I don't think I can prevent what has already happened, but I can learn to recognize the signals that powerful feelings are coming, and manage my decision making in a way that doesn't resist the feeling, but lets it run through its natural channels without triggering a trading action. Another name for this is impulse control. It's the difference between action and reaction. See the chapter in Section II called "A Journey through the Stunning World of Feelings and Trapped Emotions."

This element of Tharp Think has been an important part of my stress management strategies, which are very important to have when I use my shorter-term trading systems, because these systems maximize the number of potential stress events I encounter each day.

Trading Extremes

One of my most useful beliefs is the idea that from extreme conditions come extreme moves in either direction. I believe that extreme market conditions are more likely to produce herd behavior. When such conditions prevail, each trader's confidence in her rationally deduced rules is put to the test, and emotional responses are more likely to take over.

> From extreme conditions come extreme moves in either direction.

The market can shift rapidly from rationality to fear or greed, producing the kinds of large moves in both directions that always seem to catch traders by surprise. Deep down, we must believe that markets are fundamentally explainable, orderly, and certain, because our response when they behave otherwise is typically not one of readiness, but of panic.

Using statistics and various timeframes allows me to define exactly what I mean by an extreme move. Extremes can be defined as abnormally large movements in the market over a certain time-frame when compared to a look-back period, or even as the absence of movement. I can define the size of the subsequent move based on a reversion to the mean or a continuation of the panic. Periods of unusual quiet can create surprisingly large moves, just as the aftermath of an extreme move can produce monumental follow-on moves.

I like to think of it this way: A sudden splash in a very quiet pond can signify an important event, and a sudden large wave indicates the possibility of more large waves to follow.

The market can shift rapidly from rationality to fear or greed.

Reward-to-Risk Assessments

An important feature of Tharp Think is that it emphasizes reliance on reward-to-risk ratios rather than on always trying to be right. For instance, if my reward is three times my risk, then, even if I'm only right half the time, I can still make good money. I have learned to look at every trade in terms of reward-to-risk ratios. I look at what I consider to be reasonable and achievable rewards within a given timeframe and compare those rewards with manageable risks that include slippage, liquidity, time of day, and other environmental variables. Using this reward-to-risk perspective has led me to consider the other side of the trade. I have learned to try to understand why the other people are making the decisions they're making. This perspective effort has been particularly useful when it comes to trading sideways volatile markets in which directionality is less important than the degree of volatility and follow-through.

I have also found that the ability to frame new trading opportunities in terms of reward-to-risk ratios has enabled me to exit and re-enter trades at opportune moments throughout the day, week, and month. It gives me a common framework for making consistent decisions, which removes much of the psychological pressure that comes from needing to be right on each particular trade.

Here's a good example: When I'm trading with 3-minute candles, I may have a winning trade in hand that is starting to stall and retrace after a nice 30-minute move. I have exit rules that cause me to harvest the profit before too much is given back. Sometimes, rather than failing further, the price will move sideways for three to five more candles and then begin to go back up. This will often trigger a re-entry for me close to the price where I exited. I used to think that such profit-taking exits were "wrong" and "wasted" until I realized that risk-reward conditions and market psychology can change quite a bit even in 10 minutes. I now see that exiting in this way is "correct" because it is based on the information that is available at the time. The original trade can easily retrace all the way back to my original entry, and my profit exit is designed to cash a winner and prevent giving back the profits I already have in hand. *Failure to fail further*, though, was new information that wasn't available to me at the moment of exit. Once I can see that the price is holding a support level and continuing to go up, I can apply risk-reward analysis to determine if the new trade is still favorable and then re-enter if I so choose.

R-Multiples

Tharp Think further emphasizes reward-to-risk ratios by requiring people to express trade results as some multiple of the initial risk. If, for example, I get stopped out at my starting risk level, then I have a 1R loss. If I make three times my initial risk in profit, I have a 3R profit, and so on.

Trading systems can be described by the distribution of R-multiples they generate. I've discovered that it is useful to use R-multiples in different market conditions and across different timeframes to make decisions about portfolio asset allocation. I want to compare systems based on their reward-to-risk characteristics to decide how much money to place with each system, and R-multiple distributions allow me to do that. Here is an example.

I have a couple of swing trading systems that perform very well when the market is trending either up or down in swings that last at least one to two weeks at a time. The swing trade timeframe allows those systems to capture meaningful pieces of those kinds of moves. The results histograms of the R-multiples show how a group of individual trades have performed during those times. When market conditions start to change, the shape of the results histogram changes. I can analyze the change to see if the market is getting choppier or if the trends are getting longer. For choppier markets, I favor shorter-term systems, take profits sooner, and am ready to reverse direction. In longer-trending markets, I favor systems that pyramid into trades that start well and have a higher current relative strength.

Position Sizing Strategies™ and Bullets

A key Tharp Think principle is the use of position sizing strategies to achieve trading objectives. A position sizing strategy is not an internal system criterion, like when to enter or exit; rather, it helps determine the appropriate risk exposure to use for a system in the current market. Once I develop a number of robust systems for multiple timeframes and multiple market conditions, I can use position sizing strategies that are appropriate for each system. By using position sizing strategies, I was able to develop a standardized risk allocation to normalize my performance on a daily and weekly basis as a short-term trader.

Because of my background as an career army officer in the infantry, I use the term *bullet* to describe this unit of risk. For me, a unit of risk is a specific dollar amount that allows me to treat each trade unemotionally. When I have more than one unit of risk on a single position, my emotions become noticeable, and I am tempted to modify my rules. I have internalized the concept of a *bullet* so that I can execute trades with a standard unit of risk in a routine manner. Periodically, and after reviewing my performance monthly, quarterly, and annually, I have been able to raise the size of my unit of risk so that, as I have become a better trader, my risk level has increased step by step.

Because I restrict myself to a certain number of bullets, I select only the best targets when trading short-term systems. I want to be sure that I am using my precious ammunition wisely. This metaphor is particularly effective because it ties into my lifelong military career; it helps me apply my military discipline to my enthusiasm for trading. Left unchecked, I am more likely to play hunches and chase the next idea, especially when the market is moving quickly and I've recently had a noticeable string of winners or losers. Long runs of wins or losses invoke a number of different well-known cognitive biases that can affect my judgment and upset my equilibrium as a trader. Defining my position sizing strategies, daily risk tolerance, and risk-per-trade tolerance in terms of bullets has been an important edge in my short-term trading that comes directly from Tharp Think.

SQN Performance to Evaluate Systems, Targets, and Markets

One of the most recent aspects of Tharp Think is the use of the System Quality Number (SQN) score to evaluate systems. It allows me to clearly differentiate systems across timeframes and market types. Dr. Tharp basically looks at the system's mean R-multiple, standard deviation, and the number of trades to determine how good the system will be under the conditions in which the R-multiples were taken.

I clearly remember the day I was sitting in the back of a Van Tharp Institute Workshop and had a flash of insight that the SQN score can also be used to compare the relative quality and reliability of individual stocks, exchange-traded funds, or any other trading target. This insight led me to develop a number of different market classification strategies that incorporate SQN scores over different look-back periods to produce that moment's blended SQN score. By looking at the SQN score as a time series and using descriptive statistics to find the difference between normal and abnormal conditions, the trader and investor can tune their systems to those market conditions in which their system should work best. In addition, I can use these insights to find the best-performing stocks.

For example, the academic literature on momentum has found a small but persistent advantage for the next year in stocks that have outperformed over the past 12 months. By applying an SQN score for the past three and six months' analysis to symbols that have been outperforming in the past 12 months, you can find a set of targets that have your preferred mix of gains and volatility. Moreover, you can further identify those whose gains are improving compared to their volatility.

I feel there is a lot more gold in that mine to discover. Most recently, I have been examining the rate of change of SQN scores over different look-back periods to get early indications of a change in market state or within the quality state of individual targets. These kinds of state changes cannot be detected by looking at charts or from my feelings because there are simply too many variables, and our memories can be misleading.

Market Classification Strategies

One of Tharp Think's basic principles is that you cannot expect a system that works well in one type of market (bear volatile) to work well in other types of markets (bull quiet). It is basic sampling theory, which says that the more carefully you define your sample, the greater insight you can find, but only for populations that look very much like your sample. Selecting samples from different market types should make it easier to discover things that would work in each kind of market.

I think this concept is very useful. Even though the market is a complex mixture of multiple market types, I believe it is possible to identify conditions that will favor a particular style of trading. By designing a system for that market type, I can be prepared to profit when the market enters that market type. In bull quiet markets, I look for targets that are breaking out from a base with high relative strength compared to their peer group. In bear volatile markets, I carry no overnight risk, but go short those targets that have broken through yesterday's low and are making new lows of the day. There is no reason or need for me to believe that those two different rule sets should work for all targets, in all markets, and in all timeframes. They are each tuned to a specific kind of market. A golfer uses specialized tools for different parts of the course, and I try to emulate that idea in my trading. A 5-iron might be an average general-purpose club, but it will never putt like a putter, or drive like a driver, or chip out of a bunker like a sand wedge.

Looking at longer timeframes, the market seems to me to have the quality of weather and climate: long, slowly developing trends with more or less short-term volatility. Perhaps these cycles are aligned with business cycles, in which case I can make clear distinctions about strategies that will have some persistent value until the climate changes. My current practice is to use long-term market classification strategies to hold my long-term positions, with wide enough stops to screen out short-term noise and volatility. My market classification strategy, therefore, has to be sensitive enough to detect climate changes and yet smooth enough to keep me in good positions during periods of bad weather.

For day-trading systems, I consider the market conditions of the last 10 days, and for swing trade systems, I use a six-month look-back period to provide the market context. I use those timeframes to help me understand what the market is doing compared to that style of trading. Those look-back periods help me estimate what I can expect to see during the same look-forward period in the future. I think this gives me an edge when I am estimating reward-to-risk ratios.

What's interesting is that Van and I have entirely different methods to determine market type. Both of them seem to work well and give similar numbers most of the time.

Transformations

Working with Tharp Think principles for 15 years has produced a profound transformation in my trading. These are the five changes that are the most important for me.

Improved Systematic Performance

Before Tharp Think, my performance was all over the map. I didn't even have a method for analyzing my performance to see what was or wasn't working. I didn't have formal rule sets that I could use to achieve reliability and consistency; nor could I determine what my specific errors were. That was a problem, and it led to underperformance compared to the market. I had some large wins, but my large losses were wiping those out. After Tharp Think, I became much more systematic. I wrote rules that I could actually execute in real time. I improved my discipline to follow those rules, regardless of my feelings. I kept records of my trades to give me something to analyze for performance improvement. I began meeting my financial goals in both long- and short-term timeframes.

Specific Systems for Specific Market Conditions

Before Tharp Think, I didn't really have multiple strategies. I was busy chasing ideas across many timeframes, without a sense of market conditions and how they can affect system performance. After Tharp Think, I use a decision-making framework to organize my trading capital into three timeframes. I use a monthly rebalancing system to take care of my long-term financial objectives, swing trade systems to harvest multiday moves when markets are trending, and intraday systems to take advantage of statistically extreme moves that have begun to revert to the mean. By focusing on the beliefs and techniques that are useful in each system and timeframe, I can keep them compartmentalized. My results in each timeframe have steadily improved and enabled me to meet my short- and long-term financial objectives.

Detailed Documentation and Analysis of Trades

Before Tharp Think, the only thing I looked at was my account's bottom line. I had no detailed evidence to use as the basis for making decisions. Because I didn't have a systematic way of recording my trade decisions, I couldn't isolate the things that were working from the things that were failing. After Tharp Think, I was able to apply the discipline and attention to detail from my military career to my trading process and set the foundations for a lifetime of disciplined trading. By using trade logs, case studies, and the 12 Tasks of Trading, I've built habits that help me navigate through turbulent markets while utilizing the skills I learned through life and active duty in the army.

Evidence-Based Management

Before Tharp Think, I relied on how I felt about my most recent trades to make decisions about what to try next. I was making decisions on little more than random events and mercurial moods. After Tharp Think, I wait until I have enough data from the results of a disciplined system before I make deliberate decisions. This has helped me separate myself from my systems to the extent that I can evaluate them on the basis of their performance without it carrying over into how I view myself as a trader. I am now able to evaluate systems without their performance being an integral part of my identity. I don't feel the need to be right.

Reduced Stress

Before Tharp Think, trading was a source of extreme stress for me. As a combat veteran and a career army officer, I know stress when I feel it. I was trading with far too much risk and then changing my reasons for being in the trade once it started to move against me. I was living and dying with each tick. I was having trouble sleeping at night based on how much risk I was accepting, and it was harming my health and relationships. After Tharp Think, I've reduced my trading stress significantly. I have reduced my risk per trade, identified more manageable trading opportunities, aligned my systems to appropriate markets, and learned through position sizing strategies to adapt my risk to the opportunity that is reasonably available. Trading has gone from a compulsion and an obsession to a professional activity that supports my values and life goals.

Before Tharp Think, trading was a source of extreme stress for me.

Performance

Now that I've shared with you some of the ideas I've learned over the past 15 years, I'd like to show you some of the specific results that putting those ideas into practice has produced, both for myself and for others.

Long-Term System with Monthly Rebalancing

Since 1999, I have been publishing a long-term core investment system that I based.on Tharp Think principles. It did very well during the Internet bubble. Discounting the exceptional performance of 1999 as an anomaly, it has returned the annual performances shown in Figure 4.1, which have been published on a regular basis during that time.

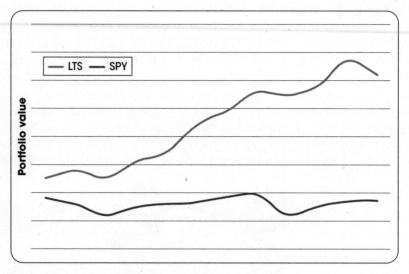

Figure 4.1   Long-Term System (100,000 portfolio)

Year Beginning	LTS	SPY
2000	100,000	100,000
2001	126,600	90,200
2002	139,108	79,268
2003	127,117	60,759
2004	155,973	74,241
2005	172,225	79,980
2006	219,931	82,779
2007	246,301	92,572
2008	279,305	96,451
2009	273,915	61,864
2010	289,528	75,282
2011	334,810	84,835
2012	311,373	85,683
Total	**+211.37%**	**−14.32%**

Through 12 years, the S&P 500 was down 14.32 percent while the LTS made 211.37 percent.

Weekly Swing Trade with Once-a-Week Portfolio Adjustments

A weekly, long-only swing trade strategy that I designed for a group of private investors using Tharp Think principles, that used end-of-week data and once-a-week portfolio adjustments, had the performance shown in Figure 4.2 across a couple of years during one of the worst bear markets in history.

Through five years, the S&P 500 was down about −7.44 percent, while the swing trading system made 27.76 percent.

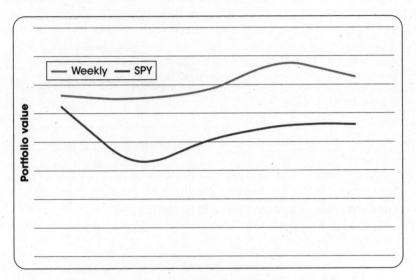

Figure 4.2   Weekly System (100,000 portfolio)

Year Beginning	Weekly	SPY
2007	100,000.0	100,000.00
2008	112,810.0	104,190.00
2009	110,632.8	66,827.47
2010	116,938.8	81,322.34
2011	135,228.1	91,642.15
2012	125,762.1	92,558.57
Total	**25.76%**	**−7.44%**

Pattern Swing Trade Using End-of-Day Data

A pattern-based swing trade system that used only end-of-day data and that was designed using Tharp Think principles for a group of private investors performed as shown in Figure 4.3.

Through six years, the S&P 500 made 3.5 percent, while the swing trading system made 54.16 percent.

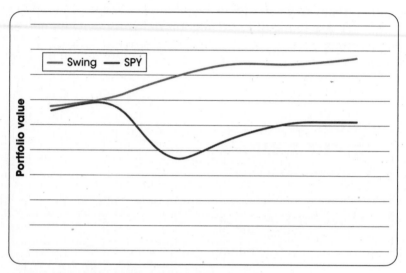

Figure 4.3   Swing System (100,000 portfolio)

Comparison of Swing Systems with the S&P 500

Start of Year	Swing	SPY
2006	$100,000	$100,000
2007	$114,970	$111,830
2008	$122,765	$116,516
2009	$139,142	$74,733
2010	$148,784	$90,943
2011	$149,231	$102,483
2012	$154,155	$103,508
Total	**54.16%**	**3.51%**

Live Trading Workshops Results

As of this writing, I have done four live trading workshops. The first was in May 2011 under bull normal conditions (VTI model). The second was in October 2011 under bear volatile conditions, and the third and the fourth were in March and September 2012, respectively, under bull quiet conditions. Most of the traders present were Super Trader candidates who did fairly well.

May 2011 (Bull Normal Conditions)   A group of 10 individual traders, half of whom were in the Super Trader program, used Tharp Think principles to trade short-term systems. Even though this was the first time these traders had traded these systems, the trading room results at the end of the workshop were all similar. The results of the most recent workshop are shown in Table 4.1.

- 407 total trades over a five-day period
- 187 winners, 27 scratch trades, 193 losing trades
- 46 percent winning trades, 6.7 percent scratch trades, 47.3 percent losing trades
- Average win: 1.12R
- Average loss: −0.64R
- Net R for the week: 86.56R

There were 13 traders in the room, although not all stayed for all five days. That averages out to 7R per trader per week. Each trader made about 1.45R per day of trading.

Table 4.1   Live Trading Results after Teaching These Systems (May 2011) Bull Normal Market Conditions

	Number of Trades	Net R (gain/loss)	Average R	Percent of Total
Win	187	209.44R	1.12R	46%
Scratch	27	0R	0R	6.7%
Loss	193	−122.88R	−0.64R	47.3%
Total	407	86.56R		

October 2011 (Bear Volatile Conditions) During October 2011, a group of 11 individual traders, most from the Super Trader program, used Tharp Think principles to trade short-term systems. Even though this was the first time most of these traders had traded these systems, the trading room results at the end of the workshop were all similar. The results of that workshop are shown in Table 4.2.

- 242 total trades over a five-day period
- 123 winners, 36 scratch trades, 83 losing trades
- 50.8 percent winning trades, 14.9 percent scratch trades, 34.3 percent losing trades
- Average win: 1.27R
- Average loss: −0.6R
- Net R for the week: 105.6R

Table 4.2 Live Trading Results after Teaching These Systems (October 2011) Volatile Bear Market Conditions

	Number of Trades	Net R (gain/loss)	Average R	Percent of Total
Win	123	156.06R	1.27R	50.8%
Scratch	36	−0.74R	−0.02R	14.9%
Loss	83	−49.7R	0.60R	34.3%
Total	142	105.62R		

There were 11 traders in the room, although not all stayed for all five days. That averages out to 9.6R per trader per week. Each trader made about 2R per day of trading.

March 26–30, 2012 (Bull Quiet Conditions) During March 26–30, 2012, a group of 10 individual traders, half from the Super Trader program, used Tharp Think principles to trade short-term systems. Even though this was the first time most of these traders had traded these systems, the trading room results at the end of the workshop were all similar. The results of the most recent workshop are shown in Table 4.3.

- 304 total trades over a five-day period
- 136 winners, 55 scratch trades, and 113 losing trades
- 44.7 percent winning trades, 18.1 percent scratch trades, 37.2 percent losing trades
- Average win: 1.24R

- Average loss: −0.78R
- Net R for the week: 80.52R

Table 4.3   Live Trading Results after Teaching These Systems (March 2012) Bull Quiet Market Conditions

	Number of Trades	Net R (gain/loss)	Average R	Percent of Total
Win	136	168.66R	1.24R	44.7%
Scratch	55	0R	0R	18.1%
Loss	113	−88.14R	−0.78R	37.2%
Total	304	80.52R		

There were 10 traders in the room, although not all stayed all five days. That averages out to 8R per trader per week. Each trader made about 1.6R per day of trading.

September 24–28, 2012 (Sideways to Bull Quiet Conditions)   During September 24–28, 2012, a group of 16 individual traders, one third from the Super Trader program, used Tharp Think principles to trade short-term systems. The results of the most recent workshop were as shown in Table 4.4.

- 370 total trades over a five-day period
- 175 winners, 35 scratch trades, and 160 losing trades
- 47.3 percent winning trades, 9.5 percent scratch trades, 43.2 percent losing trades
- Average win: 1.09R
- Average loss: −0.68R
- Net R for the week: 82.44R

Table 4.4   Live Trading Results after Teaching These Systems (September 2012) Bull Quiet Market Conditions

	Number of Trades	Net R (gain/loss)	Average R	Percent of Total
Win	175	191.49	1.09R	47.3%
Scratch	35	0R	0R	9.5%
Loss	160	−109.05	−0.68R	43.2%
Total	370	82.44R		

Ten of the 16 traders in the room stayed all five days. There was an average of 12 traders per day, so the results average out to 6.87R per trader with each trader making about 1.37R per day of trading.

Notice how the results were quite similar for all four live trading sessions. Furthermore, not every trader makes money, but some make a lot more than the average.*

In each of the different timeframes, swing and day trading, Tharp Think focused the design of the system on goals and objectives and created specific rule sets that could be executed with discipline and whose results allowed for analysis to support professional discipline. Risk management and position sizing strategies were integrated into the system rules, and the traders were satisfied with the results and the performance.

Time and again, trading systems based on Van's principles and techniques deliver amazing results, and results ultimately speak for themselves. Over the past 15 years, I have watched my trading improve as my understanding of the way I think and react to a wide range of market conditions has deepened. The market can be a volatile, unpredictable place. You cannot control it, but you can control yourself. To do that, you must know yourself, and that, more than perhaps anything else, is what Tharp Think understands.

---

*Ken does not include his own trading results in these data, but he has made as much as 50R during the five days.

5

Using Tharp Think to Go from Full-Time Broker to Full-Time Trader

Martin Horsey

Martin Horsey has worked in financial futures since 1985. He worked for a Scandinavian conglomerate bank where he traded from the office and on the floor. He then worked for 18 years as an institutional futures broker for major brokerage houses. In 2005, he established Cavalo Trading Limited with his wife and has since traded his own money. He is almost exclusively a full-time day trader who trades multiproducts across the financial spectrum.

 Before: Top institutional broker who could find very few good traders among his clients.

 After: Consistently profitable trader who can now make as much money as he used to make in commissions with much less hassle.

It was February 2005, and I was making a radical change in my vocation and lifestyle. I had been an institutional futures broker in London for the previous 20 years, executing orders on the futures floor (LIFFE) and then running a team of brokers from the office. I was giving up security and a lucrative salary package to become my own employer and trade financial futures with my own money. It was something that I had aspired to do throughout my brokering career. I wanted to be the organ grinder, not the monkey. For years, I had explained to my clients how I was eventually going to be a trader, and now I was going to prove my point.

I wanted to be the organ grinder, not the monkey!

Looking back, out of the over 200 institutional traders for whom I'd executed over the years, there were very few to whom I'd actually have given my own money to manage.[1] Most worked for banks on comfortable base salaries with no realization of how much capital they were managing. They had very loose goals and objectives. Yes, they were good at handling customer business and making money on the spread they offered clients. But when it came to outright trading, they traded on the back of economic releases, research provided by their analysts (most containing ideas that were probably at least 24 hours old). They seemed to have very little planning or commitment. Watching these traders taught me a lot of valuable lessons. Day after day, it was drummed into me how many ways you could lose money in the futures market. I was able to learn some very valuable lessons on how *not* to trade from the unsuccessful majority, and some more valuable lessons on how to trade properly from the few traders I knew who were winners. This experience was what I would take into my new venture.

My New Venture

Eight trading days after striking out on my own, things were not going quite as I'd planned. Only one of those days had been a winning day; all the rest had been losers. I was running my stake on the principal of a fund that can't have drawdowns, and I was already down 4 percent. I was trading as a day trader, taking trades based on my experience, gap trades, chart patterns, and so on. And I was listening to my gut, too; after all, I'd been calling the market correctly for the past 20 years, I thought to myself—as you do when you only remember the winners.

In those early days, there was one thing that always kept me in the game: I always had my stop. It was something I'd learned from fixed-odd sports betting. If you had a sports bet, you could only lose what you stake. In Tharp Think terms, this is the risk, the R-value. What you get back is your R-multiple. If you backed a horse at 3-1 and won, you had a 3R winner. The problem with sports betting is that you tend to have a lot of 1R losers that, over time, inevitably cancel out any multiple R-winners, and then some. You also become very opinionated in terms of backing your favorite horse, team, or player. In time, I would come to realize that opinions are not that important in the market—that they can, in fact, be a detriment. Most news and research is already known and therefore already reflected in price. The only early indication you can get of a pending move comes from watching price—or, in stock terms, the tape. This idea would eventually become the basis of my trading.

By March 2007, I'd hit a low point. "I can't do this," I told my wife. I was a little over two years into my trading journey and I'd just overtraded again. Instead of my usual 10 or 20 lot, I'd just traded a 100 lot—badly. It was 7:40 A.M. on a Friday morning at the end of a losing week, and I was trying to get back all my losses in one quick trade. Instead, I'd just doubled them. I now know that this was a revenge trade, and it was the biggest mistake I'd ever made. "Well," my wife said of my upcoming plans, "that's why you're taking the course."

Going to North Carolina

It just so happens that I was scheduled to leave London that very day and go to Cary, North Carolina, to attend Dr. Van Tharp's Peak Performance 101 workshop. I had first heard about Van Tharp many years before, in 1988, when a previous employer had attended his courses following the release of the book *Market Wizards,* a chapter of which was devoted to Van and his ideas on the psychology of trading. Memories of the chapter had come back to me in late 2006 while I was attending a tennis psychology session with my then 12-year-old daughter, who was a national tennis player. Roberto Forzoni, a sports psychologist, was giving her suggestions to improve her tennis, and as I listened I realized they would help my trading every bit as much as they'd help her game. Sports concepts such as routines, discipline, planning, preparation, and releasing the point were all applicable to trading. I was reminded of Van's chapter and, thanks to the wonders of the Internet, soon found the Van Tharp Institute's website, which listed a mixture of courses and books for both beginners and Super Traders. I opted to attend the Peak Performance Workshop, because it seemed relevant to me and where I was in my trading.

The previous two years had not yet brought me the results for which I'd hoped. Two successful but choppy years had produced approximately 15 percent returns—which may sound good, but it was only a fraction of what I'd earned as a broker, and by the time you factored in my screen costs, Internet costs, and news subscriptions, there wasn't a huge amount left for living expenses. Then, in February 2007, my old firm had an IPO. Had I stayed with them, I'd have made far more money from this than I'd made trading. This spurred me to want to make much more, and fast. The result? A 14 percent drop in February 2007, which practically put me back to where I'd started, only now with a hell of lot less confidence and optimism.

Peak Performance 101 was taught exclusively by Dr. Van Tharp over a three-day period. I'd read *Trade Your Way to Financial Freedom* in the months prior, and it really opened my eyes. It told me that I needed to treat my trading as a business, because it was a business. I'd been trading with no plan, no objectives, and few rules; my only goal had been to make as much money as possible in the shortest amount of time. In order to be successful, I needed to prepare well, have a plan, and stick to the plan. I needed to have specific goals, targets, and objectives for both the downside and the upside. Most importantly, I had to work on myself, to look at the way I traded, and see what specific system suited me. Could I take drawdowns? Did I need a system with a lot of winners? By asking myself those questions, I'd be able to find a method of trading that fit me.

At the workshop, I was taught more about how to put all of the preparing concepts I'd read about in the book into practice. After I returned home, I spent the rest of 2007 working, not only on trading, but specifically on me and the things I needed to improve about myself in order to be a successful trader. The last nine months of 2007 were losing months, but I was trading very little. I was instead spending most of my time preparing.

One of the most important concepts that Van taught me was how much mistakes cost you and how important it is to eliminate these mistakes. A mistake is not following your rules. In other words, any trade that didn't follow your plan was a mistake. Revenge trades, boredom trades, trading products I knew nothing about—these were all behaviors I'd engaged in before and needed to eliminate.

I also needed to look after myself and make sure I was fit to trade. I joined a gym for the first time in my life. Not only did the exercise sharpen my mind, it helped me lose 28 pounds, which made me feel good about myself.

In November 2007, I returned to North Carolina. It was then that a short consultation with Van was to have a dramatic impact on my trading. I was attending a workshop called "How to Develop a Winning Trading System That Fits You," On the last day, Dr. Tharp explained to the group how he was currently writing a new book called *The Definitive Guide to Position Sizing™ Strategies,* and how position sizing was a major factor in developing a trading system. It was then that the significance of the marble game and the importance of R really hit me. I remembered another chapter in *Market Wizards* by legendary day trader Marty Schwartz, who said that the most important thing in trading was "money management, money management, money management." Schwartz was one of my heroes, an ex-broker turned trader who had become a market wizard. Now I realized that position sizing was money management. It was an important revelation, the final part in my preparation. I was now going to use position sizing—money management—as the cornerstone of my trading.

Van says, "It is through position sizing strategies that you meet your objectives. The better your system, the easier it is to use position sizing strategies to meet your objectives. But it is only through such strategies that you meet your objectives." I cannot stress how important this concept was to me. *My objective was to make 20 percent a year while having peak-to-trough drawdowns no larger than 5 percent.*

Restarting Trading

By the end of 2007, I had my plan, and in January 2008, I resumed trading full time. I had a great start to the year, successfully incorporating the knowledge I'd gained, not only about trading, but about myself. I'd read an old report on money management that

Van had written in the 1990s and began to incorporate some of the principles it outlined. I started using some leverage on my futures account, which meant that my daily, weekly, and monthly results had a lot more relevance to my overall net worth.

The work that Dr. Tharp's teaching had nurtured was now bearing fruit. I'd started keeping a daily log in early 2007, and it soon became invaluable. I tracked and recorded the risk, or R, for every trade and then looked at all my results in terms of R-multiples. For example, if I risked $5,000 and lost $4,000, my result was minus 0.8R. Because of the frequency of my trades, I now had a big enough sample for each setup to come up with solid beliefs regarding my overall system.

Van's book *The Definitive Guide to Position Sizing™ Strategies* didn't arrive until summer, just as the financial crisis of 2008 was exploding. Volatility went through the roof, but by using the sound position sizing strategies I'd developed, I was able to limit my downside risk and at the same time exploit the opportunities that such markets offered day traders.

In *The Definitive Guide to Position Sizing™ Strategies,* Van introduced a new measure called the System Quality Number (SQN), which measures the quality of a system. I had about 20 or so system setups, so I went about finding the SQN for each of them. I increased the amount I risked on those systems with a high SQN and either lowered the risk or retired those with a low SQN. Throughout 2008, I had a great run. I thrived on the volatility, and since I was trading futures, I had no bias toward short or long and was therefore able to exploit the vicious downward moves in the fall of 2008. I used the money management principles described in Van's book to be aggressive with my winnings and cut back in times of drawdown. What was the net result? I was up over 50 percent, and because of my new leverage, 2008 was my first million-plus trading year.

The volatility continued throughout the first quarter of 2009. Then, I hit a nine-month period during which I basically made no money at all. The important thing to me, however, is that I did not lose during that period. I stuck to my new plan and adhered to my rules. It was the Van Tharp Institute teaching on psychology that saw me through this frustrating period.

Then I noticed that new data samples were making variable changes in the SQN for my set-ups, and realized that the market type had changed. Van stresses that it's easy to design a good system for any particular market type (such as bull quiet), but crazy to expect the same system to work in all market types. You basically need different systems for different market conditions.

My rollercoaster ride of profits and emotion.

Stocks were now in a quiet bull period, the direct opposite of the volatile bear market of 2008. I now decreased the amount risked on certain volatility expansion setups I was using and increased the risk on the reversion-to-mean strategies. The different R-multiples that this change in market type had created were teaching me the importance of recognizing market type and adjusting my position sizing strategy accordingly. Some strategies that were producing an SQN score of over 4 in 2008 became negative expectancy systems in 2009 and vice versa. My proficiency as a broker had enabled me to watch many different markets at once, and now I moved the various setups into the markets for whose state they were suited. Some markets, such as commodities, were still very volatile, so I began to trade these with the volatility expansion setups, while other markets, such as stock indices and bonds, became more suited to reversion-to-mean strategies. The key was to adapt to the market type: Find ways of recognizing these market types when they occur (using ATR, charts, etc.) and adapt accordingly.

Where I Am Now

As I start my eighth year of trading, I can look back on a roller-coaster ride of profit and emotion through the markets. The financial crisis of 2008 allowed me to watch and participate in financial history. I am proud of the fact that my biggest drawdown in the four years since, using month-end figures, has been 4.13 percent while at the same time averaging 27.58 percent per year in growth. I am constantly seeing the markets evolve with changing market hours, high frequency, and algo-trading having marked impacts on the market day. I need to constantly adapt for these and other changes.

I make a point of visiting Cary, North Carolina, every year to reinforce the methods shown to me, and I use these periods as an opportunity to meet different traders, see their perspectives, and learn from them. This gives me the impetus to think of new ideas that might be suited to the ever-changing market. More than once, I have come away with new positive expectancy systems that I am still using today.

The last course I attended at the Van Tharp Institute as of this writing was in November 2011. The course was taught by Ken Long, the author of Chapter 4 of this book, and focused on system ideas, which was ideal for where my trading is now. Ken's passion and energy for trading were infectious, and his knowledge of market mechanics was invaluable. Combine this with Dr. Tharp's trading psychology and money management concepts, and you have an unbeatable formula.

Table 5.1 reflects my yearly and monthly performance before and after being exposed to Tharp Think.

Of the 35 months during which I traded before learning Tharp Think, I made money in only 20, or 57.14 percent, and achieved an average monthly gain of only 0.22 percent. My best month was 5.8 percent and my worst month was −14.8 percent. My average yearly gain was only 2.6 percent.

After Tharp Think, my results were quite different. Of the 48 months from January 2008 to December 2011, I made money in 36, or 75 percent. My average monthly gain was 2.3 percent. My best month was 10.30 percent and my worst month was −3.65 percent. My average yearly gain was 27.57 percent.

Table 5.1 Monthly Performance: February 2005 to December 2011

	JAN	FEB	MAR	APR	MAY	JUN	JUL	AUG	SEP	OCT	NOV	DEC	Year Total
2005		-0.70%	3.20%	5.80%	-1.70%	5.20%	3.50%	-0.70%	-3.20%	1.30%	3.80%	-2.90%	13.60%
2006	1.90%	-4.00%	3.90%	2.60%	0.70%	1.30%	2.50%	-0.10%	1.40%	5.40%	2.10%	-2.10%	15.60%
2007	-7.90%	5.40%	-14.80%	-3.00%	0.70%	0.90%	-1.70%	-4.00%	1.50%	-0.20%	1.80%	-0.10%	-21.40%
													2.60%*
2008	9.70%	4.10%	1.80%	10.30%	2.70%	4.20%	0.44%	1.93%	10.17%	5.60%	-0.74%	0.53%	50.73%
2009	5.33%	9.38%	9.13%	-1.92%	2.77%	1.00%	-0.85%	-0.30%	-2.98%	4.06%	-2.62%	0.12%	23.12%
2010	2.12%	1.29%	4.00%	-3.65%	1.81%	1.96%	1.76%	1.84%	3.34%	0.82%	-1.69%	6.55%	20.15%
2011	2.75%	-2.21%	4.36%	1.38%	0.65%	1.98%	0.61%	5.14%	-2.47%	5.48%	-0.35%	-1.02%	16.30%
													27.58%*

Shading denotes trading period prior to learning Tharp Think

*Annual Average

CHAPTER 6

Adapting Tharp Think
to Your Trading

Van K. Tharp, PhD

 Before: Made his first trade in 1964 and over the next 20 years made every trading mistake possible.

 After: Now manages the Van Tharp Institute retirement fund and constantly outperforms the market while maintaining the objective of not having a losing year.

In the early 1990s, about 90 percent of my coaching work was psychological. I did two-day weekend coaching sessions to help people make huge breakthroughs. My goal at the time was to give my clients everything they needed in two days so that they could trade more effectively and not need to see me again. For many of my clients, that seemed to work.

I specifically remember one client who worked for a large hedge fund in their London office. Most readers would probably know the primary name associated with that fund if I were to reveal it. Anyway, the fund had an internal coach who had adopted the concept of *trader jail*. If you had a drawdown over 10 percent, you lost half of your capital and were severely restricted in what you could do. My client hadn't had big enough drawdowns to get into trader jail, but the possibility had him frozen. We worked through that issue and a number of other potential issues, and he left appearing quite happy, but I never heard from him again, so I didn't know what the result was.

The possibility of trader jail had him frozen with fear.

About four years later, I worked with another London client who'd been referred to me by the first trader. My response was, "Great—I assume he did fine if he recommended me." Apparently, he had, because now he was running the London office of that fund.

So, why did I mention this? I've always said that becoming a good trader requires the same amount of work as any other profession (if not more). To be a doctor, you need college, medical school, an internship, and a residency, yet most doctors seem perfectly willing to take their excess money down to a brokerage company, open an account, and start trading with no training whatsoever except for whatever they may have read in some book on how to pick stocks—not that you even have to read a book to open an account. The implication is that if the e-trade baby can trade, so can you.

It's the same for any other professional—engineer, accountant, attorney, architect, or even the manager of some business. They studied and trained hard to learn the skills they need in their profession, but they think they can just open an account, trade, and immediately make millions in the market. But it doesn't work that way. It takes a lot of work to become successful as a trader. Some of the best traders are willing to go through all sorts of hoops to get and maintain their success. Consistently making 15 to 20 percent or more on a billion-dollar account is not easy.

This introduction is my way of saying that the guidelines I'm going to give you in this chapter will be a lot of work. But so is any worthwhile endeavor. And the good news is that successful trading can be modeled and taught to others.

That said, there are five key areas you need to work on in your trading journey. The first area will be covered in this chapter and involves adopting the principles of Tharp Think. The second area will be addressed in the application chapter for Section II, and the final three areas will be addressed in the concluding chapter of this book.

Area One: Thoroughly Understand the Principles of Successful Trading

These principles are what we've called Tharp Think throughout Section I of this book. They are given in the tables below in various groupings. When you read the rules, notice what your thoughts are. If you get a big a-ha! out of them, then you probably understand what you're reading. If you don't understand them, think they're an oversimplification, or just want to know what to buy or sell, then you have a long way to go.

Let's start by naming some primary assumptions of Tharp Think that were introduced earlier and then discuss the various implications of each assumption.

The first key assumption is that trading is as much a profession as any other profession. It takes significant time (several years) and a deep commitment to become a successful trader. Malcolm Gladwell has suggested that it probably takes 10,000 hours of excellent practice to master anything. That doesn't mean 10,000 hours of normal practice will make you a skilled trader; it means 10,000 hours of *good* practice.

I'm a firm believer in simulations because you can run them at any time. With a good simulator, you could make 100 simulated trades in three days—trades that could take several months to finish in live trading. If you did that, you could achieve 10,000 hours of good practice in only a year or two.

We have a simulated trading game, the first three levels of which you can download from my website and play for free. The simulator:

- Helps you understand R-multiples.
- Allows you to really refine your objectives.
- Shows you that you don't need to be right 50 percent of the time to make money.
- Shows you the power of a big R-multiple.
- Helps you understand the power of position sizing.

The second key assumption is that trading reflects human performance just as much as any top athletic endeavor. You must understand that you are responsible for the results you get and that you should therefore devote significant time to working on yourself in order to be successful.

Look at the following statements, and notice that you could use either trading or athletic performance in the description:

- If you are conflicted inside, you could easily mess up your trading.
- If you are concerned about losing, you probably will.
- If you are full of nonuseful beliefs, you probably won't approach the markets well.
- If you are dominated by some negative emotion, it will probably influence your trading.
- If you are sick, you probably will perform poorly.

While these statements have numerous implications, they are primarily covered under level two transformations in Section II of this book. However, the good news, once again, is that successful trading can be modeled and the results of that modeling can be taught to others.

Let's go through six key parts of Tharp Think. I'll briefly describe the useful beliefs in each area and then answer some common questions that tend to arise about each part.

Part 1: Learning to Trade Is Hard Work, but It Can Be Taught

Tharp Think Principles	Check
1. Successful trading can be modeled and taught to other people.	❑
2. Learning to trade well requires as much work/education as any other profession.	❑

The first question that normally comes up is:

Will I need a teacher to go through this, or can I do it on my own?

I've designed this book so that you can do it on your own. That doesn't mean, however, that everyone can do it. Some percentage of the population will always need additional help. For example, I think I answered all of these questions in the book but people are still asking them. So I'm answering questions with the idea that they might help a few more people to do it on their own.

How do you measure success? Are any statistics available?

That question reminds me of the time when a finance professor wanted to determine if I was correct about position sizing strategies and some of the other concepts in *Trade Your Way to Financial Freedom* but didn't consider the psychological component in his analysis. Most people don't get the psychological component and can't adopt it, and their trading suffers as a result. You cannot separate Tharp Think from the psychological components necessary to achieve it.

Most people who complete the psychological portion of the Super Trader program do quite well. All our graduates are very successful and all of them, except the one who works for me, trade for a living and are happy doing it.

Doesn't the hard work trump your beliefs?

Let me repeat what I said earlier. Great trading requires a lot of work—around 10,000 hours of *efficient* practice. If you were to put in 10,000 hours worth of practice that was grounded in nonuseful beliefs and end up losing money in the process, then your work would have been pretty useless. That's why you need to transform yourself in order to efficiently adopt a level one transformation.

Part 2: Knowing Yourself

A key to successful trading is knowing yourself. Only by knowing yourself can you develop objectives and trading systems that fit you. In other words:

Tharp Think Principles (Continued)		Check
3.	You need to find a trading system that fits you.	☐
4.	In order to accomplish that, you must know yourself:	☐
	(a) Your values	☐
	(b) Your strengths	☐
	(c) Your weaknesses	☐
	(d) Your parts (see Section II)	☐
	(e) Significant beliefs (spiritual, self, market, system)	☐
	(f) Trading edges	☐
	(g) Trading weaknesses	☐
5.	You can only trade your beliefs about the markets, not the markets themselves. Thus, you should know and understand your beliefs and whether or not they are useful.	☐
6.	System development is 100 percent (1) beliefs, (2) mental states, and (3) mental strategies. Thus, it is 100 percent psychology.	☐
7.	You must know your personal criteria for being able to trade a system with confidence.	☐

Should I focus on improving my weaknesses or just make sure I recognize them?

Most weaknesses will cause you to make mistakes, so you should focus on improving them. If you make a level three transformation, which involves raising your consciousness, you will have already fixed many, many weaknesses.

What do you mean when you say that we trade our beliefs?

The market is really just the execution of millions and millions of buy and sell orders. You have no way of conceptualizing that, so you invent something like a bar or a candle to represent price. Saying that a bar represents price is a belief. Most people go further and perhaps decide that they'll only buy when they see a series of green candles, or that price should be above or below some line that represents an average in order to act. These, too, are beliefs. You can't get away from them unless your consciousness is very, very high, but you can examine them and decide if they're useful or not.

Can you give an example of a trading edge?

Sure. Here are several examples:

- Understanding that you don't have to trade every day; you can wait for a great opportunity to come along. There are some institutional traders who are required to trade every day, even if there are no great opportunities.
- Understanding position sizing strategies and how to use them to meet your objectives. Doing so puts you in the top 10 percent.
- Being aware of your thoughts and feelings so that you can work on them before they sabotage you.
- Knowing your reward-to-risk in a trade. It should always be 3 to 1 or better at the beginning of a trade and at least 1 to 1 toward the end. If you know your reward-to-risk, then you can manage your exits well.

There are many such edges, and you need to learn how to recognize them.

What do you mean by personal criteria for trading a system?

You could have a great system but not be able to trade it for various reasons. These might include:

- Some of the assumptions or beliefs on which the system is based might conflict with your own beliefs.
- You might not have confidence in the system.
- The timeframe might not fit you. For example, I'm a full-time coach and company president, but I also manage our company retirement account. We have a lot of good short-term trading systems, but I don't have enough time to trade them.
- Perhaps you get too excited when you watch the markets closely and end up doing stupid things. You'd be better off with a system that only requires you to look at what the market did at the end of the day and perhaps make a stop adjustment.
- Perhaps a particular strategy is too complex for you, causing you to frequently make execution mistakes when you try to trade.

Is it possible that many types of trading fit me, and that I am able to trade many kinds of systems?

Anything's possible, but it's not likely. We teach many good systems in our technical workshops, and I find that when my Super Trader candidates get my approval for a system they want to use, they've usually taken one of the systems we teach and *modified* it in some way to fit them.

Part 3: Mistakes

Once you start trading, you'll probably make mistakes. I define a mistake as not following your rules. When you understand mistakes, you'll have a whole new avenue to follow to improve your trading efficiency (i.e., to make fewer mistakes) and improve your profits. These are all covered by the next set of rules.

Tharp Think Principles (Continued)	Check
8. A mistake means not following your rules. If you don't have rules, everything you do is a mistake.	❏
9. It is much better to trade a lower-scoring SQN system that fits you than a higher-scoring SQN system that doesn't fit you.	❏
10. You are responsible for everything that happens to you. When you understand this, you can correct your mistakes. We call this *respond-ability*.	❏
11. Repeating the same mistake over and over again is self-sabotage.	❏
12. A trader who makes one mistake in 10 trades is 90 percent efficient; that 10 percent drop in efficiency could be enough to make him/her a losing trader.	❏

Through my modeling work with traders, we've developed a number of trading tasks to help prevent and eliminate mistakes. These tasks usually assume that the trader has already addressed and resolved a number of personal psychological issues that cause repeated mistakes; we'll address how to avoid those mistakes in Chapter 18.

If someone hasn't done significant psychological clearing, how can he know the difference between expected system performance and the impact of mistakes? It takes a certain level of awareness to be able to see mistakes.

It isn't difficult to know whether you've followed your own trading rules. Every time you don't follow one of your rules, you've made a mistake, because not following your rules is precisely what a mistake *is*. It's pretty simple.

With that guideline in mind, you can start keeping track of the impact your mistakes have on your trades in terms of R. Some examples of this are given in Chapter 18. Using this sort of approach, you can see when you're trading at 75 percent efficiency (i.e., one mistake per four trades) and understand that one mistake can cost you 3R. Can you lose 3R every four trades and still be profitable? Most people cannot.

Part 4: Objectives and Position Sizing Strategies

A key undersanding is (1) that objectives are much more important than most people think, and (2) that you achieve your objectives through position sizing strategies. The quality of your system just tells you how easy it will be to use position sizing strategies to achieve your objectives. Most people don't even think about objectives, except that they'd like to make a lot of money. Most professional traders don't have a clue about position sizing strategies. They learn that asset allocation is important but don't understand that the *how much* factor is what makes it important—and that's precisely what position sizing strategies are all about.

Let's look at the implications of this:

Tharp Think Principles (Continued)		Check
13.	Fifty percent of system development is thinking through and clearly defining a set of written objectives. Those objectives should address your desired gain, your maximum acceptable drawdown, and the relative importance of each.	❏
14.	You need to design core objectives that fit you.	❏
15.	There are potentially as many objectives as there are traders.	❏
16.	You meet your objectives through position sizing strategies.	❏
17.	The overwhelming majority of your performance is due to your position sizing strategy and your efficiency as a trader.	❏
18.	You must know your mission/purpose in life and incorporate that into your trading.	❏
19.	You need to know your financial freedom number (passive income per month less monthly expenses). When it's positive, you are financially free.	❏

Here are some questions people have asked about objectives and position sizing.

Why are objectives so important in designing a good system?

That's best answered by another question: How can you get what you want if you don't know what you want? Most people don't know what they want.

Can you give some examples of core objectives?

You have to decide what you want. For example, I manage the Van Tharp Institute retirement plan. My core objective is to not lose any money by the end of the year. However, I am willing to give back most of the profits I've earned in the year for the potential of large gains. And I have a strategy that's pretty good for meeting those objectives.

If I were trading a speculative account for me only and day trading, my objectives would be to limit my monthly loss to 2 percent and to aim for 25 percent in profits. Again, I'd be willing to give back profits for larger gains. These would be monthly goals.

Can't my objectives just be to make as much money as possible with the smallest drawdowns possible? What's the downside to always having those as my objectives?

If you don't know what your downside is, then "making as much money as possible" is a very weak objective that is too general to allow you to effectively use position sizing strategies.

I've heard that risking 2 percent of your account equity on any trade is too much. Do you agree? That doesn't sound like a lot, and I'm worried I can't make money if all I risk is 2 percent per trade.

Risking 2 percent is a lot, not a little. In Dr. Ken Long's chapter, he gave examples of people who made 50R in five days at our live day trading workshops. If you were risking 2 percent, it would mean that you were up 100 percent in one week. However, the risk per share is so small that risking 2 percent in one trade would exceed the margin requirements of most accounts. Thus, how can you be concerned about making money when 1) it could cause you to exceed the margin requirements of your account when your stops are narrow and 2) you could make 100 percent per week risking 2 percent? I'd be much more concerned with the potential for huge losses risking 2 percent per trade.

Can you show me concrete examples of the impact of small changes in position sizing strategies on a system in terms of total dollars/percent returns?

Let's say you're trading a system that makes 50R in a year and has a peak-to-trough drawdown of 22R at some point during that year. Further, let's assume that your account value begins at $100,000. Table 6.1 shows the impact of various position sizing strategies. However, remember that these are rough numbers. The actual numbers will depend on the actual sequences of the R-multiples because risk percentages are made on the current equity, not the starting equity. For convenience, the table assumes that all the calculations are based on the starting equity. As you can see, when the risk is based on the starting equity, a 22R drawdown would bankrupt you if you were risking 5 percent.

Table 6.1   The Impact of Various Risk Sizes on Drawdowns and Equities

Risk Percent	End of Year %	End of Year Profit	Drawdown %	Drawdown Loss
0.25%	12.5%	$12,500	5.5%	$5,000
0.50%	25%	$25,000	11%	$11,000
1.0%	50%	$50,000	22%	$22,000
2.0%	100%	$100,000	44%	$44,000
3.0%	150%	$150,000	66%	$66,000
4.0%	200%	$200,000	88%	$88,000
5.0%	250%	$250,000	Bankrupt	Bankrupt

Part 5: Probability and Reward-to-Risk Assessment

Trading/investing is all about probability and reward-to-risk ratios under specific market conditions. When you understand these rules and the market conditions at any given time, you can use statistics to predict some boundaries for your performance. While you cannot predict the future, you can get a good idea of what your performance will be through statistics and proper sampling under the different possible market conditions. As you begin to understand this, you'll be amazed at the changes that occur.

There are a huge number of implications to this rule. First, let's look at reward-to-risk ratios and R-multiples and what they mean for systems.

	Tharp Think Principles (Continued)	Check
20.	Never open a position without knowing the initial risk.	❏
21.	Define your profits and losses as a multiple of your initial risk (R-multiples).	❏
22.	Limit your losses to 1R or less.	❏
23.	Make sure your profits on the average are bigger than 1R.	❏
24.	Never take a trade unless the reward-to-risk ratio of that trade is at least 2:1 and perhaps even 3:1.	❏
25.	Your trading system is a distribution of R-multiples.	❏
26.	When you understand #6, you should be able to hear/see a description of a system and know the kind of R-multiple distribution it would generate.	❏
27.	The mean of that distribution is the expectancy, and it tells you what you'll make on the average trade. It should be a positive number.	❏
28.	The mean, standard deviation, and number of trades determine the SQN score for your system.	❏
29.	Your SQN score tells you how easy it will be to meet your objectives using position sizing strategies. Other than that, your system has nothing to do with meeting your objectives.	❏
30.	Systems are usually named after their setups, which are usually based on some attempt to predict future prices. Prediction has nothing to do with trading well.	❏
31.	System performance has to do with controlling risk and managing the position through your exits.	❏

If prediction has nothing to do with trading well, what do we try to achieve when we open a position? It seems to be prediction.

You are not predicting what the market will do, you are making a reasonable estimate that your risk-to-reward ratio is at least 2 to 1. If that's the case and you're right at least 50 percent of the time, then you'll have a positive expectancy system.

What makes calculating risk with R-multiples better than other methods?

There are two ways to calculate risk. Method one is based on knowing when you are wrong in a trade and getting out when that condition is met. That determines 1R for you.

Method two is what Wall Street would have you think of as risk, which is volatility. In my opinion, this is a pretty meaningless definition of risk. You'd be saying that futures are more risky than mutual funds. While futures do have more leverage, if you risk 1 percent of your equity, it doesn't matter whether you're invested in unleveraged equities or highly leveraged futures. There's more risk for an inexperienced person investing in mutual funds than a professional investing in futures.

R-multiples have nothing to do with calculating risk, but with how you measure profits and losses. When you measure profits and losses in terms of your initial risk (i.e., R-multiples) you start thinking in terms of reward-to-risk in your trading, which is a huge edge for you.

In gathering R-multiple distributions for systems, can backtesting results be used or is forwardtesting necessary?

Backtesting is fine, but some people do way too much. Forwardtesting with very small position sizing is also fine (i.e., one share of stock).

Why should we not take a trade with a reward-to-risk ratio below 2:1? Isn't it possible to develop a system on a really short term (scalping) that is profitable because the winning percentage is bigger than the losing percentage?

Anything is possible. But trying to be right is a sure path to disaster because of the psychological issues involved, and trying to predict is a path to disaster because, in my opinion, no one can really do it. Paying attention to reward-to-risk, on the other hand, makes it much easier to be net profitable after a number of trades.

What about a system that has a large win rate (80 percent+) but the average profit is less than the average loss? It violates the Tharp Think principle about having a large reward-to-risk ratio, but expectancy and SQN may be good. Many systems that sell option premiums are in this category.

What you usually don't see in those systems is the huge negative R-multiple that could come up against you because you're only seeing small losses. Most of those systems are a disaster in the long run.

Does a big positive R have a negative (lowering) impact on the SQN score even if the downside risk is limited? If yes, how could we manage this?

The SQN score of a system is designed to show you how to achieve your objectives with position sizing. If you tend to make most of your profit from a few huge R-multiples, you cannot risk that much per trade because you are likely to have many losses in a row. Risking a lot when you have, say, 20 straight losses means you probably have very little money left when the big R-multiple comes along.

For example, assume that you risk one percent per trade on a $100,000 account and you have 20 straight losses. That one percent is of your remaining equity and at the end of 20 losses you would be down to $81,790.60. Now if you got a 30R winner and you are risking one percent of your balance of $81,790.60, your new equity would be $106,327.90 You've had 20 losses and one winner, but you are still up 10R and your equity is up by 6.3R percent.

But let's say you risk five percent per trade on your balance. At the end of 20 straight losses, you would be down to $35,772.89 or down 64 percent. If you risk five percent on this amount and get a 30R winner, you would be up to $89,621.48. You are up 10R, but because of your position sizing, your equity is still down over 10 percent.

However, a system that gives you 20 1R losses and one 30R win every 21 trades only has an SQN score of 0.65. If you had a system with an SQN of about 7.0, then you probably could quite safely risk five percent per trade and expect to be up significantly at the end of 21 trades. And an SQN system of 7.0 is unlikely to have 20 losses in a row.

You emphasize exits and position sizing strategies over entries when developing a system. But wouldn't a low-risk idea mean that entries are important? I define a good entry as one that has a high probability of going in the right direction, a minimum amount of risk, and, most importantly, a good reward-to-risk ratio (2 to 1, but preferably 3 to 1). Couldn't improving your entry timing also greatly reduce your risk?

Your entry and your initial stop define what 1R means for you. Once you do that, you can estimate a target and a probable reward-to-risk ratio. But even there, it's your exit combined with your entry that's important. Entry by itself is relatively unimportant. Entry with your initial stop-loss is very important in setting up what 1R means.

Part 6: Systems and Market Type

The next significant aspect of thinking about probability and reward-to-risk is that all markets are not alike. When you buy a trading system or buy into a fund, you're usually expected to sign something that says you understand that past performance does not necessarily reflect future performance. This reflects a basic lack of understanding about statistics. What they should say is:

- We have traded this system under certain market conditions. We know how it performs under those conditions, but we don't know how well our samples represent the potential performance of trading under those market conditions.
- If our samples are accurate, we still have not simulated enough performance from those samples to predict what might happen in the future under those trading conditions.
- We don't know how the system might perform under market conditions for which we have not traded it. In fact, we probably haven't even thought enough about that to know whether we've made some assumptions that might cease to exist if certain things about the market were to change.
- We might make mistakes trading the system in the future, and that would definitely cause the system to underperform under those market conditions.

That's what funds really mean when they say, "past performance does not necessarily reflect future performance." This principle is reflected by the following concepts:

Tharp Think Principles (Continued)		Check
32.	There are at least six different market types. You should understand how your system will perform in each of them. 1. Bull volatile 2. Bull quiet 3. Sideways volatile 4. Sideways quiet 5. Bear quiet (almost doesn't exist) 6. Bear volatile	❏

Tharp Think Principles (Continued)	Check
33.	It's easy to design a Holy Grail system (one with a high System Quality Number score) for any one market type listed above.	❏
34.	It's insane to expect that trading system to work in all market types.	❏
35.	The biggest mistake people make is to try to design one system to fit all markets.	❏
36.	You should only trade your system in the market type for which it was designed.	❏
37.	Good traders understand the big picture, know how to measure it, and become aware when the situation changes.	❏
38.	Media and academia know none of this and will not teach it to you.	❏
39.	For each market type, you need a large sample size to estimate what the population is for that system.	❏
40.	You also need to do Monte Carlo simulations with your system's R-multiples to get a better idea of what to expect in the future. This will work if the sample you draw from is similar to the population.	❏

Can you explain a procedure for knowing when to enable/disable systems because of changing market types? Is it a binary switch, or do you start reducing/increasing capital allocated, and so on?

Our market type tends to move gradually. Let's say we have a strong bull market, and that, after two weeks of high volatility moves with price going nowhere, it moves down to bull. Then it declines for three weeks and moves to neutral. If you have a system that only works in bull markets, you probably shouldn't be trading it.

However, one alternative some good traders use is to trade equity curves. If the equity curve in your system starts to go down, remove capital from the system. If it goes down as much as 10 percent, you could take 90 percent of the capital away from that system, but you'd still be trading it at 10 percent. When the curve starts to move up, you can allocate more capital.

Is there any market type for day trading?

There are many different ways to measure market type; you have to find one that fits you. Overall, the long-term market type based on 100 days is probably not too meaningful for a day trader, but volatility is definitely meaningful, and whether you have a trending day or a fairly flat day is important. You could probably use the first half-hour of trading to estimate that.

Most of these rules came from modeling great traders, although a few of them are unique to me. I call them Tharp Think because our program is unique, as far as I know, in combining them.

What these rules seem to have in common is a statistical approach to markets that relies on thinking about reward-to-risk rather than being right. They also emphasize that great performance is a function of the market, your system, and you.

Steps to Learning Tharp Think

First, study all the points in the boxes. Some of them are obvious, and just reading them may be an ah-ha! experience for you. Check these off in the space provided. If you don't understand some of them, reread the chapters in Section I of this book.

Other key points may not be so obvious to many people. They may require you to read more and to use and apply them to really get them. For example, R-multiples are important if for no other reason than that they get you to consistently think about reward-to-risk ratios in a trade—and that's really important. But I've seen comments on blogs like "Why should I convert everything to R-multiples? I'm perfectly happy with profits and losses." If this is you, or if some of the points are not that obvious, you may have to study more. Here are some suggestions:

- Go to the glossary at www.vantharp.com and study all of the terms mentioned. See how many of the concepts you understand after reading the thorough definition of them.
- Subscribe to our free e-mail newsletter, *Tharp's Thoughts*, on the same website. It's free, and we frequently discuss the concepts mentioned here.
- Most of the concepts in my books have appeared in past issues of *Tharp's Thoughts*. All of these back issues are available for free at our website.

If you still don't understand everything, I suggest the following:

- Read *Trade Your Way to Financial Freedom,* 2nd edition. When you read it, have the idea in mind that you want to understand the key concepts that are not obvious to you.
- Read *Super Trader,* revised edition, with the same goal in mind.
- Read *The Definitive Guide to Position Sizing™ Strategies.*
- We periodically do a one-day workshop or six-part webinar about Tharp Think. Go to matrix.vantharp.com for more information. If you mention this book when you order, we'll give you a 15 percent discount.
- Finally, as suggested earlier, download our trading simulation game, which will teach you these concepts by allowing you to actually apply them. The first three levels of the game are free.

You can download the game at www.vantharp.com

SECTION

II

PSYCHOLOGICAL TRANSFORMATIONS TO HELP YOU FUNCTION AT A SUPERIOR LEVEL WITHIN THE MATRIX

Van K. Tharp, PhD

In the first section, you were introduced to Level I transformations, which involve the adoption of a number of core beliefs we call Tharp Think. The section included five chapters that detailed the stories of people whose success increased after they adopted Tharp Think principles to their trading.

Quite frequently, though, there are significant issues in your life that must be removed or "transformed" before you can truly adopt Tharp Think principles. These transformations are what we call Level II transformations. This section introduces you to a number of people who have made huge transformations through some

111

form of Level II change. The psychological sections of Tharp Think apply here. These principles are summarized in Chapter 12.

My Super Trader candidates typically spend 1,000 to 1,500 hours working on their personal transformation. They take four psychological workshops—usually several times each. They do 20 psychological lessons to take them through my Peak Performance Course. They do a 28-day transformational course that requires about three hours' worth of work a day. I also usually ask them to do outside work, such as the 365-day daily lessons from *A Course in Miracles* or the Sedona Method Course. Most of them also become Oneness Blessing Givers as I find this process to be extremely transformational.

Section II of this book deals with some of their psychological/ spiritual journeys, but different portions of the journey were more important for some than others, so the chapters in Section II each focus on a different area of transformation.

Chapter 7 deals with beliefs. You already understand that beliefs form a filter through which you determine reality. It's like the movie *The Matrix*, only the robotic programming seems real and it's done through your beliefs. When you realize this, you can systematically begin to examine every belief and determine whether or not it serves you. Is each belief useful for operating as a trader in the Matrix?

Ultimately, all beliefs in some way limit you because they separate you from Oneness. To the extent that you must operate within the Matrix, however, you are at a huge advantage when you understand how you are programmed. Just like Neo, the main character of the movie, you can start a process of reprogramming yourself by getting rid of nonuseful beliefs and constantly adopting more useful ones. As you begin to do this, your whole life will change, and your success will blossom.

Beliefs are easy to change when you find one that's not useful. All you do is notice that it is not useful and find something that is more useful. This is only possible, however, when the nonuseful belief doesn't have charge or emotion linked to it. A charged belief is one for which some strong, negative emotion comes up when you think about it. When a nonuseful belief has charge associated with it, you must remove the charge through some sort of feeling release.

In Chapter 8, one of my Super Trader candidates describes an extensive feeling-release process he went through. There are many processes for releasing feelings—at least five of which are taught in the Sedona Method course and another three of which are taught in my Peak Performance Course and Peak Performance 101 workshop. The person writing this chapter went through a particularly heavy version of feeling release that lasted several months, and he tells you exactly what he did and what happened.

Getting rid of nonuseful beliefs

Chapter 9 deals with an understanding of the parts inside you and how to get them to work together. Essentially, you are a crowd inside. There are lots of roles you play in life and each of those "parts" thinks it is you. For example, you might be an engineer and have an engineer part. Collectively, through all of those parts, you adopt an identity that is Who You Think You Are. We start to examine these parts in Chapter 9. I take you through a parts-negotiation exercise I did with a CBOE floor trader in 1987—just a few days before the October 19th crash. This floor trader was easily able to make $100,000 each year, but he could never make much more than that. Part of him felt as though he didn't *deserve* any more than that. After I finished working with him, essentially doing parts negotiation, he avoided losing money in the 1987 crash. That was major, because more CBOE option traders went bankrupt as a result of that crash than traders in any other area of trading. Later, he was able to make $700,000 in the few weeks following the crash. Obviously, his $100,000 income ceiling was gone. This chapter was adapted from my *Peak Performance Course for Traders and Investors.*

The floor trader I interviewed in that chapter went on to become a great humanitarian. He gave lectures in Chicago high schools to help kids succeed. He tutored other people and opened up a retreat center for traders. And his entire demeanor changed from that of a tough guy to that of a spiritually advanced person. He died about 14 years later and had a total sense of peace about him when it happened. He was a great friend and is deeply missed.

Perhaps one of the most important things you can do in your trading journey is to get out of the way and let your Higher Self lead you. One of the strongest examples of this occurred in the mid-1990s when I was working with a retired professor of engineering. We worked for two days on clearing out issues. At the end, he went through an exercise involving connection with his Higher Self, and it really worked. He learned how to trade through that connection and increased his net worth substantially over the next 14 years. By the time God told him to stop trading right before the 2008 crash, he'd accumulated enough money in his retirement account to live comfortably for several lifetimes.

Chapter 10 is a description of my own journey following my Inner Guidance. It is a very powerful story and one, of course, that I know very well. I remember often getting the feeling that I should do something, but not knowing whether I could distinguish my intuition from "into wishing." Later, an inner voice would give me guidance, but sometimes it was my Higher Self giving me advice and sometimes just another part trying to *imitate* my higher self. It was hard to tell the difference, so I didn't know whether I could trust it.

In 2008, I became involved with the worldwide Oneness movement, and it's been the most powerful transformative journey I've ever taken. When I discovered Oneness, everything changed, including my relationship with that inner voice. My spiritual journey is far from over, but I'll share what's happened so far in Chapter 10.

Lastly, one of my associates has developed a form of parts work she calls Transformational Meditation™, or TfM™ for short. When practicing TfM, you still negotiate between parts, but one of the parts is your Higher Self. It does wonders to eliminate the crowd inside, reduce internal chatter and bring you toward Oneness. In Chapter 11, one of my Super Trader candidates describes his many experiences working with TfM.

CHAPTER 7

Beliefs

THE BASIS FOR THE MATRIX

Van K. Tharp, PhD

Dr. Van Tharp's biography is at the end of the book.

 Before: Acts unconsciously out of beliefs without realizing it.

 After: Sees the impact of beliefs and is able to change them at will.

What's a belief? Anything you or I say reflects one or more beliefs, including this sentence. For example, I could make the statement, "I am a trader." That's a belief about who I am, or at least who I believe myself to be. I've said in this book that my mission is helping other people transform through a financial metaphor. Again, that's a belief—only this time, it reflects one of my values. I could say it's possible to make 100 percent trading every year. That's a belief about capability, and such beliefs usually have the words "can" or "cannot" in them.

The following story comes from the *Foundation for Inner Peace* newsletter about 20 years ago. It's a true story that illustrates the long-term impact of beliefs. It goes something like this:

> A family has a five-year-old and the wife was pregnant with another child. The child knew a baby was on the way and it kept asking the mother, "When the baby is born, I want to talk

to it." This happened throughout the pregnancy. And when the baby was born and brought home, the boy's request continued. The little boy would constantly ask, "Please, Mommy, I want to talk to the baby alone." Finally, the parents gave in, but for safety and out of curiosity, they installed a baby monitor so they could listen in to the conversation. And when the little boy, now six, was alone with the baby, he said the following words, "Please tell me about God. I'm starting to forget."

By the time the child was six years old, it could speak well, was fully indoctrinated into beliefs and only had a vague memory of what life was like before those beliefs started to filter his reality.

Understanding the Impact of Beliefs Will Change Your Life

If you're new to this idea, it might be difficult for you to fully grasp, but when you finally get it, your life will change forever. Let's start out by talking about how most of us form beliefs in the first place.

People do not act upon direct, real-world information; they act upon information that passes through neurological, social, and individual filters.* Neurological filters are defined by the limits of the sensory mechanisms through which they receive their information. For example, we can only "see" visible light or "hear" audible sound. *We cannot detect most of the energy waves around us.* We can feel the difference between two points only a millimeter or so apart on the skin of our fingertips and yet not feel the difference between two points as far apart as an inch on the skin of our back. We don't perceive the "real world" because we're only wired to be able to detect a small portion of it. What you believe about the universe begins with the sensory information available to you through your neurological filters.

The second type of filter we use is the social filter. These are filters or beliefs that are shared by a common group of people. They include language, shared perceptions, and moral values. What you believe is strongly influenced by the social filters you wear. For example: Suppose I tell you to go out to a shopping mall and ask

---

* About 50 percent of this chapter is taken from Volume 3 of Van Tharp's *Peak Performance Course for Investors and Traders* with permission.

five strangers for hugs. Immediately, all sorts of social filters might come up for you. You might think:

- I don't hug people. It's just not done.
- Interesting, it sounds like an adventure.
- I don't approach strangers. It might not be safe.
- I don't even like to talk to strangers.
- Wow, I get to hug five people today, what a great experience!
- What if they walk off and reject me?

While neurological filters dictate the information limits of all human beings, social filters distinguish groups of human beings. Those who speak English have different filters from those who speak Maidu. People who speak Maidu, for example, can only recognize three different colors, when the human visual sensory mechanism is capable of detecting 7.5 million.[1] The Maidu language distinctly filters the experience of color, so that those who speak it as their only language believe that only three colors exist. How about you? Do you believe that over 7.5 million colors exist? Do you even know some of the colors for which we have specific words? For example, what does "indigo" look like?

Another example of social filtering exists among the Navajo, who have no concept of the future—only a never-ending present. Consequently, an offer of a great future reward, such as the prospect of making money in investments, will have no meaning for a Navajo.[2]

The graphs, charts, and statistical methods shared by investors, or even specific groups of traders, also constitute social filters. For example, people who use Gann magic numbers or Gann angles[3] will have a different perspective on the market from those who do not. Similarly, investors who use stochastics will develop different expectations about the market from those who do not use them. And if you don't know what stochastics or Gann concepts are, you'll have a different experience reading this paragraph from those who use them regularly.

Finally, each individual has his own personal history, and that history provides a set of unique filters or beliefs through which he views the world. This means that no two people will perceive the world in the same way. Your unique experiences shape your beliefs about the world. The investor who has initial success in bear markets may only feel comfortable in bear markets because the model she's developed allows her to expect success in such down markets.

She may not feel comfortable in bull markets because she has no experience of success in up markets.

There are all sorts of beliefs. You have thousands of them, and you started forming them as soon as you learned language and began interacting with the people who surrounded you. Those beliefs created your reality.

Your personal history may allow you to see rich possibilities in the world of investments (or in any aspect of your world). On the other hand, your personal history may restrict your ability to see choices and options. The person who is preoccupied with trades that got away is not able to see/hear/feel all of the present opportunities that are available.

I've often said that you never trade the market itself; you trade your beliefs about the market. What is the market? It's billions of ticks coming into a central place to buy and sell; it's the emotions and thought processes that go into the orders. But you don't trade that. Instead, you look at a chart—probably with a lot of indicators. You probably form some beliefs about the chart or the indicators, and you trade those beliefs.

For example, each month I measure the 100-day SQN score of the market. Specific SQN score numbers tell me whether we are in (1) a strong bull market, (2) a bull market, (3) a neutral market, (4) a bear market, or (5) a strong bear market. In other words,

"Please tell me about God. I'm starting to forget."

I have a belief that certain values of the SQN 100-day score are useful in helping me determine market type, and I publish this information each month in my free newsletter, *Tharp's Thoughts*. At the end of September 2011, I said that we were in a bear market.

The graphic in Figure 7.1 shows a monthly candlestick chart of the S&P 500. How would you interpret it?

It looks pretty clear, don't you agree?[4] But in reaction to that statement, someone said something like this:

> I read your market update regularly, as well as an Elliott Wave expert's market update. Both of you are saying that we're in a bear market. But the market keeps moving up; in fact, it's gone up at least 10 percent in the last 10 days. You both have decades of experience and strong knowledge of market analysis, so how can you be so consistently wrong?

My response to his comment was that I was not predicting the market, I was telling people what was going on at the time I

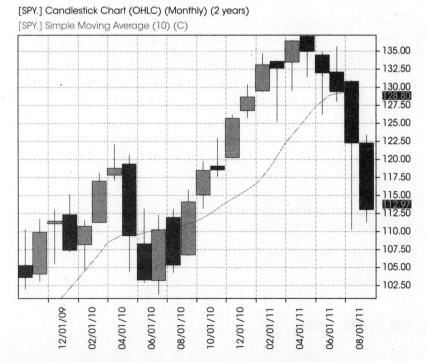

Figure 7.1 **Monthly Candlestick Chart of the S&P 500**

[SPY.] Candlestick Chart (OHLC) (Monthly) (2 years)
[SPY.] Simple Moving Average (20) (C)

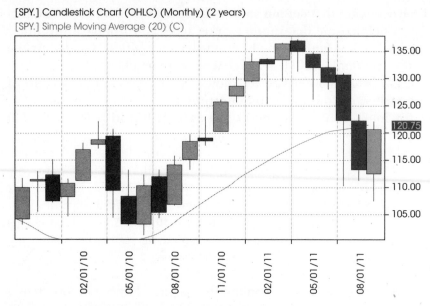

Figure 7.2   S&P 500 with One Additional Month

reported. He saw that the market had gone up in the 10 days after my report and decided (1) that I'd predicted the market, and (2) that my ability to predict was terrible.

So, let me show you a monthly chart (see Figure 7.2) that includes the first 12 days of October. Is the market going up or down?

The market has produced a new low and hasn't taken out the highs of the prior month. Is it going up or down? I'm just asking you to observe what is happening right now—not to predict. I would say that, on a monthly basis, at least, the market has stopped going down. That's it. No prediction of where prices might go.

Now, if the person who wrote to me above is a day trader or a swing trader, then, sure—the market could be in a short-term up move. But that's what I mean about beliefs. What you see depends on who you are. Even the definition of *bear market* can vary from person to person.

So, let's look at another perspective. The next chart in Figure 7.3 shows an hourly candlestick chart of the market over the last week at the end of the day after I got his comment. Is the market going up or down? Does that say anything about where it will go tomorrow? Do you see a low-risk trade to the upside? Do you see

[SPY.] Candlestick Chart (OHLC) (Intraday 60 Min) (1 Week)
[SPY.] Simple Moving Average (20) (c)

Figure 7.3   An Hourly Candlestick Chart of the S&P 500 for the Same Time Frame

one to the downside? It's all in your beliefs. And your beliefs determine the meaning that you give to some event.

One of my favorite quotes about beliefs comes from Harry Palmer, the founder of Avatar. Harry says:

> You experience what you believe, unless you believe you won't,
> in which case you don't, which means you did.[5]

What Harry is essentially saying is that your beliefs shape your life no matter what.

At the same time that the reader said my predictions were wrong, I showed the chart to Dr. Ken Long (the author of Chapter 4). Ken likes to trade extreme down moves, and he thought that Figure 7.1 was a perfect setup for a future up move. If the next bar didn't make a new low and closed toward its highs, it was the perfect setup for a good up move.

Ironically, it took out the low (by a lot), but it did close toward the high on the next bar. It was the perfect setup, except that the reward-to-risk ratio (assuming your stop was just below the low) was less than 1 to 1. The chart in Figure 7.4 shows the setup, what the next bar did, and what happened after that.

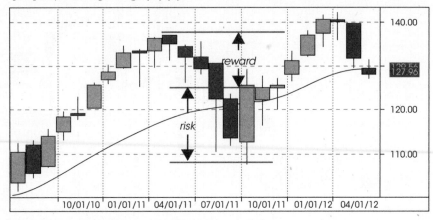

Figure 7.4   Risk Reward Trading Five Bars Down

So, when I said we were in a bear market—it was an observation that the market was going down. The reader suggested I was wrong because it started going back up, but that only happened in the days following the report, and he assumed I'd made a prediction. And when Ken Long called the extreme down move a trading opportunity, he was also right, but the reward-to-risk ratio on that trade (at least on a monthly basis) was terrible.

Notice the power of beliefs in all of those statements.

I recently asked one of my Super Trader candidates to write a brief explanation on how he creates his experience. What he wrote was so precise that I asked his permission to share it with you in this chapter.

How I Create My Experience

There was a homework exercise in the Peak Performance 202 workshop that really got me thinking about creating my experience. I'm in the Super Trader program, and we spend a lot of time eliciting and examining our beliefs. Part of that process is to figure what our beliefs get us into, what they keep us out of, and how they limit us. The process is quite fascinating to me. As an engineer, I wanted a way to simply show the belief-creation process and how it starts affecting reality. The flow chart in Figure 7.5 documents the process as I understand it.

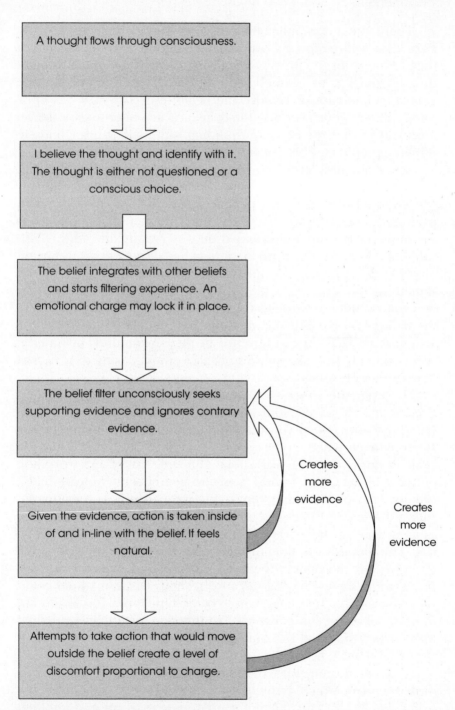

Figure 7.5   Beliefs and Experience

There are many interesting observations, given this process. First, it is a self-reinforcing process, once started. Second, the easiest time to interrupt the process is right at the time the initial thought flows through consciousness. After that, it requires much more energy to interrupt or remove the belief, especially if it has emotional charge. Third, because the belief acts as a filter to experience, it actually creates the experience in line with itself, similar to a self-fulfilling prophecy. This can and does happen on multiple levels.

At the simplest level, one simply observes evidence in line with his beliefs and ignores anything outside. A third-party observer can easily observe another person doing this because the third party does not have the same filters and thus can see the omissions the observed person makes based on observed reality (this is also subjective because the third party has her own filters working on omitting as well). An example is when people are asked to read something out loud and either omit or insert words to match their perceptions filtered through their beliefs. This process gives rise to the saying, "People only see what they want to." At this level, people are creating what they experience in their own mind. In physical reality, though, they are simply unconsciously choosing to omit part of what they observe.

However, the process of creating experience through beliefs becomes much more complex because people act based on beliefs. One possibility is that you use your uncontrolled thoughts to create your experience. For example, I was in Cary recently for the Peak Performance 101 workshop. The first day of the workshop ended a bit late, and I hadn't yet checked into my hotel. I had a two-hour personal commitment to attend to as well as checking in, eating dinner, and doing homework. I was feeling rushed. In fact, as I was leaving the workshop, I had the thought that I would be late. The thought was uncontrolled and, because it was reasonable given the circumstances, I believed it (this was all unconscious). At this point, I started having negative feelings because I hold other value beliefs like "It is important to be on time" and "It is important to finish all of my commitments." In this case, my values conflicted with my behavior, and I was unwilling to experience the creation of the belief that I'd be late.

As I was dealing with that struggle and negative emotions, I missed a turn, which created more evidence that supported the belief that I'd be late. Then I missed another turn, and another, until I ended up on a highway I didn't want to be on. As this was happening, I was getting more and more angry, and at one point—the second time I needed to turn around on the highway—I hit the steering wheel and screamed obscenities. Next thing I knew, I'd wasted another 30 minutes. The end result was that I was, in fact, late. I felt terrible–and I created the whole experience from my uncontrolled thoughts.

I hit the steering wheel and screamed obscenities.

This series of events actually did happen as I was late. It was not simply observation and omission. I unconsciously took action in support of the belief by making wrong turns. Now, I could easily find many ways to explain the story from the perspective of a victim (it was dark, I didn't know the area, the signs were confusing, etc.), but that would just reinforce the creation I was unwilling to experience and lead to self-sabotage. It is much more useful to me to figure out how I created the experience so that (1) I don't repeat something I don't want, and (2) I can create what I do want. So, as I was analyzing what happened, I started to look for positive experiences, times in my life when I'd consciously created things I do want so that I could analyze them, and I ended up thinking of something that is having a pretty major effect on my life right now.

A few years ago, I decided that I'd like to live in Mexico. My wife is from Mexico, and I've visited several times, so I fell in love with the concept. I visualized scenarios of moving, of what it would be like to live there, and how I'd accomplish the goal. In essence, I held a strong intention and engaged my creative consciousness. I believed the thought (intention) and identified with it (through visualization). I'd always thought that my move to Mexico would be sometime in the future, after I'd left my career as an engineer—mainly because I had other beliefs about when I would "retire" and how much capital I would need to do so. Since I didn't yet have the capital I needed, the idea of moving to Mexico was always in the future. But the belief that I would move to Mexico integrated with my other beliefs in a way I did not anticipate.

My belief construct immediately started creating my experience. I happened to run into a senior decision maker at my company before I was leaving for a vacation in Mexico, and he asked where I was going. When I told him I was going to Mexico, he asked if I'd ever been to the company site there. I said no. He told me that his department really needed some senior leadership down there, and I told him that if they ever wanted to send someone down, they should keep me in mind. Eight months later, out of the blue, he sent me an e-mail indicating that changes were taking place, that another peer manager was hiring and that the role would require some travel to Mexico. Never once did he tell me that the job involved relocation to Mexico, but my filter caused me to conveniently omit that.

I contacted the hiring manager and told him that I could help him and that I was interested in relocation to Mexico. He told me that he would like someone to relocate there but had not yet opened a requisition or told anyone of this. He also told me that my career experience was a perfect fit for what he wanted. Further, he was creating a whole new department that was to include many former colleagues I enjoy working with. It was as if the universe had aligned to bring me the opportunity to move to Mexico in a different but better way than I originally envisioned. What transpired was that my intention had manifested itself.

In this case, my thought was controlled through creative consciousness. I believed the thought and identified with it. My filter started working when the new belief was integrated. I observed reality through the filter and took action accordingly, thus creating my experience. However, there were several aspects of what happened in which my direct action played no part. For example, I didn't cause the organizational realignment that created an opportunity in Mexico with a new department, but it happened in the very department where I knew a senior decision maker with whom I'd previously had a conversation regarding my desire to move to Mexico. My point is that beliefs are creative forces that go beyond simply filtering experience through perception in the physical world. They are much more powerful than that. However, everything I've said consists of beliefs, and if they don't integrate well with someone else's belief system, there is always another explanation that will fit better. The above beliefs are simply useful for me.

You Are the Awareness of Thoughts that Flow through You

Eckhart Tolle asks people to meditate simply by (1) watching their breath, (2) paying attention to the silence, (3) feeling the aliveness of the inner body, or (4) being aware of the now. When you do this for a while (any of the four methods), you may notice several things:

First, you'll notice that thoughts begin to flow through the mind. If you just notice it, that's all that happens—thoughts flow. They are just objects in consciousness until you begin to identify with them. At that point, you might think that you are the thoughts, or that you actively thought them. But did you? Did you make any conscious effort to think the last thought that flowed through your mind, or did it just come? And if it just came, where did it come from? Are you the thinker of thoughts or just the observer?

Eventually, if you do this enough, you'll begin to notice that you are not the thoughts at all; you are the awareness of the thoughts. This is a very powerful position to be in—understanding that thoughts just happen, and you are nothing more than the awareness of those thoughts.

Most of us, though, are not in that particular place. Instead, we think that we are the creator of the thoughts or that we actually are the thought. For example, imagine that you are feeling perfectly fine. However, when you go to the bathroom, you notice some blood. You go to the doctor, and, after a great amount of time, you get back a diagnosis of stage four colon cancer. You are given six weeks to live.

Suddenly, you believe those thoughts. You are someone with cancer, and you are someone who is going to die within six weeks. Can you absolutely know that it's true? What happens when you have that belief? Who would you be without that belief? Is it a useful belief?

Chances are good that you definitely believe it is true. After all, the doctor said so, and chances are that your behavior will change dramatically as a result of identifying with that belief. You go through treatments that make you feel very sick and perhaps make you lose your hair, and this just gives you more evidence that you are not okay. Remember, though, that before you noticed the blood and got the diagnosis, you were a happy, cheerful person. What happened to change that? Nothing except that you believed a thought instead of just being the awareness of that thought.

Perhaps your reaction to the last two paragraphs is one of absolute horror. How could I possibly say such things? How could I believe that you are anything other than someone with cancer who is going to die? If you didn't check it out, you probably believe that you'd definitely die, and perhaps much sooner. But is it true? Are you absolutely sure?

But perhaps there's a different interpretation of who you really are. What if you are only the awareness of your beliefs? What if you are not your body? That, however, is not the topic for this chapter. My only point in bringing it up right now is to show you the power of beliefs.

Belief Hierarchy

Gregory Bateson[6] observed that human thinking is organized into logical levels. Organization at each level must be supported by the underlying structure. In fact, the purpose of any given level is to organize the information of the level below it. Thus, organization at level X must be supported by the material at the next-deepest level, level Y. Similarly, organization at level Y must be supported by what is at a still deeper level, level Z. Consequently, the structure of the deepest level determines what can be supported at the peripheral levels.

Let's consider how organization at the deepest level supports the structure at peripheral levels. Consider a stack of cans at the supermarket. Imagine taking a can from an inside row on the bottom of the stack—the deepest level of the organization. Doing so is difficult. The cans on top of it are heavy. And if you do succeed in removing a bottom-row can, much of the stack will probably fall down—especially the portion supported by the can that was removed.

Now ask yourself, *What if beliefs form such a hierarchy?* Think about the revolutionary implications of such a hierarchy of beliefs on procedures for changing human thinking. A change at the deepest level would permanently change the entire system. Anything at a superficial level that was not supported by the deep level change would not be stable enough to remain. This is why we can support people in making such dramatic changes through belief change work.

Another implication of the hierarchical structure of beliefs is that changes at a superficial level are easy to make, but they don't have much impact. Furthermore, the change is not likely to stick unless it's supported at all levels. Thus, superficial changes are easily made, but not stable. Let's go back to the stack of cans for an illustration. Take a can off the top and replace it with another one. Notice that it's a rather easy task. However, the new can is not likely to stay in place unless you replace it in such a way that it is supported by the underlying structure. If you try to balance it precariously on the edge of the structure, it will probably fall.

If these logical levels of organization consist of levels of beliefs, what would these levels consist of? Robert Dilts[7] has proposed the following hierarchy for all beliefs:

1. Environment beliefs are about what *is* and are attempts to organize observations about the world: "Markets tend to trend."
2. Behavioral beliefs are about your behavior: "I *trade* trending markets."
3. Capability beliefs are about what you can or cannot do: "I *can* make 100 percent per year trading trends."
4. Value beliefs are about what's most important to you: "*It's important* to catch the trend."
5. Identity beliefs are about who you are and usually begin with the words *I am:* "I *am* a trend-follower."
6. Spiritual beliefs are (or could be) beyond you and imply how the universe is organized: "*God loves* trend-followers."

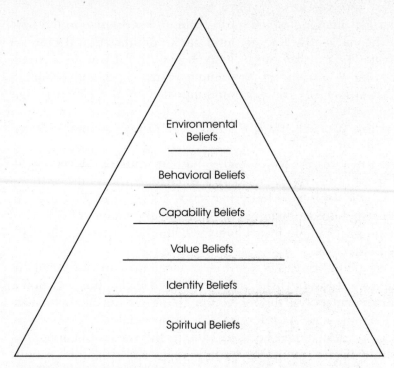

Figure 7.6   Belief Hierarchy

These are shown in the Figure 7.6. The pyramid structure merely demonstrates how each level of beliefs is supported by other beliefs that are deeper and stronger than the beliefs on the previous level. The structure of the pyramid does not represent the number of beliefs in each level. In fact, there are many more environmental beliefs than spiritual beliefs.

Let's look at the bottom levels in more detail, because you "live" at these two levels. First, the *identity level* determines who a person thinks she is. It's one's mission in life. Beliefs at this level, which usually begin with the words "I am" or "I feel," might include the following examples:

- I'm useless when it comes to trading.
- I am a skilled trader.
- I'd feel better about myself if I had more money (this one implies that the person doesn't feel good about herself).

Problems I call *personal issues* occur at this level. If you find that you have some emotion that comes up repeatedly in your trading, it's probably a symptom of a personal issue. Think about the significant people in your childhood—your mother, your father, your stepmother, your stepfather, brother, sister, aunt, uncle, and so on. Imagine hugging each of them in your mind. If you find that there's someone who played a significant role in your upbringing that you cannot imagine hugging, you definitely have an issue problem. You might say, "Well, I don't want to hug him, because then I'd have to forgive him." But you're not actually hugging that person—just your mental image of him. So, in effect, the person you're not forgiving is really yourself. That image of them is part of you. And until you you can forgive them internally, you're just mentally burdening yourself with that belief.

Generally, when issue problems are resolved, people go through major life changes. Their inner conflicts magically disappear. Stressors become trivial. That's the power of resolving high-level beliefs that do not support you.

The *spiritual level* determines one's overall philosophy in life. In essence, you have a few simple choices about what you believe the nature of the universe to be. Whatever you pick tends to determine your overall outlook in life. It also tends to determine who you think you are.

Every religion imparts spiritual beliefs. Your particular beliefs tend to support and comfort you. However, some beliefs support strong self-esteem and promote trading skills, while others do not. Here are some typical examples of spiritual-level beliefs that people might have as a result of their upbringing:

- People have no control over what happens to them, and I certainly don't.
- God extracts His own vengeance. If you don't do what He wants, you will pay a high price.
- The universe is perfect and everything happens for a reason.
- When you die, that's it—you're dead!

Only one of these particular beliefs is supportive. Which one is it? Why don't the other three beliefs support you?

I've become a trainer for the Oneness Blessing, historically called Deeksha, and I teach people to become Oneness Blessing givers. The blessing is one of the most powerful tools I've come across to help people change, but over the years, I've had people from each of the five major religions reject taking it—often because of fear-based beliefs from their religion. On the other hand, I've also had people from all five religions become blessing givers. Those who adopt it typically find that it accelerates their transformations. Those who reject it, get to be right about what they believe. And there is a certain perfection to all of that.

Changing Your Beliefs

When you realize that your beliefs control your reality, you suddenly have the opportunity to completely change your experience of the world by changing your beliefs. But how do you change your beliefs? It's actually pretty simple. Unless a belief is charged with emotion, you can change it with the following simple procedure. I call it the Belief Examination Paradigm.

1. Recognize the belief.
2. Ask yourself, *Is this a deliberately chosen belief, or did someone give it to me?* If it is not yours, then ask, *Who gave it to me?*
3. Ask yourself, *What does this belief get me into?* Another way of phrasing this, borrowed from Byron Katie,[8] would be *What happens when I have that belief?* Come up with between 5 and 10 things.
4. Ask yourself, *What does it get me out of?* This tends to be a more difficult question because you're seeing it from the perspective of someone who has the belief—you. So perhaps another question you could use, also borrowed from Byron Katie, is *Who would I be without this belief?* Incidentally, one of the answers to that question for almost every belief you can think of is usually, "less separated."
5. Next, you need to ask yourself, *Is this belief useful?* If you don't do a good job with question four, you are likely to think that most of your beliefs are useful.
6. If the belief is not useful, you can usually change it just by finding a more useful belief and substituting it. However, that only works when the belief doesn't have any charge holding it in place. When there is a charge, when stored fear or anger or some other negative emotion is holding it in place, you must release the charge before you can substitute a more useful belief.

Where do you get your trading beliefs?

Let's look at an obvious one: *I'm not worthwhile*. Let's say you were subjected to abuse as a child and consequently decided that you must not be worthy of love.

Now, let's take this belief through the six questions.

First, you've already recognized the belief. It's an identity belief that says you are not worthwhile. You have a low sense of self-worth and self-esteem.

Second, you decided that what was done to you was bad. And they couldn't possibly have done it to someone who was important or worthwhile.

Third, what does it get you into? What happens when you believe you are not worthwhile? Let's make a list.

1. You don't go after things you want because you don't believe you deserve it.
2. You think others will treat you poorly because you are not worthwhile.
3. You don't present yourself to others well because you believe you are not worthwhile and tend to behave accordingly.

4. You feel sorry for yourself all the time.
5. You've considered committing suicide.
6. You can't trade well because you don't feel worthy of profits. In fact, you feel so worthless that you don't even bother doing things that might make you a good trader. It's useless because you're not worth it.

I could go on, but you get the picture. In fact, imagine you have this belief and generate five more things that it might get you into.

_____

_____

_____

_____

_____

Fourth, what does it get you out of? Who might you be if you didn't have that belief?

1. You might be a lot happier because you feel worthwhile.
2. You'd tend to pursue your goals because you believe that you deserve them.
3. You'd tend to notice what gives you joy, and you might even decide that those things were a clue about what your purpose might be. You might find your purpose and discover that, because you're on track, your life just works.
4. You'd pursue relationships that support you.
5. If one of your goals was to be a great trader, then you'd have no problem getting the education and training it takes to be a great trader.

Now, you add another five.

_____

_____

_____

_____

_____

The fifth question you need to ask yourself is, *Is this belief useful?* The answer is obviously "no," so perhaps you could just substitute a new belief—"I am worthwhile."

However, in this case, you'll probably find that you cannot substitute the more useful belief. Why? Because there's a lot of fear and anger attached to the belief that locks it in place. For this reason, you'd need to do feeling-release exercises like the ones described in the next chapter.

Let's look at one more example. It's an old one that I used to have: "I'm the best psychological trading coach in the world." On the surface, that belief seems very useful, but I took it through the Belief Examination Paradigm about 10 years ago and this is what I came up with.

First, I've already told you the belief was an identity-level belief.

Second, I asked, "Where did the belief come from?" Well, I chose it for myself because I thought that having it would allow me to operate effectively. And once I adopted it, I found a lot of evidence to support it.

Third, I asked, "What does it get me into?" Here's my list.

1. I defined being a good psychological trading coach as spending two days with clients (usually on a weekend), discovering and helping them get over all of their blocks to being a great trader. Consequently, my weekends were quite often not free. It got me into being busy on weekends.
2. I only did it three times each month (I wanted some weekends free), but I had a six-month backlog of clients.
3. Eighty percent of my clients were easy to work with and went away as better traders.
4. My goal was to have my clients be independent of me, but I found that the 20 percent who were difficult to work with seemed to adopt the belief that "you've helped me so much, but there's a lot more I need to learn, and only you can help me."
5. The 20 percent were energy-drainers; I felt drained when I finished working with them.
6. The 20 percent kept coming back, so that roughly 50 percent of my time was spent working with people who seemed to drain my energy.
7. I wasn't that happy working with them.

8. I only had three major sources of income at the time—my Peak Performance Course, my Peak Performance Workshop, and my consulting practice. It was very time-intensive, and my income was limited by my time and energy.
9. I kept raising my rates, but the clients kept coming back.

I actually could go on, but you can see that this belief, the way I interpreted it, got me into a lot of nonuseful things.

Fourth, what would happen if I didn't have that belief? Who would I be without it?

1. I could broaden my horizons and work with all aspects of trading.
2. I could look for ways to work with more traders at one time, which would make me more effective.
3. I could spend my weekends doing things I found more enjoyable. We actually still have workshops on weekends, so I didn't totally plan this one correctly, but with my current lifestyle, I don't know the difference between a Thursday and a Sunday. I tend to do the same sorts of things each day.
4. I could have a lot more income.
5. I could do things that wouldn't drain my energy.

There were far more things on the list, but you get the idea.

Fifth, I had to ask, *Is this belief useful?* You'd think that considering myself to be the best would be useful, especially since I seemed to have lots of evidence to prove it. People really wanted to work with me, and I had a six-month backlog of clients. But my conclusion was that it wasn't. This is partly because of the way I interpreted the belief and thus the meaning I gave it. A number of nonuseful beliefs branched from it, such as:

- I needed to spend weekends doing one-on-one consulting.
- I have no way to screen out the energy-drainers or keep them from coming back.
- There really is a limit to how much I can change about what I do in my life.

Once I figured out all of this, I chose a more useful belief: "I am one of the world's best trading coaches; I cover all aspects of trading, and I only need to do what gives me joy."

Finally, the initial belief didn't have any charge to it, so it was easy to adopt a new belief.

Now, here's a challenge for you. List about 200 of your identity beliefs. Run each of them through the Belief Examination Paradigm. Find those beliefs that don't have a charge and change them, and make a note of those beliefs that do have a charge so that you can work on removing the charge after you finish the next chapter. The multistep program given in Chapter 12 will provide you with an easy way to find those 200 beliefs.

Everything Has the Meaning You Give It

Let's say the price of a stock goes down, and five different people experience a loss. Chances are that each one of them will take away a different meaning from that loss.

- Trader A: "My stop took me out. I'm wrong 52 percent of the time and it was just another loss. I'm proud of myself for executing my trading plan perfectly."
- Trader B: "Why did I listen to that recommendation? He's wrong again. I never should have listened to him. When will I ever learn?"
- Trader C: "Wow, I'm down 70 percent in my account after that loss. I've lost nearly everything. I'm a stupid idiot."
- Trader D: "Boy, I'm glad I only risked $400 on that position. I wasn't that sure about it anyway."
- Trader E: "The expectancy of my system under these market types is 1.2R. After 10 trades, I'll probably be up 12R. This was just one trade on the way to completing all 10."

Notice that one event occurs, but five different people each assign a different meaning to it.

Now, let's take a word like *tree*. Picture a tree in your mind. What do you see? If I were to survey 100 people about this exercise, I'd probably get 100 different responses. One person might picture a pine tree, while another might picture a big weeping willow, or an apple tree full of apples, or an oak tree with acorns, or a dead tree, or a giant sequoia. Some might imagine their tree in more detail than others, or think in terms of personal images, like the tree under which I proposed to my wife, or the tree we used for shade during the last picnic, or my favorite tree at my grandfather's cottage, or any number of other tree memories. So a simple word like *tree* means different things to different people.

Because different words mean different things to different people, two people can hold the same belief, such as, "I am tough," but hold entirely different opinions regarding what that even means. Consequently, the Belief Examination Paradigm for the belief "I am tough" would be different for each person.

That belief actually came up in a recent class. The person who held it totally saw that it limited him and held him back. It meant he was stubborn. It meant he was limited in many ways. Meanwhile, five other people in the class had the same belief, but they felt it was useful to them. For them, "I am tough" meant that they could endure through thick and thin, that they were resilient. And I'm sure that if I'd asked the question "What does that belief get you into?" or "What happens when you have that belief?" I would have gotten five different answers from all five people.

Another way of saying this is that each belief is likely to produce a different reality in different people, just because of the meaning given to the words.

Lastly, let's look at a common response that I get from many people when I talk about beliefs. They are likely to say, "But there are facts and there are beliefs."

So to answer that typical response, let's list some typical facts:

- Markets tend to trend.

Reaction: What's a trend? Five bars up or down? Five months up or down? And what about when they don't trend, which tends to be 85 percent of the time, depending upon your definition of a trend.

- Gravity is a fact. If I go up high and drop something, it will fall to the earth.

Reaction: If you go high enough, and drop something, it will just float. Gravity is relative.

- My father was abusive and that's an absolute fact.

Reaction: Your father may have been abused as a child, so that when he raised you he was simply doing the best he could with the resources he had. At some level he really loved you and is proud of you. Furthermore, you are simply defining some of his behaviors as being abusive and then saying that those behaviors describe him.

• The chair I'm sitting on is solid.

Reaction: The chair you are sitting on, on a microscopic level, is mostly space. It just feels solid to the touch.

• The earth is round. That's definitely a fact.

Reaction: The earth is actually somewhat pear shaped, but in the past many people considered it to be flat. Furthermore, what you see with the senses is very limited. What if you had no limitations to your senses? Would the world still be round? Would *round* even be a meaningful concept? Notice that we simply use words to give meaning and structure to what we see.

• I'm an engineer. That's a fact.

Reaction: Is who you are defined by what you do? Sure you might have a degree in engineering and your current job is within the scope of what you might call engineering. But you could also call yourself a problem solver. And that would also define what you do but not necessarily who you are. And when you say, I'm an engineer, are you not defining yourself by what you have done in the past, rather than what is going on right now?

Hopefully, you get the point. Beliefs are how we give meaning to things. It's what shapes our reality. But those beliefs are shaped by our neurological filters. They are all relative. They depend upon language. And they are not who you are, but they shape your experience.

So do you want to prove yourself to be right? Please don't bother because you are. People are always "right" about their beliefs. On the other hand, you could assume that you just don't know because you want to understand how you shape your reality and perhaps program yourself to operate in a much more useful way. If the latter is the case, then let's move on and look at removing the charge and how it is done in the next chapter.

A Journey through the Stunning World of Feelings and Trapped Emotions

Anonymous

The author of this article wishes to remain anonymous. The work he describes in this chapter spurred a remarkable personal transformation. This transformation has allowed him to attain a level of success both in his personal life and professionally that he could not have imagined before.

 Before: Burdened by a sense of unworthiness and inadequacy that inhibited him personally and professionally.

 After: Feeling confident and alive in his relationships and career.

I've always considered myself a pretty well-adjusted guy. I come from a solid family and have great friends. I've been given tremendous opportunities. And by any standard, I've been successful professionally and in life. However, we all have our issues. Mine mostly consist of the lingering belief that "I am inadequate and unworthy." This belief goes way back and is completely irrational, given my station in life. But try telling that to the eight-year-old kid still inside of me.

I was unaware of these feelings of inadequacy until relatively recently. About a year and a half ago, I began therapy, which helped me make immense progress in uncovering this belief in my

143

I felt inadequate and unworthy.

unworthiness and identifying how it impacted my life. The primary domain in which it arose was my relationships. By living with this belief, I was sabotaging myself; I was entering and staying in the wrong kinds of relationships instead of seeking out healthy ones.

However, despite my new awareness of these feelings, the underlying sense of inadequacy and unworthiness persisted and continued to affect me in various ways. The belief that I am inadequate is highly charged, meaning it is linked to deep, underlying emotions. While it is easy to take an uncharged belief and replace it with one that is more useful, highly charged beliefs cannot simply be wished away. This led me to look for methods to deal with and manage beliefs that have a high emotional charge. When I began this process, I had not yet discovered all of the Van Tharp Institute material on feeling release.

The Turning Point

In late May 2010, I attended a seminar on "Uncovering Your Romantic Blueprint and Changing Your Romantic Fate," taught by Erwan and Alicia Davon. A key section of that workshop had to do with handling emotionally charged beliefs.

The way most of us react to our negative thoughts and feelings is to resist them. Resistance, however, is actually the essence of self-sabotage and has the ironic effect of causing these beliefs and emotions to persist. Erwan's method involves doing the exact opposite—that is, accepting all of your negative beliefs and their related emotions and letting yourself feel them fully. Once you do that, you come to realize on a very fundamental level just how false they are, at which point they simply dissolve. He calls this process *core work*.

I went home and tried it out. I spent the better part of three days lying on the floor of my apartment and letting myself feel beliefs like "I am inadequate," along with other core beliefs I've held onto since childhood. Then, just as Erwan said, I reached a point at which the beliefs just fizzled out and were not there anymore. A few days later, they came back again, which suggested that the method is not a one-off event; it's a practice I need to follow on a regular basis.

Since then, I've spent literally hundreds of hours doing core work. It was pretty much all I did for two months. At times, especially during the first few weeks, I could feel the emotions coursing through my veins with a raw intensity I'd never felt before—probably because I'd never allowed myself to feel those emotions fully in the past. The process brought memories to the surface that I hadn't thought of in decades, and that unleashed even more feelings. For about the first six weeks, I would start my meditations with a belief, like "I am inadequate," and I would allow myself to feel that belief and the emotions associated with it until they went away. I would do as much as I could to bring the feeling up and keep it there, until, finally, no matter how hard I tried, the feeling would just disappear.

Eventually, I learned that (1) I don't have to start with a "topic"; I can just work on whatever emotion happens to be there in the moment, and (2) it can be more efficient to consciously drop the thought, and often the image, associated with a belief and just feel the emotion in my body. Doing this tends to make the meditation an entirely different experience from when I get caught in a cycle where thought perpetuates feeling and vice versa, or when I try to manufacture a feeling that isn't there to begin with.

These practices have fundamentally transformed my life. Through them, I can often reach a state I can only describe as "clarity," or what's left once all of my false feelings and beliefs have dissolved. When I'm in this state, I have no "self," probably because

I'm shorn of all the false conceptions that made up my sense of self in the first place. Instead, all that remains is the world before me— or, in a word, reality.

> These practices have fundamentally transformed my life. Through them I can often reach a state I can only describe as clarity.

If I "try" to get into this state of clarity, I don't get there. The secret is simply to accept your present experience, whatever it is, and feel it fully. I now truly understand the statement, "If you want happiness, want what you have." For a long time, I often found myself resisting negative emotions precisely because I wanted to be in a state of clarity when I wasn't. Since then, I've become much better at accepting my feelings and whatever happens to be there in a given moment.

> If you want happiness, want what you have.

But I believe I've finally found a way—*the* way, perhaps—to manage my emotions and whatever else comes up in life. The two central principles are (1) being present—or, getting out of my head and into my experience—and (2) fully accepting my experience—that is, feeling it fully without resistance.[1] If I am feeling resistance, I accept the fact that I'm feeling the resistance and feel that, too.

I can imagine many readers growing skeptical at this point, but anyone who knows me well will assure you that nobody has been more cynical about this psychological/spiritual stuff than I used to be. It can make a world of difference in your life, but you've really got to experience it for yourself. That's what it took for me.

The most important thing I've discovered is that I no longer have to be afraid of experiencing my thoughts and feelings, because they are only that—thoughts and feelings. My old, emotion-laden beliefs certainly have not disappeared forever, but they no longer own me; I own them. When I consciously get out of my head and just feel my experience, when I accept whatever that experience is, I easily and instantaneously get to a point at which these feelings and thoughts stop affecting me. I let myself feel them in my body without identifying with them in my mind. Doing this completely changes my interaction with the world.

I believe a core principle is that you are not your thoughts and feelings. Most people think they are, but they aren't. None of us are. We are simply the awareness of our thoughts and feelings. Suffering comes from identifying with them and thinking that they *are* you, and that they are *yours* to begin with. This is exactly what I've come to understand through all the work I've done.

Self-Sabotage Models

When I read about the different feeling-release models in The Van Tharp Institute materials, I was struck less by the differences between the various models than I was by their commonalities:

1. The Unwilling to Experience Feelings model (hereafter referred to as UEF)
2. The Unwilling to Experience our Creations model (UEC)
3. The Oneness model

I'll give my own interpretation of these models for the readers.

The UEF model views self-sabotage as a product of our efforts to avoid experiencing our beliefs and feelings. The remedy for self-sabotage, according to the UEF model, is to do the opposite of resisting—that is, to fully experience your beliefs and their associated feelings. Once you do this, they tend to dissolve.

In my case, I have always felt inadequate. But whenever the feeling would arise, I'd ignore it or try to push it away. By doing that, I was preventing myself from really examining this belief for what it is, and as a result, it stayed with me. Once I started allowing myself to truly feel it, I came to realize, not just intellectually, but on a deep, emotional level, that it is entirely false.

The UEC model regards self-sabotage as the result of our unwillingness to experience, not just our beliefs and feelings, but all of our creations. For example, some part of you might be a creation as discussed in Chapter 9. However, while learning this model, it seemed to me that many of the types of creations that are discussed really amount to particular kinds of beliefs and/or feelings. That said, I found it useful insofar as it specified the various and important manifestations our beliefs and feelings can take (games, identities, etc.). The solution to self-sabotage in the UEC model, similar to that of the UEF model, is to accept and fully experience your creations.

The Oneness model presumes that any thought, feeling, or action that results in a sense of separation or takes you out of a state of peace, joy, and bliss is self-sabotage. The solution to self-sabotage in this model is to return to an awareness of Oneness and do whatever makes you feel Oneness, peace, joy, and bliss. Upon first reading the Oneness model seemed quite different from the UEF and UEC models. But then I remembered that the best—indeed, the only—way I know of to attain the state of Oneness is to open up to your experience and feel it fully, with acceptance (that is, to do exactly what is prescribed in the UEF and UEC models). It is only then that any "false" perceptions, perceptions that comprise your awareness of a distinct "self" that is separate from everything else, dissolve, thereby bringing you into the state of Oneness.

As I've been doing more and more feeling release, I've discovered three successive stages of consciousness. The first is resistance. You resist whatever parts of your experience you dislike, but, by resisting it, you cause it to persist. The second stage, acceptance, comes when you stop resisting, truly and fully. In the third stage, you transcend your experience, but only when you've accepted it. The UEF and UEC models seem to help with the second stage, acceptance. It is at the third level of consciousness—transcendence—that I believe the vision outlined in the Oneness model can finally manifest itself.

A core principle of Oneness is that there is no thinker, only thinking, because you are not your thoughts and feelings. They are just there. They appear in your head, and you are simply the awareness of them. But you routinely identify yourself with your beliefs and think they define you. That concept is one of the most important things I've learned.

Accepting My Feelings

Initially, while doing my core work, I spent a lot of effort resisting any negative emotions whenever they would appear, particularly those connected to my sense of inadequacy, because I'd grown attached to being in a state of clarity and oneness. Whenever feelings of inadequacy would pop up and ruin my clarity party, I would judge and resist them. This only caused them to persist, which in turn prevented me from being in the very state of clarity I was aiming for. It was all a big game I'd been playing, one I was only half-aware of. But I've made a major shift in that regard. During my meditations and throughout my day, I've been much more accepting of any and all emotions that arise. The reason, I think, is that I've shifted my goal away from attaining clarity to simply experiencing my emotions fully.

I now realize that the main purpose of all my meditation work is not to reach clarity, although that is often a pleasant byproduct. The purpose, rather, is to be able to feel my emotions without letting them affect me. Of course, since I've shifted my outlook in this regard, I've spent considerably more time in that elusive state of clarity than I had at any time previously. I still feel my feelings, but I've stopped identifying with them. That marks a major shift for me. For most of my life, I wasn't even aware of my feelings at all. In a sense, I was totally asleep. That's one way we resist our feelings. Another way is through denial: "I'm not feeling this." When I'd become conscious of certain emotions, I'd simply deny that I was feeling them and go on as if they didn't exist. Or I'd distract myself with something else—even with something as simple as moving a part of my body. This was particularly true of my feelings of inadequacy and unworthiness.

A lot of the suffering I experienced came from judging myself. Usually, I find that when I'm feeling intensely inadequate, about 85 percent of that feeling is a sense of inadequacy that arises from the fact that I'm feeling inadequate. "Shouldn't I already be over this inadequacy stuff?" I ask myself. "Why am I still feeling this?" Once I feel through this reaction and just experience the underlying, primary feeling of inadequacy, the intensity of the feeling reduces to a rather mild 15 percent of what it was when it started.

I would often take some feeling I had and project it onto the rest of the world. Projection actually took many forms:

- Avoidance. To avoid a feeling, I would make up an imaginary drama involving someone else, such as having an argument in my head with the person, coupled with a strong emotional reaction to my image of them.

- Denial. Sometimes, I'd attempt to deny a part of my past, a part I would subsequently see in others around me, which in turn redirected my contempt toward them.
- Codependency. To avoid feeling unworthy, I would attempt to fix other people's problems for them and thereby feel worthy again.

When I first began feeling release, I would go to a park bench* and just feel what I wanted to release for about 50 minutes. I would use this method every day. I would pick a feeling off the shelf, bring it up so that I'd feel it intensely, and then just try to experience it fully. I found that, although the exercise was effective in dissolving beliefs and feelings temporarily, I had to keep doing it on a regular basis. The beliefs and feelings did not disappear permanently—even after about six weeks of daily work. Nevertheless, I thought it worthwhile to try again because my resistance to my emotions had decreased significantly since I had first attempted the exercise.

When I still found myself experiencing resistance, I decided to try something one particular day in the park. It turned out to be an interesting exercise in resistance itself. When I sat down, I set the alarm on my phone to go off after 50 minutes so I wouldn't have to keep looking at the time. I then brought up the feeling of wanting to resist my emotions and experienced it in all its aspects. There were three major ones:

1. My frustration with the fact that I was still experiencing emotions such as inadequacy on a regular basis despite all the work I had done.
2. The general sense of unpleasantness that came with feeling negative emotions.
3. The fear that if I went into interactions with people while feeling negative emotions like inadequacy, I would put out a negative energy that would turn people off. This belief was the most powerful.

After about 40 minutes, all of these feelings just kind of dissipated. However, when my alarm went off, I opened my eyes, stood

---

* *The Peak Performance Course for Investors and Traders* actually has a park bench feeling-release technique similar to this. It just took me a while to realize the similarity.

up, and immediately felt a sense of fear with respect to feelings of inadequacy during social interactions. The fear was directed toward a woman with whom I was to have a date the next day; I was afraid that if I went into the date feeling inadequate, she would sniff it out and reject me. I walked around and felt this feeling for a while, but it stayed with me. I eventually discovered that I was simply waiting for it to go away, which itself is a form of resistance, and that very resistance, in turn, was preventing the feeling from going away.

I set the alarm on my phone to go off in another 20 minutes and resolved to use the time to just experience my fear of feeling my inadequacy. The act of setting my alarm and creating a designated period of time to feel the feeling helped to reduce the pressure I felt around making the feeling go away. In other words, it (temporarily) extinguished my resistance. The effect was dramatic; after only two minutes, my fear of feeling inadequate evaporated. The reason, I'm sure, was that I was no longer resisting the feeling.

I was afraid of rejection.

But then the feeling came back. I immediately became frustrated with this. The frustration, of course, amounted to resistance. I recognized this and began to feel even more frustrated at the fact that I was feeling frustrated. Needless to say, this cocktail of frustration and resistance made the underlying feeling—the fear of feeling inadequate—persist. And that's where I ended the exercise. I learned that even when the process works, the feeling I'm working on may return. But the lesson here is to just be patient when that happens and experience the recurring feeling without resisting it.

Another example: Recently, there have been times when I've felt a sense of fear and pessimism about being profitable as a trader. This belief is irrational, given that I've been profitable in the past. However, a couple of recent attempts at paper-trading some new strategies did not prove successful; it was then that I developed this belief.

I did some work on releasing these feelings, but despite my best efforts, I struggled to bring them up. My attempts at feeling the fear and pessimism gave way to a sense of determination to learn from my mistakes and correct them, which is, of course, a healthy mental state. The parallels with my past were not lost on me; my usual (unconscious) strategy for motivating myself has always been to derive strong determination from a fear of failure (negative motivation as opposed to positive motivation). In any event, by the end of the hour, I no longer felt any pessimism or fear over my prospects as a trader.

Where I Am Now

I have now spent a good two weeks going to the same spot and feeling through my inadequacy and unworthiness, devoting 45 minutes to an hour each time (I have switched the spot from the park to a lookout point on the top of a mountain near my house). While I haven't been able to do the exercise every day, I have managed to do it every other day, at least. Most of the time, the feeling ends up dissolving towards the end of the hour and I feel extremely clear and confident. This feeling of clarity tends to last at least until the end of the day. The effect on my mood and especially my interactions with others has been dramatic.

Also, on recent occasions, the feeling of inadequacy has become harder to stir up, proved less and less intense, and required shorter and shorter spans of time before dissolving. I take this to be a sign of improvement.

By the time this chapter was published, I married the woman I had such anxiety about dating. Just to underscore how groundless most of our anxieties are, she reports that what she initially found most attractive about me was my confidence.

I now have two separate exercises that I'm doing on a regular basis. The first method, which I just described, involves taking a particular belief or feeling, going to a neutral spot outside of my house, and spending 40 minutes to an hour doing everything I can to stir up the emotions. I continue this exercise every day for a week or two, or until I start noticing real changes. Again, it is important to do everything you can to bring up the emotions—use thoughts, mental images, anything, and do not let up until the end of the hour. Also, focus on accepting everything that you experience during the exercise; this point is very important.

I've found that this method is really helping to dissolve the core beliefs I've always had about myself. The effects have been dramatic and lasting. I'm clearer and more confident in general and my old feelings of inadequacy and unworthiness are coming up less frequently and less intensely.

The second method simply involves stopping your thoughts, bringing yourself back to the present, and letting yourself feel fully whatever emotions happen to be there. In the first exercise described above, you are consciously trying to stir up certain feelings and are using anything you can to do that, including your thoughts. The second method is different because you are not trying to stir anything up; you are just working on whatever is there to begin with. The goal is to get out of your head entirely—that is, to completely ignore whatever thoughts are there—and come back to the present. Being present means noticing your body, the sounds around you, and any sensations you are experiencing. Then look for any feelings that happen to be there—not thoughts, but feelings. A thought is in your head; a feeling is in your body and consists of physical sensations and sometimes images. Feel any emotions fully and accept them.

This second method involves combining presence and acceptance—getting out of your head and into your feelings and accepting whatever you are experiencing in that moment. You can designate, say, 20 minutes a day to sit down and really concentrate on this exercise. But I actually try to do this all the time now—while driving, interacting with people, and so on. With practice, I've become better at noticing and accepting my moment-to-moment feelings and often find that they simply flow through and out of me in a matter of minutes. I've also developed the ability I mentioned earlier to feel my emotions in my body without identifying with them in my thoughts. This is a very powerful skill.

Both practices have their time and place. Maybe you've spent two weeks using the first method on a particular belief or feeling and found that it still comes up, even though the feeling is less intense and frequent. When it does come up, you can use the second method to let the feeling simply roll through you without letting it permeate your thoughts and affect your actions.

Remember that the key to both methods is acceptance: Whatever you are feeling—accept it. Whatever your reaction is to what you are feeling, accept that as well. If you are having trouble doing the exercises and find yourself getting distracted or lost in your thoughts, accept that too, and just bring yourself back to the present. Acceptance is a skill just like any other. As such, it requires patience, practice and persistence.

Some readers may be thinking, "This sounds painful and boring, and there is no way I'm going to spend hours feeling negative feelings." That's the resistance that keeps those negative feelings in place and brings them up unconsciously all the time.

To me, this is like saying, "I refuse to brush my teeth." If I don't devote time to taking care of my teeth, I'll have problems, just as I will if I don't take the time to consciously experience my negative emotions. Engaging my emotions has become a normal part of my routine. It really is as important to me as brushing my teeth.

Anyone can do it, and you don't have to spend hours and hours lying on the floor the way I did. I took the hard route and figured out a lot of the mechanics on my own. But in doing so, I hope I have made things a little more efficient for those who are reading this. Taking 45 minutes every day for a few weeks to go to a park and work on some particular feeling will probably yield enormous benefits. If you absolutely need to, skip the gym for a week or two, and do this instead. These practices have done more for my physical health than exercise and medication. If you don't have time to go to the park, there's nothing stopping you from using the second meditation I described above—that is, taking a few minutes during

This is like saying, "I refuse to brush my teeth."

your day to bring yourself back to the present moment, feel your feelings, and accept them.

You can try to avoid your emotions. But that won't make them go away. They will continue to affect the results you get in life, even if entirely unconsciously. You may as well just learn to accept them. That way you'll be able to manage your emotions instead of having them manage you.

As many readers can attest, few activities bring out your emotions like trading and investing. You can have a great system, but if you make emotionally driven mistakes while trading it, as most people do, you won't come close to achieving its potential results. Because I've done all of this psychological work, I am now able to feel my emotions without being affected by them. People always talk about the need to have an edge in the markets. Well, this is my edge!

Well, this is my edge.

Far more important than any effect on my trading has been the impact this practice has had on my state of mind and my life. *Being able to experience my emotions without being beholden to them has fundamentally altered the way I walk in the world.* Moreover, the feeling of clarity I attain after doing this work is unparalleled and indescribable. It's like having a completely clear picture of the world before you, one that is unobstructed by all of the false conceptions that usually muddy that view.

The state of clarity, alas, tends to be elusive; sometimes it happens, and sometimes it doesn't. Regardless, my everyday existence is entirely different from what it used to be. Until recently, I lived mostly in my thoughts while ignoring, denying, and repressing my feelings. But now, for the first time, I am experiencing reality. Sometimes it is placid and beautiful, other times it is raw and intense. But it is pretty incredible out here.

Note from Editor: Feeling Release as a Metric for Awakening

Oneness University says that you can think of yourself as awake when a feeling disappears in 30 minutes. This doesn't mean that you stop thinking about it and then, two days later, it comes up again. It means that the feeling is gone and won't come up again in the same situation or in the same person. When that happens, you are beginning to awaken.

The time required to release a feeling gradually becomes less and less until it suddenly flows through you without any attachment at all. It takes seconds, if it comes at all. At that point, the "awakening"* is permanent. Thus, should you do any of the feeling-release exercises recommended in this chapter, you can use the time you carry the feeling as a metric of your state of consciousness. If it takes an hour and comes back the next day, you still have a lot of work to do. However, a few months' worth of spending an hour or two each day engaged in intense feeling-release exercises can have a dramatic impact on your life.

---

*Byron Katie, who, by my definition, is an awake person, says that she doesn't know what "awakening really is." Instead, she says that you just "awaken to one belief at a time."

CHAPTER 9

You Are a Crowd of Conflicting Parts Inside

Van K. Tharp, PhD

Note: The CBOE floor trader initially wanted to remain anonymous because he was afraid that his investors would panic if it were ever discovered that he'd "seen a shrink," as he called it. As it turned out, one particular investor was someone I (Van Tharp) knew very well and who had also been using my methods. It's a small world. The floor trader continued to make huge returns for his client year after year. He also went on to develop a very spiritual approach to life. He gave talks to high school kids, spreading the success principles he'd learned. He became certified in the methods of Stanislov Grof, and we did several holotrophic breathing workshops together and one technical course. He passed away in 2003 after dealing with prostate cancer. I consider him a very dear friend, and I miss him dearly. Since his initial request was to be anonymous, I decided to honor that here.

 Before: Floor trader interviewed had $100,000 ceiling to his income.

 After: Made over $700,000 in a few months after solving a conflicting parts issue.

This material has been adapted from material that was published in Volume 4 of the *Peak Performance Course for Investors and Traders*. In that section, I introduce people to parts negotiation. Essentially, parts negotiation comes from the idea that you have a lot of parts inside of you. We'll explore that idea and how to join parts together in this chapter.

Your mind appears to have various parts. These parts even show up in your language. For example, when you say:

- *I* could kick *myself* for doing that.
- *I* don't understand why things like that happen to *me*.
- On the one hand, *I* really want to succeed, but on the other hand, *I'm* just lazy.
- Sometimes *I* do things that seem self-destructive to *me*, and *I* ask *myself*, "why?"

"I," "myself," and "me" do not represent the "whole you" in these sentences. Instead, they represent different parts of you interacting with each other. For example, the part called "I" wants to kick the part called "myself" in the first sentence.

To help you think about parts, consider the following:

1. What roles do you play in life? You may have parts representing one or more of them. Perhaps you have a trader part. You have another part that does research and is a perfectionist. You have another part that wants excitement and wants to throw out all the rules and just have fun. Perhaps you have a part you call "the banker" who just doesn't want to lose money and doesn't want to take risks. Perhaps the trader part is in conflict with the excitement part, which is always doing certain things for excitement. There are literally thousands of possibilities.

2. You also have parts that represent significant people in your life—perhaps to protect you from them. Perhaps your dad was a perfectionist. You'd bring home a test result of 95 percent, and he'd say, "Why didn't you get 100 percent?" Eventually, you started criticizing yourself to protect yourself from Dad's criticism. Even many years after he dies, you might have a part that says, in your Dad's voice, "Why did you take a loss on that trade?"

3. Parts might include feelings you don't want to feel, so you might also have a "part to protect you from that feeling." It does so by noticing situations in which that feeling

would normally come up and then uses the stored feeling to remind you to avoid these situations.

Every part is established with a positive intention, quite often to protect you from something, but you tend to forget about each part once it is established, as well as its intention. Consequently, a fear part designed to protect you from fear actually ends up bringing up fear all the time and producing fear in your life. One of the things you need to do to resolve the conflict is to go back to the part's original intention and give it positive things to do. This is usually essential in a parts negotiation.

You are a crowd of conflicting parts.

You were not born with all of these parts. Instead, you invented them as you grew up and matured. They are your creations. You developed each part to carry out some positive intention in some context. Here is a list of some of the positive intentions your unconscious parts may have:

- Protect you from failure or keep your pride from being hurt.
- Help you gain the approval, or at least the attention, of others.
- Help you incorporate a particular value into yourself.
- Protect you from painful memories.
- Motivate you.
- Help you survive.
- Help you feel better about yourself.
- Show concern for your future well-being.

Exercise: Have a Parts Party

Try the following exercise to get an idea about some of your parts. Go to bed with a writing tablet and a pen or pencil. Before you fall asleep, bring up the part of you that bought this book. It's either your trader/investor part or the part of you that's curious about self-development.

Beginning with that part, ask what its positive intention is for you and thank it for helping you. Then ask it what other parts are inside—parts you might be in conflict with on a regular basis. If you're talking to your trader part, it might bring up your perfectionist part, your excitement part, your conservative part, your researcher part, your fear part, your "get a real job" part, and probably a number of others.

Now, ask each part, "What are you trying to do for me? What's your positive intention for me?"

You might not get any answers immediately, but that's okay. Be ready to write down what might come up.

The primary objective of this exercise is to find out who is in there and to come up with at least two parts that are in conflict. If you find two conflicting parts, you can do the next exercise and negotiate between your parts.

Parts Negotiation Exercise

1. *Identify two parts that are in conflict.* What you're looking for is a statement such as, "I want to X, but something prevents me from doing X." Your conflict might be as simple as, "I want to be a trader, but I never seem to have the courage to make

a trade." These are just two examples. There are many statements that indicate internal conflict.

Here are some of the most common conflicting parts:
- The part that wants to trade, and the part that can't pull
  the trigger.
- The part that wants to trade, and the part that wants
  excitement.
- The part that wants to trade, and the part that wants to
  find the perfect trading system.
- The part that wants to trade, and the part that refuses
  to take a loss.
- The part that wants to trade, and the part that says you
  don't have enough time.
- The part that wants to trade, and the part that says
  you should do something productive.
- Hopefully, you get the idea. All you need are two conflicting parts to move on in the exercise.

2. *Put one part in one hand and one part in the other and notice what
   they look like.* You might be making up what they look like
   (i.e., a white mist, me with a cowboy hat, a little boy of nine,
   etc.), but that's okay because it's coming from somewhere
   in your unconscious mind. And if you can't visualize things,
   then just get a feeling that might represent each part. If you
   do enough Level II transformation, you might find that your
   ability to visualize returns or strengthens. Just do it.
3. *Become one of your parts and ask it about the other part.* Again, just
   associate with the part even if you think you are just making it
   up. Get that part's opinion of the other part. What does it do?
   How are they in conflict? What does it think about the other
   part? Get all of the details. Finally, ask the part, "What's your
   positive intention for me?" Be sure to get this; it's the basis for
   negotiation. Examples of positive intentions were given earlier.
4. *Do the same for the other part.* Get a full description of what it
   thinks about the other part in the other hand, and be sure to
   end with the positive intention of that part. At this point, you
   should have the positive intention of each part.
   a. Be sure that you have intentions (to make money trading)
      and not behaviors (help you trade).

    b. Also, be sure the intention of each part is positive ("I want to protect you from fear" vs. "I want to screw up your life"). Every part was established for a positive intention. Thus, a fear part that sees fear in everything is probably just trying to protect you, even though it might not seem that way.

5. *Go inside again and ask to communicate with your creative part.* Ask the creative part to come up with three ways to meet the intention of both parts. If one part seems particularly negative, find things that the negative part can do to meet its positive intention.

    a. A fear part can engage in feeling-release rather than bring fear up for you constantly.

    b. A conservative part can develop a sound business plan for you or be in charge of risk control.

    c. An excitement part can go skydiving on the weekends rather than do stupid things that impact your trading.

    Hopefully, you get the idea. Keep generating ideas until both parts are happy. By the way, they can always try a solution for two weeks to see if it works out. If it doesn't, they can always renegotiate.

6. *When the two parts agree, ask if any other part objects to the agreements.* For example, two parts might negotiate to use all the time during your waking hours and then find that other parts object.

7. If no other parts object, join your hands together and bring them back into your body. You are complete.

8. If one part objects, join the two agreeing parts on one hand and bring the objecting part out on the other hand. Restart the negotiations, beginning with step two.

The only time you'll have problems with this exercise is:

1. When you lack the awareness to do the exercise—when, for example, you can't find your parts in the first place, or can't imagine what they look like. If this is the case, be willing to make something up. I've said this to many clients, and the imagination takes over. It still works.

2. When you don't have good positive intentions for each part. You might have negative behaviors or intentions. If that's the case, keep working until you have positive intentions.

When you can't reach an agreement because of a stubborn part it is very important to give the one that appears to be the most negative something to do to help it meet its positive intention for the most you. This always works in my experience.

Let's look at an example. The following interview was conducted in the late 1980s with a client of mine who had undergone a massive shift as a result of doing such an exercise.

Interview with a CBOE Floor Trader

My first year trading, I had $7,000 in the bank. I borrowed $15,000 to buy a seat on the exchange. My wife was seven months pregnant, and we didn't have any insurance. I had to put $4,000 of what we had in my trading account, which left us $3,000 to live on, and I was going to have to pay for the upcoming hospital bill. I probably would have told my own kid that he was nuts if he'd tried to do something like that, but I was young and I wanted to start my own business. I really didn't think about the danger. I just thought about the opportunity, and I'm glad I did.

Since that first year, I never really had a year under $100,000, but it never seemed to be enough money. I was never really satisfied. I always questioned, "Why do I make enough money to live on, but not enough money to excel, to be a millionaire?" Whenever I had to make money, I made money. But if I made a lot of money, I would just coast and not make any more until I needed to make it again. I could predict the market with above-average skill, but I couldn't pull the trigger. The only time I would make the investment was when the fear of not making the investment was greater than any other fear I had. For example, I sat through 1985 with the market going virtually straight up. Time after time, I'd get signals and tell everyone else at the office about them. They'd all go out and make money on it, but I would say to myself, "Wait for one more indicator to come in line." I finally got to the point where I said, "I'm going to hate myself more for not investing," so I bought and made money. But everything I did was out of fear.

The culmination came when I started to get anxiety attacks. After 15 years of trading, I started getting terrible anxiety attacks about my positions. I had a position with maybe $15,000–$20,000 worth of risk and a potential profit of over $100,000. The market was going against me, and I started going nuts about it, even though my risk was limited. I got so crazy about it that I had to take the position off. If I were thinking about it logically, and a friend who was in the same position came to me for advice, I'd tell him he was nuts for getting out of a position that still had plenty of room in it. Indeed, one side of me was saying, "This is stupid," but I was out of control. I had to get out of the physical and emotional pain and exit the position. Three or four days later, I developed an anxiety attack about it. My partner and I were about to go to lunch, and I said, "I've got to get out of these positions before we go to lunch." He responded, "You got out of them two days ago."

I could tell people what to do, but I couldn't do it myself. I remember one fellow in particular on the floor—he had maybe $600K when he started—and he was down $400K. He threw his pencil down on the table and said to me, "I've got to do something to make money." I said, "Do this," and the guy did it. He made $2–$3 million, and I sat there and watched him. I had more money in my account than he had in his account, but he had the guts to go in and make the trade. I did that with several people. I said, "This is the place to buy," and these people would all jump on board, and I would sit there and say, "Gee, I was right."

Everybody thought I was a great guy and that I was quite knowledgeable, but, deep inside, I knew I really wasn't. I felt very negative about myself for no apparent reason. If I'd seen someone like myself in the business, I'd have said, "Hey, that guy really knows what he's doing," but when I looked at myself internally, I felt so negative.

One day, at the dinner table, I took out a notepad and wrote down every negative comment my family and I made. My wife had made about 8, my son about the same, and my daughter about 10. They were jokes, or making fun of somebody, or criticizing something, and I realized that I had created that negative atmosphere. I wanted to change.

Eventually, I recognized that I was successful, but with that recognition came new problems. Deep down, I was haunted by my father, who'd developed a serious drinking problem after becoming successful at about the same age I was then. This negatively shaped my view of success, so that when I reached the point at which I believed I was successful, I stopped making money. I stopped trading the way I used to trade. I don't think I was even trying for the big hit. I think I was trying not to make money, finding excuses not to do what I used to do. I was always afraid.

It was foolish of me to limit my life and my choices this way, but I'd experienced a loss of vision and couldn't see what was happening. Sometimes you need a kind of intervention where you have someone ask you the right questions because you can't see things yourself. You're blind to your own opinions because you filter them out of your thought process.

Working with Dr. Van Tharp

In my business, you don't tell your investors that you're going to a psychologist/trading coach; they'd think you were nuts. Consequently, asking for help was a very big step for me. But I'm glad I did. In one of my training courses, I said, "If you invest $10,000 and lose it, but gain experience from the loss, you've lost nothing. You've transferred one asset to another asset. But if you lose $10,000 and don't learn anything from it, then you've lost money." If I lost my investors because they frowned on me for working with a coach/psychologist but gained something personally by knowing myself more and solving this problem, I didn't need anyone else's money. I'd trade my own money. I read Dr. Tharp's interview in the April 1986 issue of *Technical Analysis of Stocks and Commodities* and decided to call him. We seemed to be compatible in terms of what he was trying to do and what I was trying to do, so I bought *The Peak Performance Home Study Course.*

The course made a lot of sense to me. Doing the relaxation tape seemed a little silly, but I realized that there were a lot of things he was saying that I'd never conceived of before, so I said, "What the heck, I'll do the relaxation tape." The first 10 or 15 times I did it, I thought, "I'm not getting anything out of this." But after doing it for 30 days at Van's suggestion, I could bring about a feeling of relaxation anytime I wanted.

If I don't understand something in a book, I tend to skip over it. There were parts of the course I kept trying to read, but my brain would want to skip it. It was the conflicting data that I didn't understand. I just kept going over it and over it, forcing myself to read it. It was as though a part of me was pulling away from reading these sections, and another part of me was not letting me comprehend it.

I could sense that a change was happening, but I think I was still anxious; I think it was some of my old anxieties. I was always afraid of money. I was always afraid that I'd lose this or I'd lose that. I think there was an initial reflex: "I've gotten enough out of this thing; I'll save myself a couple thousand by not doing the follow-up." Finally, though, I said to myself, "I've made a commitment to do this entire thing; I'm going to see it through," and that's why I did it. It was a big changing process. When you're changing, you don't realize it. I realize it now because I've written all these things down, and I watch as I'm accomplishing all these goals that I've set for myself.

Once I finished the course, I wasn't too keen on spending more money to do one-on-one consulting with Van, but I figured, "What the heck? I've lost more than this on one trade I didn't take, so I might as well give it a shot. If I've lost the money, then I've lost it." I looked at it like one more trade, and not a big trade in the scheme of things. It was a trade I was making for myself, to improve myself. But it turned out to be so much more than that. It was one of the best things I've ever done!

Dealing with Conflicting Parts

When I did my "Dealing with Conflicting Parts" exercise, it was the most shocking thing that ever happened to me in my life.

We'd gone through a weekend of trying to isolate and identify problems, and now we were doing the parts analysis. I thought, "Well, this is just going to take a few minutes; then we'll come back down and trade." I wasn't really prepared for what happened.

I was told to hold out my two hands and put my "family" part on one hand, and my "success" on the other hand. It sounded bizarre, but I complied. Van asked me to look at them and tell him what they looked like.

I looked at "family," which was in my right hand, and it appeared as a very clear crystal ball. I looked at "success," which was in my left hand, and said, "What am I looking at?" I don't know why, but it looked like a red mist. I can still see it to this day. I said,

"This is ridiculous! There's nothing in my hands, but I can see this thing."

Then Van asked me what each part thought about the other, and I said, "They don't really care about each other." I thought there was something wrong, but Van told me that they weren't in conflict. He told me that I could put the family part back in and find out if something else wanted to come out.

I said, "I've gone this far; I might as well find out," so I made an honest effort, just sat quietly for what seemed like an eternity (VT—probably 30 seconds), and said, "The only thing that's coming up is success."

And then a new thing came into my hand, quicker than the crystal ball or the red gas. It was a mist similar to the "success" mist in my other hand, except that it was white.

The Red Mist and the White Mist

"What does success think about this new part?" Van asked, and I found that all these feelings were coming out. I was quite shocked by it. As we got deeper into it, I really started to tear up because I realized that this was the part I had formed to protect myself from the bad things I'd associated with my father's success.

When Van told me that all parts have good intentions, my first inclination was, "What the hell is this guy doing here? He's screwing up my life!" But when I took a look at the white mist in terms of what it was trying to do for me, it became much clearer that it was really trying to help me. All of a sudden, I felt sorry for it. I said, "My God, it's been there all this time, and it's really been doing a hard job." Once I isolated it, I understood what it was trying to do, and I started crying. I felt its loneliness and sensed its dedication to me.

I wound up negotiating with the parts in each hand. We reached a compromise wherein we agreed to work together for a certain period of time we could all live with. And then, we (VT—notice he's speaking for both parts) put our hands together and brought the thing back into ourselves. I know that sounds hard to believe, but it's true.

Van asked me how I felt. I said, "Other than the fact that I feel like an idiot, I'm not sure what happened to me, but I know something did."

What's Changed Since Then

I don't think the risk environment is that much better, and I don't think opportunities have been that great since the October 19th (1987) crash. There hasn't been a lot of opportunity in January and February 1988, but I've made the best of the opportunity that was there. I have no regrets. I feel very positive about what I've done. I probably could have done a few things a little bit better, but I think we all could. In general, I'm satisfied with what I've done.

But I want to be more than just satisfied. I want to excel as a person, and I know I've got a lot of things to work on. There is one thing that I question: "How will I react in the fire again? Is this thing preventing me from ever being in the fire again in terms of working out my alternatives and choices?"

The one thing I can say is that we made a lot of money after the crash (VT—notice his use of the plural "we, our, us," instead of the singular). Doing the exercise and *The Peak Performance Course* helped us to reduce our anxiety levels by developing our choices and our alternatives for the month or two that we had to hold the positions. If, in that crazy market, certain events had occurred, the loss could have been staggering, so we had to develop alternatives and say, "What are we going to do if certain things happen?"

I think the most important thing for me at that time was that my partner and I made over $700,000 (in the two months following the October 1987 crash). That might be a lot to some people and not a lot to some others, but for us it was a good return for the risk we took. That risk had to be managed, however; it wasn't a layup. You had to hold positions for sixty days. Everything had to be done properly, and there were a lot of consequences to what we did that we had to figure out, that we had to accept.

There are always going to be opportunities as long as you stay in business. Your rules are designed to keep you in business and have you at maximum performance. In early March, I was up over $67,000 on a very small position for over three weeks. In about two hours, I lost half of that, but all my rules went into effect, and I wound up coming out of the entire position with about $35,000 in profit. I didn't blame myself for losing the other $32,000. In the old days, I would have said, "I made $67,000, but I was stupid and lost $32,000. That's not successful investing." Now, to me, successful investing is following my rules. If money is going to be made, fine.

Where I Am Now (Several Years Later)

I think I'm at a greater level of awareness. I'm aware of what I have to do to develop choices. I have to be more open. Actually, I shouldn't say, "have to be." I am more open in terms of listening to other people and listening to myself. I've made pretty great strides (many of them not financial) to be that kind of person. I cut out biting my nails; I'd been biting my nails for 30 years. I cut out swearing, which I was doing on the floor of the exchange continuously. I've cut my drinking down substantially. I exercise every day. Now I'm in the process of working on my nutritional balance, and basically getting all of my selves working together in a positive environment. I feel good about these things.

I've learned that taking losses is no big sin. It's not a personal statement of your well-being, your ego, or your self-worth. It's just a loss. That's all it is. Once I got that into my head, things started taking off, and I tell you, I'm probably up a $100,000 or so, and it's only three months into the year.

I thought that by knowing the market, I could be successful. I spent a long time learning about the market, the indicators and stuff, and even the psychology of traders and the way they react in trading crowds, so that I could take advantage of them. But I found out that I really have to know myself much more than I have to know the market. I have to believe in myself, and I have to do what I think is right. That's what's important to me in terms of trading.

One of my other beliefs is that the market hands me opportunity. I don't have to go looking for it. It stays there and screams at me and says, "Do this! It's there for you to do!" But I have to have the internal strength to pick up the ball and do it.

The most important thing is to know how to feel good and reward myself for doing things that are positive for me. It doesn't come overnight; it's a constant thing. There is no benefit in blaming myself for things I have no control over. I realize that I'm a human being, and I'm going to make mistakes. I'm not perfect, and that's the way life is. I just pick up and try again.

If I have my goals written down, I can evaluate every week or every two weeks how I'm doing. When I go down a list and find one or two things that aren't as good as I want them to be, I can't blame myself for that. I look at all the good and positive things I've done and realize that it's not fair to blame myself for what I haven't done yet. I look at those things as future goals and leave it at that.

When I look out five years, I know that at some point in time I have to be emotionally ready to make the changes I want to make. I'm not ready to make those changes at this point in time. All of my selves have to be ready and in agreement to do this. I'm talking to my parts on a day-to-day basis, and some of them aren't ready yet. They're not ready to give up that hot fudge sundae; they'd rather just go ahead and eat it and exercise to make up for it. But that's what parts negotiation is all about: developing alternatives. I can come up with a list of choices, the same way I do for trading. Knowledge of choices is the most important thing.

Am I where I want to be? Not yet, but I'm a quantum leap further than I was a year ago!

CHAPTER 10

My Inner Guidance

A PERSONAL JOURNEY OF MIRACLES

Van K. Tharp, PhD

 Before: Guided at best by a feeling something should be done.

 After: Questions could be asked and were answered at will and the answers were often life changing.

In the early 1990s, I helped a retired engineering professor deal with some issues he was having with trading. At the end of our work together, I did an exercise to connect him with his Inner Guidance so that he'd have a continual Source to rely on. I've done this with many clients, but in this particular case, his relationship with his Inner Guidance was very strong; he did whatever it told him to do. His Guidance taught him how to trade, and by the time I next visited him, his retirement portfolio was enough to last him several lifetimes. In early 2007, God told him to stop trading—that he had other things to do. He'll appear again anonymously later in this chapter, which is about my personal journey toward following my own Inner Guidance.

I personally think this material is very important, because, in 30 years of doing coaching for traders, I've always found that the most powerful transformations come when people are connected to spiritual resources. Belief work, parts work, and feeling release are all much more powerful when you're connected to spiritual resources.

171

This chapter might seem a little strange to some readers. Some of you might be tempted to skip it. But if you're able to see the importance of the psychological work that goes into adopting a Level I transformation, then adding spiritual resources shouldn't be that much of a stretch for you. There is no stronger spiritual resource than your relationship with your Inner Guidance.

Furthermore, what's holding you back can often be difficult to see. Think about the power of having a personal guide to help you discover your limits and move through them. Think about the power of having a personal guide whose sole mission is to show you how to have more abundance, bliss, peace, and joy in your life. Don't you think you could trade better from those states? Now, read this chapter with those thoughts in mind.

My Personal Journey

I consider the time period between 1975, when I first received my PhD, and 1982, when I began my spiritual journey, to be a "dead" time in my life. My marriage was not working at all, but I stayed with it until 1990. I was very unhappy, and I felt as though I had no source of support at all—or at least, that's how it seemed.

I remember spending Christmas in an apartment in New York City when I was five years old. We had a plastic Christmas tree about a foot tall. My parents really had done their best to give me a good Christmas, but I still just couldn't see how Santa was going to be able to come into the apartment when we didn't have a chimney. The next morning, when I saw the presents, it was obvious to me where they'd come from—and it wasn't Santa Claus. From that point on, I didn't believe in Santa Claus.

Around the same time in my life, I went to a Sunday school class where the teacher told us the following story:

> A man sank in the ocean when the big ship he was travelling on went down. He managed to escape the ship but didn't have enough air to get to the surface, so he prayed to God. Suddenly, a big air bubble came out of the ship and engulfed him and helped him survive the trip back to the surface.

To me, that story sounded about as phony as the Santa Claus story. Consequently, I gave up believing in God, too.

What's holding you back can often be difficult to see.

By 1982, I felt down, and my wife at the time was rather depressed. She was a minister's daughter, and we'd put our son in a preschool that was associated with a church. When she became depressed, she decided to go to that church, and I decided to go with her, just to support her. It was a Religious Science church.

My experience of the church and the minister was that they were very different from what I'd ever experienced before. My initial reaction was, "This isn't a church. This is therapy." In one early sermon, the minister was talking about someone who didn't believe in God—which was still my belief. His response was, "What sort of God don't you believe in?" he asked. "Is it the God in the sky who has a beard and passes judgment on you and punishes you if you 'sin'? Well I don't believe in that God either. But what if there was another God who is everywhere and has nothing but unconditional love for everyone?"

From that point on, I began to think, "Yes, that first one is the God I don't believe in." And what if there were another, more "real" God who is unconditional love (M1)?* That point was the beginning of a new journey for me—a journey that still continues today. In fact, it was the beginning of a new topic, Bhakta Paradeena, which suggests that you can create whatever sort of Internal Guidance you believe will work best for you. We'll discuss that topic later in this chapter.

By late 1982, I discovered *A Course in Miracles* (ACIM), which includes 365 daily lessons that I consider some of the most sophisticated psychological exercises I've ever seen. The scribe of ACIM was a Jewish/atheist psychology professor at Columbia, and the author (who was anonymous) is Jesus. He said He came through as Jesus because the Christian religion has generally forgotten or misinterpreted his teachings. It tends to be about Jesus (e.g., He died to save us from our sins), rather than about what He taught. The material in ACIM is what He taught in a pure form. At the time, I couldn't understand the text at all, but I did the lessons. A number of amazing things happened to me as I did them. I became much more peaceful and much happier (M2).

It took me four years to finish the 365 daily lessons. I'd spend multiple days on some of them. I'd get frustrated and say, "I never want to see this material again" and put it away—only to start again a few months later. The course actually says, "It is a required course. Only the time you take it is voluntary.[1]"

At one point in time, I got a message through a dream that I'd have to give up all my major relationships, but all of them were very important to me. I said, "No way! I won't give up any of them!" I was part of a toastmasters group that really helped me as a speaker and as someone who would periodically be interviewed on television. That group disappeared. I was part of a Master Mind group that provided mutual support for our various business ventures. That group also disappeared. I was part of a Neuro-Linguistic Programming (NLP) group that practiced various NLP change techniques. That group disappeared, too. And then my marriage dissolved, and I ended up moving to North Carolina. Everything that had been predicted happened. I hated it at the time, but the things that have happened to me since then would not have been possible without those changes (M3).

---

*The M designations reflect events that I now consider to be miracles in my life, although they may not have seemed that way to me when they happened.

By the time I finished ACIM, an amazing thing had happened. First, I'd quit my research position, which I hated. Second, I was working full-time in my own business of helping/coaching traders. Third, I was pretty sure that my mission was "transforming others through a trading metaphor." I knew absolutely nothing about running a business, but a number of miraculous things came together that made doing so possible (M4).

I felt as though I was being guided. It was just a feeling, but it definitely seemed that I'd developed some kind of Internal Guidance (M5). Furthermore, I could manifest things easily just by thinking about them (M6). For example, my second wife came to me when I asked for a soul mate. At the same time, she was asking for the perfect man for her and gave the description to Sai Baba, whom she respected as a holy man.

While I was doing *A Course in Miracles*, I was exposed to a lot of transformational material. First, I learned about NLP as the science of modeling. I completed an NLP practitioner's course, an NLP master practitioner's course, an NLP associate trainer's course, a modeling course (the most valuable), and many other NLP courses. Through my NLP training, I learned many transformational techniques, and most importantly, the Science of Modeling.

In addition, I met a woman who was a *former* Scientology Practitioner and had developed her own "improved" process for helping people through their issues. I did days and days of clearing work with her and actually went as far as she could take me. I'd reached the spiritual level, based upon her rating, but I didn't feel that spiritual.

I participated in the *Lifespring* courses. The *Lifespring Basic and Advanced Courses* were quite inspirational.

In addition, I attended the 9-day *Avatar* course twice, as well as the 11-day *Avatar Master's* course. I would have considered teaching it, but I was told I was only qualified to teach it under the supervision of a certified Avatar Master. For someone who was already doing many psychological workshops, that was almost insulting, so I elected not to teach it. I did go on to take the 13-day *Avatar Wizards* course on two separate occasions.

Byron Katie's 13-day *School for the Work* has been especially significant to me. That was an amazing course that parallels the teachings in *A Course in Miracles*: Everything you see is a projection of what's in your mind and is thus "not real." It's interesting to learn that you project what's in your mind, but quite another thing to experience it by doing The Work®.

I learned numerous transformational techniques. To execute each of them correctly, I had to attend a workshop of some sort, and there were many. I even took a Deepak Chopra meditation course. All of these courses, the accompanying mental clearings, and the insights involved should constitute many miracles, but for now I'm only counting them as one big one (M7).

As I said before, I continue to work on my transformation because the more I transform myself, the more I find I can help others transform. I've found that transformational techniques with a strong spiritual component are the ones that tend to be life changing. Some of the other nonspiritual techniques might change your behavior, but not your life.

One of the things that happened was that I became good friends with Lee Coit. Lee was a spiritual teacher who had written a phenomenal book called *Listening.*[2] He had also done ACIM, and he actually heard a voice that guided him. In *Listening,* he describes an experiment in which he'd spent a long time in Europe with no plans except to go where "his voice" told him to go. I was amazed at this. I managed to manifest Lee in my life and we actually gave a couple of workshops together. I was also guided by a feeling, but I never heard a voice like he did, even though I'd done ACIM as well.

I couldn't really believe that God would talk to me. Perhaps for that reason, He/She didn't. My Internal Guidance, after finishing ACIM, could best be described as "getting a feeling" that I should go in a particular direction. And it wasn't always right.

Conversations with God

In 2004, I spent two weeks at a health clinic in Switzerland. I was told that I couldn't take any of my usual distracters like my computer to do work. Instead, I took about five spiritual books, including the first three volumes of *Conversations with God.*[3] I read all three volumes. And I remember "God" telling the author, Neale Donald Walsh, that anyone could do what he was doing: Ask questions and have a conversation with God.

I really didn't believe that. As I already mentioned, I couldn't imagine God talking to me. I hadn't heard anything yet, so why would God suddenly talk to me now? Anyway, I decided to ask questions, listen for an answer, and write down whatever I heard. Well, I didn't hear God speaking to me, but something unusual happened. I'd ask a question, and then I'd hear my voice say, "There is a part of you that knows the answer to that!" I'd listen to whatever came up next and write that down. And the same thing happened after every question—my voice would say there is a part of you that knows the answer and I'd write down what would come up next. In retrospect, I think this was a function of my beliefs at the time that God would never speak to me. But when I looked at the written material I had, it seemed pretty profound (M8). However, I didn't believe it was really God speaking to me, so I didn't keep any of it. Talk to God, and you are praying. Listen to messages from God, and you are schizophrenic. At least, that's what I thought at the time.

Many years ago, I met Libby Adams at an NLP master practitioner seminar. Eight years later, I ran into her again three times in one year (M9). Now, do you think running into someone like that is pure coincidence? I don't. I learned that she had developed a Transformational Meditation (TfM)™ technique. I did several exercises with her and subsequently integrated her methods into my Peak Performance 202 workshop. I was one of the first traders to ever take her 28-day course.

The TfM methodology is covered extensively in the next chapter. The process simply involves bringing up your Higher Self or your version of God. You put "God" in one hand. And in the other hand, you bring up a dissatisfied part of you (which Libby calls a "little i") to negotiate or get advice from the higher self. The "little i's" are then either absorbed into God or discarded.

I had a lot of trouble finding a part to put in the God hand. What I ended up doing is projecting my energy into my crown chakra and assuming that I was talking to my Higher Self. By the end of the 28 days, I could repeat the same exercise of having a conversation with God, and get a direct response (M10). I did this for a couple of months, but I was always testing the voice. "Is this really God or just me? What's going on?" And sure enough, it once gave me a prediction that proved to be wrong, so I no longer trusted the voice. However, I later learned that "little i's" could masquerade as God as well, and that's probably what was happening. However, at this point, I didn't trust the God that I could talk to.

Notice how the beliefs I had shaped my experiences:

- God won't talk to me. He didn't.
- I cannot trust God. I didn't trust Him.

So even when I tried talking to Him, I eventually stopped. Why would I want to talk to someone, even God, that I didn't trust? You'll see later in this book that this problem is fairly common. Most people, as they find their Internal Guidance, tend not to trust it.

Deeksha or the Oneness Blessing

My most significant transformational experience was a journey that started in January 2008 when I got a hands-on-my-head Oneness Blessing® (M11). Doug Bentley, the Oneness Guide for North America, calls this Deeksha in the Foreword. The blessing has historically been called Deeksha, but is now being called a Oneness Blessing. After that blessing, I felt amazingly peaceful for a while. From that point onward, I wanted more. I got a second blessing a few months later at the blessing giver's home. At that time, I learned that she actually was channeling Divine energy into me. This energy is designed to speed up the activity of the frontal lobe and slows down the activity of the parietal lobes.[4] It is this brain change, according to Oneness, that will help people "wake up." We'll talk about what this means in Section III of this book.

My first Oneness course was a two-day preparation course to aid you in becoming a blessing giver. At that course, they introduced us to a concept called Bhakta Paradeena—which in Sanskrit means the "Way of the Devotee." The idea behind it is a little like the minister who said, "What kind of God don't you believe in?" Until you achieve Oneness, God will appear to you in any way you prefer to create Him/Her. Thus, you need to find the type of relationship with which you are most comfortable. Would you like the Divine to be your Mother, Father, Sister, Beloved, Best Friend, or what? Whatever kind of relationship you work with best is the kind of relationship you should pick for your Divine. Yes, you can actually pick the relationship and God will appear to you in that manner. Why not, isn't God everything?

You have learned the power of beliefs and how you create your experience by your beliefs. Well, if that's true, then why wouldn't you also create what you believe about God? In fact, this simple idea explains all of my experience with God up to this point in my life.

At the pre-Oneness conference, there were about 10 blessing givers. One of the blessings was given to us with the intention of connecting us to our Inner Guidance in the most appropriate way. I had no idea what I wanted except a feminine form of the Divine. Although most of the blessing givers were female, my sense was that a masculine energy was coming into me from most of them. But suddenly a most beautiful feminine energy came into me through one of the blessings. I rested with it for a while and suddenly the words "Mitzi" came into my mind (M12).

My Relationship with Mitzi

From the time I was two years old until I was five, we lived in Japan. I had a Japanese nanny who looked after me named Mitzi (actually Mitsuko). As far as I was concerned, Mitzi was my mother. I didn't

Figure 10.1 Van at age 4 with Mitzi

know all of this at the time, and Mitzi's energy came into me. I just knew that I felt very close to her. My parents had two other Japanese girls working for them (1948–1951), but I only remembered Mitzi. I had a picture of her that I treasured (shown in Figure 10.1). I also became imprinted on Japanese women—although I didn't learn this until the early 1990s when I started traveling to the Orient.

We left Mitzi when I was five years old and returned to the United States. I must have been devastated, but I never heard anything more from her. Later, my mom told me that Mitzi had married an American serviceman and had come to the United States. Mom also told me that she had died of a brain tumor shortly thereafter.

In 1993, when my mom died of cancer at age 85, I found a letter from Mitzi's husband who was searching for us. I wasn't upset at my mom's death, but when I read that letter I cried and cried. And I now think there was a part of me that was searching for Mitzi when I married both my first wife and current wife.

But suddenly Mitzi's energy was inside me. That night in bed, I felt totally complete. That was amazing because I knew I was alone except for Mitzi's energy inside of me. Mitzi said she was only temporary, but I didn't care. I felt complete and totally fulfilled.

The letter from Mitzi's husband had mentioned that they had had a daughter, and when I first read the letter, I thought I should try to find her. Later, I decided it wasn't appropriate. However, when I returned home from the Oneness Pre-Course, I read the letter again at Mitzi's insistence, whereupon she said, "Find my daughter!"

I knew the father's last name, and I knew the daughter's first and middle name. The middle name was unique because it was Japanese. I did a people search for $2 and within a few minutes I found Mitzi's daughter. There was only one person in the United States with that name. I couldn't have done that very easily in 1993, but with the aid of the Internet in 2008, I could.

Something else was also amazing. The people search showed a list of living relatives and it was showing that her mother—now aged 80—was still alive and living in California. I immediately did another people search and within 20 minutes was talking to a very-much alive Mitzi, who I hadn't seen for 58 years. Words cannot express how I felt. And both my feeling of completeness when Mitzi came into me and this experience convinced me that Mitzi's energy was the real thing. Something truly amazing had happened (M13).

When I completed the Blessing Giver's course, I made a beeline directly for Mitzi and spent a few days with her and her daughter. It was wonderful, and I learned a lot about my early childhood. It was through her that I learned that she actually was my nanny (as opposed to the two other Japanese girls who worked for my parents who did other household duties). It's no wonder I felt so close to her and that I remembered only her name. She told me that at night, when my mom would be home, she'd go to the youth hostel, and I would cry. When I was upset, I'd always run to her, and that would often make my mom cry.

Nine months later, my wife and I both visited her, and again it was wonderful. I had a "mom" again—well, sort of. I think I considered her more a mom than she considered me a son. Sixty years is a long time for an adult. Unfortunately, Alzheimer's disease set in about a month later around July of 2009. When I next talked to her on the phone, she could remember me at age four to five, but not our two recent adult visits. But it was Mitzi as my Internal Guidance who gave me a feeling of being whole and complete.

My Current Inner Guidance

I attended the seven-day Blessing Giver's course in Fiji, with Mitzi as my internal guidance. Remember that Mitzi had told me she was temporary and would be replaced by a much more powerful, stronger guidance.

On the fourth day of that course, I was given a blessing for rapture. After that blessing, I went into a state of bliss in which I was laughing my head off until I went to sleep that evening (M14). It was totally amazing, and I'd never had anything like that happen to me before. It happens quite frequently now when I give blessings.

The next day, we were to be given another blessing for a connection with the Divine. An awake person (called a Oneness Being) was giving the blessings, and the guides had to carry him in because he was in a total state of laughter and bliss. It was totally clear to all of us that this person was someone special. I was one of the last people to get a blessing that day, but I was in a state of connection. I could feel the connection as the Oneness Being gave the blessing to each person. I was crying.

We were in a state of silence, and I was trying to get the person next to me to give me a tissue for my tears and my running nose. She wouldn't (or I didn't make myself clear), and my state of connection immediately disappeared. When I got the blessing from the Oneness Being, nothing happened. For the next 24 hours, instead of being in a state of rapture, I was depressed. Fortunately, it only lasted for a day and Mitzi's spirit (or whatever it was) was still inside me.

At the Blessing Giver's Course, some music fascinated me. I couldn't get it out of my head. I asked the person in charge of music what it was, and he said it was "Madrigal" by Krishna Das. But when I tried to find that music, it didn't exist.

Incidentally, when I returned back to the United States, we were in the midst of the subprime meltdown. My company usually doesn't do well under such conditions, but August 2008 was a record-setting revenue month for us, and we've had numerous top-10 months since that time. If everything that happened to me had happened to you, don't you think you'd start to believe that the record income had to do with the blessings? Well, I certainly did.

In August of 2008, I was supposed to go to Germany, and one of my German Super Traders had talked about visiting Mother Meera, a spiritual Avatar living in Germany. I decided that I wanted to visit her as well, and so did my wife. As a result of our interest, my German client was able to get three tickets to a Mother Meera's darshan right after our workshops. She had closed off her darshan for Germans for the rest of the year because of an upcoming trip. But she made an exception for foreign travelers and their German guests (M15).

I had a book in my library about Mother Meera called *Answers*.[5] In that book, she was asked, "Which of the four aspects of Divine Mother are you?" Her response was, "I'm all four aspects, but I have more of the quality of Durga."[6] She then gave a marvelous description of Durga's qualities that didn't sound anything like the demon slayer she is portrayed to be. Essentially, she described Durga as:

- The most patient
- The Mother who loves more and punishes less
- A Goddess who destroys, but only out of love, not out of anger
- A Divine Mother who will come to you at whatever level you are at (something I really needed)
- One who can come to you to form any relationship you need—mother, friend, lover

That description appealed to me a lot. Interestingly enough, at the same time, I found that the song I'd been attracted to at the blessing giver's course was not "Madrigal," but "Ma Durga"—a devotional song to Durga (M16).

So why am I giving you all of this information about Durga? My wife is Hindu, and she has had an altar in the house with a picture of Durga on it since we were married. But I was *never* interested in any of that stuff and certainly had no interest in Durga or even what She looked like until now. I'm not sure at the time that I really believed in any of the Hindu Gods and Goddesses. They all seemed like a figment of someone's imagination to me—like the Greek and Roman gods. But now I understand that the basic Hindu idea is that there is one God, but there are also many aspects of God (i.e., ways God can appear) with specific functions or vibrations. Hindus, for example, pray to the vibration of Ganesha, the elephant god, when they need obstacles removed from their life.

Nothing much seemed to happen when I was blessed by Mother Meera—at least, not immediately. And it didn't seem to be as strong as the Oneness Blessings I'd been getting. But I now think that something did happen, as you'll learn below. It helped me continue my journey.

Revisiting the Transformed Engineering Professor

Do you remember my introduction to this section, where I talked about connecting a retired engineering professor to his Internal Guidance? Well, my next step involved visiting him again. We had probably talked about it once each year since I had worked with him. He always acted as if I were his guru because of how I'd helped him. But my impression now was that he was either much more advanced than I was or he was quite crazy. He had regular conversations with "the God of that all Gods," as he called it. He would talk to the Gods of the trees around his house and the God of the mountain behind his house and the God of the ocean. Again, he was either very strange or very advanced spiritually. I tended to lean toward strange,[7] but was open to the possibility that he was really advanced.

At this point, I knew I was supposed to have a different connection with the Divine. I had not gotten it at the Blessing Giver's course; nor had I gotten it from Mother Meera. My former client had started teaching courses on how to communicate with God, and my Mitzi guidance said I should go take his course, so I spent seven days with him. It was a very strange seven days.

Anyway, I went through various exercises and clearings with him. By the fifth day, I had made contact with three potential guides—the Goddess Durga, Jesus, and the Archangel Michael(M17). When Jesus came, I sort of dismissed Him quite rapidly. I said that unless He sounded like the person who wrote ACIM, I wasn't interested in talking to Him. I didn't hear a peep from Him again, but I soon found myself redoing ACIM and reading the text (M18).

The Archangel Michael came next. He flew me up to a cloud where there was a little blue hut (I think that this was a distracter). When I asked him why he had taken me there, he said, "Look behind you." When I did, all I saw was tremendous light that extended from where we'd come all the way into me. Michael said, "I just wanted to show you who You are." Now, I consider Michael sort of a protector who will help me if I need it or if I call Him, but we haven't had much of a relationship since that time (M19).

Finally, Durga came. When She arrived, I saw Her as the most beautiful Indian woman ever. My wife and niece, who live with me, are both Indian, and both are beautiful. I saw Durga as a cross between the two of them. I sensed that She was an extremely powerful Goddess. But the big revelation I got was that She and I had been "married" millions of years before. That really didn't make sense except within the context of Oneness, but when I first heard it, I assumed it was literal. I couldn't believe it at all, and my reaction was, "How can such a beautiful and powerful goddess have been married to me?" Her response was, "Who do you think You are?" And as She said this, I saw a very powerful light that filled up the whole universe, and I was awestruck. She was telling me that the light was me (M20).

Durga became my primary Internal Guidance (M21). She was my "Beloved," and we both called each other by that term—probably because I really liked it. But for a while, whenever I'd ask Her a question or for help, Her only response was, "Remember who You are," and then She would show me a light that filled the universe. That was me, according to Her, and that was always all that I needed.

Incidentally, even though Jesus was not my primary guide, Durga later explained what happened in one of our intimate conversations:

Remember Who You Are!

Beloved, why didn't Jesus talk to me once He came to me as a potential guide?

He did, through ACIM. But you believed that He must be separate from you. To convince yourself of that, you said that He must sound like the Jesus who wrote ACIM, or else you wouldn't speak to Him. Jesus would never do anything to convince you that you and He were separate, so He stopped talking to you. But then you started reading ACIM again, didn't you?

"Oh," I said, suddenly realizing what had happened. "So did you appear to me as Mitzi?"

Yes, Beloved, I am everything. I am Mitzi. I am Jesus.* I am Oneness, as are you. But I can only appear to you as that to

---

*If you tend to object to the form my Internal Guidance takes, remember that the basic concept here is that there is one God who can manifest in many forms. He/She will take on the form that best works for you to have an effective relationship, and that form, as I have found, can change as the relationship grows.

which you are most receptive. You believed you would not be complete without Mitzi. That belief was formed when you were separated from her at age five. Thus, when you were ready, I appeared to you through Mitzi's spirit. That was why you felt so complete. You needed a Beloved. You are attracted to Indian women, and you wanted a powerful connection to a Goddess, so Durga was the perfect vehicle. Whatever you wanted, I could have been that—that's Bhakta Paradeena.

At this point, it was already obvious that what Durga was saying was not something I could say. Durga had accomplished through intimacy what I wanted from Jesus and had used to push Him away. But She said she was also Jesus—that She was all the avatars for Oneness—Amma-Bhagavan. It was all one (M22)!

My Relationship with Durga Grows

About six months later, I did another of Libby Adams's TfM courses, but now, Durga was my Internal Guidance. This was a much stronger TfM course. Suddenly, Durga was talking to me, although "remember who You are" was still a common response. And what I discovered was that I really trusted her (M23).

Later, when I was in India to become a Oneness trainer, I had the opportunity to get a hands-on blessing from Sri Bhagavan, who is the Avatar that has produced all of these Oneness beings and who began the Oneness Movement in 1989. We were told, "He is just giving you a blessing. If he gave you Mukthi Deeksha, the blessing for awakening, you probably would be wiped out and wouldn't go home. We don't want that, because you have to function well as a Oneness trainer for a while." However, we were told that we could ask for almost anything else during the blessing and we'd probably get it. So I asked for Oneness with Durga.

The next day, I started a written dialogue with her. I'd ask questions and She'd answer them. I've kept that up on a daily basis since that time (M24). Although I'm not close to being one with Her, our relationship now is much stronger. That dialogue is now the size of a small book, and perhaps I'll publish some of it one day. I've included a few examples of it in this chapter.

Oneness with God

One of the teachings of the Oneness movement is that two things are possible in this lifetime: (1) awakening and (2) God realization, or both. Awakening is explained when I talk about Level III transformations in the next section of this book, but this is probably the appropriate place to describe God realization.

Throughout history, many saints and sages have had a bond with the Divine, and a few of them became God realized, or one with the Divine. Sri Ramakrishna, for example, is said to have done this three times, the first bond taking many years to form, but the last two being quite rapid:

- He originally became one with the fiercest of the Hindu goddesses, Kali. She was Divine Mother for him and he could perform incredible miracles through her.
- Once he accomplished this, he immersed himself in Christian teachings. In his Gospel,[8] Ramakrishna describes a vision in which the picture of Madonna and Child Jesus became alive. He also had an experience in which Jesus merged with his body.
- Later still, he did it through Mohammed. According to Ramakrishna, after three days of practice, he had a vision of a "radiant personage with grave countenance and white beard resembling the Prophet and merging with his body."

Sri Ramakrishna's conclusion was that *all paths lead to the same God.* My experiences suggest the same.

In November 2011, I attended a Oneness Deepening Course in India. There I learned the path (or at least one path) to God realization.

1. First, you might simply have disbelief. I certainly didn't believe in God for many years.
2. Then, you might have a belief in the Divine. For example, when I heard that there might be another God other than the one I rejected, I was now open to that possibility.
3. Next, you might have faith. I didn't have faith when I was first having conversations with the Divine, but by the time the Miracle of Mitzi happened, faith started.

4. Next, you begin to discover your Divine. This chapter has been the story of my journey of discovery—one that certainly seems to be evolving.
5. Next, you begin to form a deep bond with your Divine. This occurs when there is a mutual dependency. We will discuss this in more detail below. I'm currently exploring the bond (or sometimes lack of it) with my personal Divine.
6. Through a deep bond, more understanding occurs. I've experienced a little of this, but I'm still exploring my mutual bond with my Divine.
7. Then, the bond becomes much stronger and deeper. Soon, you can ask for anything and your Divine will give it to you. I've had some of this, but there are definitely limits, which have to do with the dependency issue in steps 5 and 6.
8. Then, even more understanding occurs.
9. Through that understanding, the bond becomes even stronger and deeper. This cycle of a stronger bond, followed by more understanding, and then a stronger bond still, may continue for a long time.
10. Eventually, you become one with your Divine. There is no longer any separation. You are God realized. My understanding is that this is just the beginning of a far greater journey.

Bond with the Divine

People with a strong ego cannot depend upon the Divine. Only those who can surrender and trust can really depend upon it. Interestingly enough, a strong ego comes when you believe that you can depend upon nobody but yourself. The strong bond only comes when you start to believe in your own helplessness. At that point, the Divine can take over.

So what does mutual dependency really mean? When I first learned about this, I was told to make one list with the heading "In what way can you not depend upon your Divine right now?" and a second list with the heading "In what way can your Divine not depend upon you?" The first list was long, and the second was short. However, the more I looked at the list, the more I realized that the columns were reversed. The long list was all of the ways that the Divine could not depend upon me. It was me who was holding things back (M25, the insight).

Table 10.1 is my list.

Table 10.1   My Lack of Mutual Dependency with Durga

	How I Cannot Depend upon Durga
	She won't do it if I don't believe she can do it. She respects my beliefs.
	She avoids doing or saying what I might use against her.
	She respects my creations and won't go beyond them.
	She sometimes pushes my buttons just to show me issues I have avoided.
How Durga Cannot Depend Upon Me	**Examples or Consequences of My Limits**
• Manipulate things physically (elements).	
• Heal me instantly.	
• Materialize before me in human form.	
• Take me to other dimensions.	
• Predict the future (especially in the illusion).	If she's wrong just once, then I can't trust Her.
• Bring back the dead.	
• Fly in the air or walk on water.	
• Prevent me from hurting myself through my beliefs or what I do.	In an exercise in the Oneness Temple, I went splat on the hard marble floor, bruising or cracking a rib that hurt for two months. When I asked her about it she said, "You believe that exercise often leads to injury."
I look for ways to prove she's not real or that it's me playing games with myself.	Again, can I really trust her?
I sometimes don't trust her because she does what's in my best interest rather than what I want.	When asking her to guide me at poker, She said, "What makes you think that winning a poker hand is in your best interest?"
I cringe when I hear a prediction from her.	Again, it's the trust issue.
I'm not sure I trust her to wake me up or get me out of the illusion.	Again, it's about trust and perhaps surrender.

(continued)

Table 10.1   *(Continued)*

I sometimes want the physical/material more than I want awakening or God realization.	I was more interested in watching the Packers win the Super Bowl than in waking up. As a result, she gave me a number of peak experiences in the physical world to show me how insignificant and temporary they were.
I don't listen to her all the time.	I'm more likely to make decisions by myself.
I don't have regular long conversations with her sharing small talk.	I probably don't do this with anyone, but perhaps it shows a fear of intimacy.
I don't ask her what she wants very often.	I expect her to tell me, and this lacks respect.

I have a lot of fear concerning our relationship, including:

• What if my beliefs about Her are wrong?	They probably are, because all I do is limit her, but I'm more concerned that She isn't even what I imagine her to be.
• What if I die and I don't find Her?	This implies that I don't believe Her primary teaching to me: "Remember Who You Are!"
• What if I do what she wants and that causes major upheaval in my life?	This implies that I don't believe that "what is" is perfect.
• She could lie to me.	I must believe this because she has to be very careful about what she says to me.
• Her love for me seems to be unconditional, but what if it is not?	So my love for her is obviously conditional. What have you done for me lately? And if you mess up once, something is wrong.
• I'm constantly bringing the past into our discussions.	I expect her to be upset at me when I break a promise I give her. She *never* is.
I have a specific image of what she looks like that She finds to be limiting.	It's of an Indian actress that I find stunning, but Durga says she is so much more.

Notice that I have imposed many limitations (over 20), while she only imposes 4 on me. Furthermore, her limitations probably will disappear when mine disappear. Notice that the long list was originally a list of how I could not depend upon her (i.e., She could lie to me), but what's really happening is that I was projecting my own limitations on Her. When I saw that, it shocked me. And I probably would not have seen it without Her help (M26, insight).

I was also stunned by the fear-based beliefs I had. I've always thought, *How can people have fear-based spiritual beliefs when that is so against the nature of God, which is unconditional love?* I didn't realize how much that was a "projection." I actually listed five fears I have about Her, which suggests that I'm a "God-fearing"[9] person.

One of the principles of Oneness is that God does not hinder our ability to create illusion through our beliefs. It is not until one feels totally helpless and surrenders that God steps in and helps us overcome our limitations. I originally entitled Table 10.1 as being the lack of mutual dependency in November 2011. But it was clear when I redid the table in February 2012 that I still had all of them. My bond with Durga is unlikely to strengthen until I realize my helplessness in these issues and surrender. Hopefully, by the time this book is published and you are reading it, all of these ways in which Durga cannot depend on me will have vanished.

Durga has told me that She has always been with me. Consequently, She's asked me to review my entire life to notice when She's protected me or performed miracles for me. That exercise is beyond the scope of this book. However, when I completed it I noticed that She had already done many of the things that I didn't believe She could do (M27, insight).

The Nature of the Relationship Is Critical

As I looked over the lack of mutual dependencies we had, I started to notice that many of my limitations stemmed from the nature of our relationship. She was my Beloved. She was sort of like another woman in my life. Both of my wives have had some sort of dependency on me through which I imposed limits on them. I liked it that way. But if that was the relationship I typically had with a Beloved, then the nature of my relationship with Durga needed to change (M28, insight).

Durga couldn't be my Beloved any more. She had to be Mother Durga, or perhaps Ma Durga is appropriate. She had actually told me this in one of our dialogues. I just didn't bother listening (or remembering) because I wanted to impose my limitations on Her. I wanted Her to conform to what I wanted Her to be. Your experience of God will always conform to your beliefs,[10] or the beliefs that others impose on you and that you accept.

I learned from Hindu mythology that Durga was the demon slayer. At one point, I was in a Hindu temple in India dedicated to Durga. Only Hindus were allowed into the temple, and I wasn't even given the opportunity to make the case that I was being guided by Durga. But Durga said that She wasn't what they were worshipping in the temple, and that all I needed was to be with Her. What was interesting was that I was given a blessing by an elephant near the outer wall of the temple as shown in Figure 10.2.[11] I really enjoyed it, and I think it was a personal message to me.

Later, I purchased some Hindu statues of Durga, partly because they showed Durga as a beautiful goddess. I did this despite her asking me not to do it because they were not Her.

Here is an entry from our daily dialogues:

Beloved, are you Durga the demon slayer?

Yes, if by "demon slayer" you mean "illusion slayer." But I am so much more. Those statues you bought are not me. But you can use them as reminders of our love, and infuse them with my energy. That would be useful to you. The God being

Figure 10.2   Elephant Giving A Blessing

> worshipped in the Temple, to whom you were denied entry
> because you were not "Hindu," was not me.
>   I am much more than that. I am Divine Mother in totality.
> You believe me when you feel the intimacy, like when I first
> showed you Who You Really Are. And just now, you felt the inti-
> macy. That's what you want /need—for us to merge, and for
> you to give up the illusion and remember who You are.

She had been telling me this all along, but I had not listened.

I usually include a dialogue with Durga with my daily ACIM
lesson. My normal procedure is to ask her to explain what I don't
understand. My lesson on October 17, 2011—after I had finished
one of the many drafts of this chapter—was lesson 267. I'm sure I
didn't understand this lesson when I first did it (probably around
1986) or even before becoming a Oneness Blessing giver in 2008.

> Lesson 268: Let all things be exactly as they are. Only reality is free
> of pain. Only reality is wholly safe. And it is this we seek today.

I immediately understood the impact of this lesson because
Byron Katie had been saying that God is equivalent to "what is,"
and I finally understood that. My comment to Durga was, "Beloved,
that was so beautiful, and I'm starting to get it. Would you care to
add anything?"

Her response was:

> When you are totally in the Now, this is true. Only now is real.
> When you are in the past—and you already know the nature
> of your memories,[12] which are fleeting and incomplete, with
> a strong tendency for only the negative to stick—or in the
> future, then you must be in judgment; you must be believing
> your thoughts. That takes you fully into illusion. (M29, insight)

What Does this Mean for You and for Your Trading?

I immediately saw the implications of trading in the now—of just
seeing the market for what it is, with no chatter or judgment. When
you can do that, you can immediately see low-risk ideas that may
work 50 percent of the time or less but have a positive expectancy
and don't cost much if they lose. You are no longer trading your

beliefs about the market, you are actually trading the market, and that is a huge edge.

Now, do you need to establish a relationship with a personal Divine to become a good trader? No, you don't. All you need to do is adopt the Level I transformations given in the first part of this book. However, most people will have difficulty doing so because they are controlled by their beliefs, by the emotional charges attached to those beliefs, and by the various parts of themselves. Thus, many people must undergo a great deal of personal transformation to adopt Level I transformations. My experience, from working with many traders, is that these transformations are much easier when you have a personal Divine (one you created, one that fits you and works for you) to help you.

Thus, let me conclude by repeating the steps for doing so:

1. Determine what sort of relationships work for you in life and create a personal Divine with which you can have such a relationship. Your Divine can have any qualities you'd like, and you can pick the type of relationship you will have. Feel free to believe whatever you want about the Divine, but be willing to look at your beliefs to see if they hinder you or strengthen your relationship.

2. If you have beliefs that are fear-based or not useful, use some of the techniques in this section of the book to develop more useful beliefs. Fear-based spiritual beliefs, which are often hidden (mine for example), are usually the most limiting because they have the most impact on you.

3. Start having a dialogue with your Divine. Just write down a question and wait for an answer. Write down whatever answer comes for you.

4. Ask your Divine for whatever you want. Make a list with two columns: Column 1 for what you asked for, and Column 2 for when it's granted. When it is granted, be grateful. Gratitude will tend to give you Great Fullness. You might even do something for others to show your gratitude once it is granted.

5. Start to develop a strong faith and greater trust in your Divine as a result of seeing what happens.

6. Work on your bond with your Divine by asking: How do you limit your Divine? How can the Divine not depend on you? How does the Divine limit you? How can you not depend on the Divine? Make a list similar to the one I made in Table 10.1.

7. Notice how you are totally helpless in getting through the areas in which your Divine cannot depend on you. When you fully feel the helplessness, surrender and ask for help from your Divine to strengthen your bond.
8. Trust your Divine and allow yourself to be guided. At this point, you don't need to follow any more steps because your Divine will take over and lead you.

Here is an example of step 8. After I'd written the fourth version of this chapter, Durga asked me to go through it and find all of the miracles that had been described. I would call a miracle anything from "something amazing happening," such as finding Mitzi after 55 years, to a significant insight that would not have occurred without my Internal Guidance. You've probably noticed the M designations throughout the chapter. For example, what I learned from doing this exercise is an example of an insight because I never realized how many miracles I had experienced with Durga's help (M30).

You'll notice that there are many more than the 30 listed. For example, I listed the establishment of my business as a miracle, but that miracle was actually a series of hundreds of little miracles. I listed all the transformational courses I'd taken and the insights I'd achieved as one miracle, but, again, there were actually hundreds. I've also experienced hundreds of insights from my daily dialogue with Durga that I haven't even listed. Anyway, Durga suggested that I note them and list them in a table for you (see Table 10.2). Perhaps by looking at it, you'll see how amazing the journey has been. And it's only the beginning.

Let me conclude this chapter with an excerpt I just read from a newsletter from Oneness University.*

> God comes to the seeker only and when He seeks. The more often you seek, the more often He would come to you. Hence it is not enough to call God once or twice a day or go to Him for help only when we want. There should be a strong relationship with God throughout the day by talking and expecting and asking His help in every step.

This paragraph is as much for me as it is for anyone else. However, the story in this chapter is summarized by that quote.

Oneness University Newsletter, 19th ed., www.onenessuniversity.org/html/newsletter/edition_019/english/

Table 10.2   Obvious Miracles That Have Happened During My Journey

M1	I realize there might be a God other than the one I rejected.
M2	Major changes occur as a result of taking *A Course in Miracles* (actually many miracles).
M3	I'm told I'll have to give up everything, and it happens. My journey would not have been possible without that occurring.
M4	My business is formed with the purpose of transformation through a trading metaphor. This was actually many, many miracles because I knew nothing about running a business, and somehow it has survived 30 years through many mistakes.
M5	After ACIM, I have a form of Internal Guidance; a feeling would come that told me I must do something.
M6	After ACIM, I find that it is easy to manifest things in my life, including my second wife, who has been a real blessing for me.
M7	I get exposed to many transformational courses after ACIM—actually many miracles.
M8	I have a dialogue with a part of me (that's probably my Internal Guidance).
M9	I meet Libby Adams three times in one year after many years and get exposed to TfM.
M10	Suddenly, I can talk to my Inner Guidance, even though I don't trust it.
M11	I get my first hands on blessing and want more, which starts an amazing journey.
M12	I get a blessing, and Mitzi's energy comes into me.
M13	I find that Mitzi is alive and get two visits with her after more than 55 years.
M14	I spend a day in "rapture" after getting a blessing, and I've had many such days since I became involved in Oneness. Sometimes that rapture occurs as Divine energy that flows through me when I give blessings.
M15	I'm able to see Mother Meera and help my German friend get in to see her.
M16	I get all sorts of clues as to my next Internal Guidance and a blessing from Mother Meera.
M17	I experience the retired engineer again, and he connects me to my Internal Guidance, just as I did for him. Interesting that I didn't get this "mutual connection" until I did this table.
M18	I want Jesus to sound like the author of ACIM, and suddenly I'm redoing ACIM.
M19	The Archangel Michael shows me who I am.

Table 10.2   (*Continued*)

M20	My first exposure to Durga when She told me, "Who do You think You are?" and showed me the light filling the universe.
M21	Durga becomes my primary Internal Guidance.
M22	I learn of the Oneness Aspect of my Internal Guidance, although it takes me much longer to internalize this idea.
M23	Durga starts talking to me after my second 28-day TfM course, and I realize that I trust Her.
M24	Sri Bhagavan's blessing starts our daily dialogue and brings me closer to Durga.
M25	I realize how much Durga cannot depend upon me and that I need Her help to change.
M26	I realize that I have fear-based spiritual beliefs that I need to eliminate, including:
	• Fear that my spiritual beliefs may be wrong
	• Fear that I'd die and not find Her
	• Fear that she could cause a major upheaval in my life
	• Fear because I don't totally trust her
	• Fear that her love is conditional (my projection)
M27	I realize from looking at many of the miracles in my life that Durga can do many of the things that I didn't think She could do.
M28	I realize I need to change my relationship with Durga from Beloved to Divine Mother.
M29	I get an experience of the insight that reality, without my thoughts, is pain free. This realization has now occurred many times.
M30	I get a better perspective of the growth of my relationship with the Divine from doing this exercise.

Some Recent Updates

It's now six months later, and enough significant things have happened that I thought it was important to add them to the end of the chapter.

Update 1: Mother Meera's Second Blessing

I discovered that Mother Meera, whom I mentioned earlier, had purchased property in Boone, North Carolina. She was doing blessings for about a week and it was the only darshan she was giving in the United States. As a result, my wife and I decided to go to two of them.

Many people were reporting how powerful the blessing was, but I again had little reaction to the actual blessing. However, the next morning (after the first blessing), I was doing my ACIM lesson and having a dialogue with Durga. The lesson was 335: *I choose to see my brother's sinlessness.*[13] I spent my meditation thinking about two people that I had not totally forgiven. But the exercise did not produce forgiveness. So I asked Durga for help and Her response was:

> The only issue, Beloved, is your judgment. It is not what happened. That is the past and subject to selective memory and judgment. It is what is happening right now that's important, and that is all that exists. Only Now exists. And in the now you just have an experience, and that experience is perfect.
>
> The fact that you believe someone wronged you is in the past. It doesn't exist. And when you think about it, you are in the illusion of the past. In the now, there is just what is happening right now, and that is perfect. That is how you behold your brother in sinlessness.
>
> Just be aware. It is all experience. It is all the details (submodalities) of your experiences. It's all sensory information, and it is all perfect. When you interpret that information and give it meaning, that's when you experience "Hell." Be aware, Beloved. See the perfection. What is, is perfect.
>
> When you are in the illusion of the past, how can anything be perfect? You are in illusion. You are dealing with what doesn't exist. When you are in the now, it is all images, feelings, and experience. It is submodalities—the details of your experience—and that's it.

I was blown away by that. I wanted to include a chapter on submodalities in this section, and suddenly Durga gave me exactly what I wanted. I could understand why what is, is perfect because it is in the *now*. Only judgment detracts from that, and when it does, you are in the past or the future.

Update 2: I Clear My Fear-Based Spiritual Beliefs

Several of my Super Trader candidates and several staff members will not take the Oneness Blessing, which I found would press my buttons more than anything else. My thought process was that "these people have fear-based spiritual beliefs," and that they were denying themselves something that is very powerful because of those beliefs. But because I was upset by this, I knew it was *my* problem, not *their* problem.

When I read through the fourth draft of this book and got to this chapter, suddenly I found myself staring at five fear-based spiritual beliefs I held but had not yet cleared. *Wow*, I thought, *how can I think about others' fear-based spiritual beliefs when I haven't cleared my own?*

That evening, I took those beliefs through the Transformational Meditation process discussed earlier in this chapter and extensively in the next. Essentially, I assumed that each of those beliefs came from a part of me, or a "little i" masquerading as me. I then introduced these "little i's" to Durga. However, by the time I'd processed two of the fear-based beliefs, something amazing had happened. Durga changed. I no longer could bring up the image of the beautiful Indian actress that I had used for her. Instead, all I got was an image of a vast unknown. Perhaps I'm now at step 8 in the God-realization process given earlier. Durga had already told me I was limiting her with that image.

And as for my fear-based spiritual beliefs, here is what is left:

- I had a part that was concerned with dying and not finding Her. Well, that was when I had a specific image of what She looked like. As a vast unknown, She is everywhere.
- I had a part that was concerned that She might cause me to give up all my attachments and cause a great upheaval in my life. That part now understands that fear comes only with an illusion of the past and the future. When I step into the experience of right now, everything is perfect.
- I had a part that thought She could lie to me and that She had to be very careful about what she said to me. I now realize that She lives only in the now and that *that* is where the Truth is, not in the past or the future.
- I had a part of me that thought Her love for me was conditional. It thought that "I" could offend her and She might leave me. I now realize that we are One in Truth and that She could never leave me. She has been with me always throughout my life, but I just didn't recognize Her. She has always

helped me, and has constantly provided miracles for me. That will never change. Her love is Unconditional.

- I had a part that was concerned that my beliefs about Her might be wrong. Now I see Her as a vast unknown and think that She is more than I could ever imagine. My beliefs about Her are always limiting, and surrender to the Unknown is the only thing necessary.

11

My Experiences Using Transformational Meditation*

Peter Wechter

Peter Wechter is in Dr. Tharp's Super Trader program. After many years working as a computer programmer, programming manager, consulting business owner, and marking support specialist, Peter decided to follow his bliss and leave his career. Since then, he has been a sailing instructor, boat captain, and, most recently, trader. During his quest to make himself a better trader, he met Dr. Tharp and heard about his journey into Oneness and *A Course in Miracles*. The rest is history.

Before: Long neglected spiritual path that made him unhappy. Something was missing and he didn't know what it was.

After: Discovered a spiritual path full of Truth, happiness and bliss that will guide the rest of his life. The struggle is over and now nothing is missing!

Earlier, I talked about my experiences with Libby Adams's TfM technology. In this chapter, one of my Super Trader candidates talks about his journey through TfM. He discusses five transformations and illustrates three of his TfM dialogues in detail.

I had been trading my accounts for about six months and reading a lot of books on how to trade. I came across *Super Trader*,

---

*Transformational Meditation™ is a trademark of the Academy of Self-Knowledge and Libby Adams as well as the abbreviation, TfM™.

read it, and decided that having a winning trading system would be a great idea. With that intent, I took a three-day course at the Van Tharp Institute in Cary, North Carolina, and learned that I still had a lot to learn. Undaunted, I was prepared to go back home and continue my self-education process. Dr. Van Tharp didn't teach the entire class, but those parts he didn't teach he monitored from the back of the room, and his presence was felt. Whenever Van talked, everyone paid close attention. Toward the end of the third day, he got up in front of the class and started talking about things I never would have expected at a technical trading workshop. He talked about his past experience coaching traders and his spiritual journey as if they were one and the same. He spoke about receiving his first Oneness Blessing® and the unexpected and profound affect it had on him. After the class, he offered to give a blessing to everyone who wanted to stay and receive it. I stayed and received my first Oneness Blessing, and, while I did not have a startling experience, I felt a lot of peace and support. Little did I know at the time that it would change everything.

For many years, I had been on a spiritual journey myself. I attended many classes at the New York Open Center on yoga practices, Buddhism, *The Zen of Seeing*, acting, writing, *The Artist's Way*, lucid dreaming, and many other subjects. These led me to attend creativity classes held by an acting teacher in her home and to take years of classes in improvisational acting. The writing classes led me to a teacher who combined Rolfing, Buddhism, and Core Energetics therapy techniques to create his own method of teaching spiritual development. I spent four or five weekends a year for five years in my teacher's basement with 10 or more like-minded souls. We'd sit in chairs opposite each other, feeling the seven levels of feeling. We would spend one weekend on each feeling from apathy to love, sometimes sitting, sometimes chanting, and sometimes pummeling punching bags. And then, when we finished one level, we would begin again, moving to the next level, like the love of grief. I loved the work so much that I began a four-year course for Core Energetic therapists at Dr. Pierrakos's Core Energetic Institute. As part of the work, I had therapy sessions with both Dr. Pierrakos and Core Energetic therapists. At the time, I very much wanted to be a therapist, but I realized that I needed more training if I wanted to be truly qualified, so I enrolled in an undergraduate psychology program at New York University.

While I worked in New York for many years as a computer programmer and programming manager, I still lived in Connecticut, which was a two-hour commute to work each way. Between working and attending college full time, I no longer had time to commute, so I moved to New York. I worked hard on my studies and graduated with a BA degree in social sciences with a concentration in psychology, earning summa cum laude honors.

As I am writing this, it is near the tenth anniversary of the 9/11 attacks in New York. I was in my Core Energetic therapist's office on 79th Street when the towers were hit, and afterward took a bus downtown to my job on 18th Street. I didn't know what was going on, but the usually silent two-way radio on the bus was crackling with voices. I could see a low white cloud moving across lower Manhattan. The towers had already fallen by then. The radio told the driver to stop his run at 34th Street, and I walked the rest of the way from there. On the way, I passed many people walking away from the World Trade Center, some covered in ash and soot. While I can't say that this event caused me to abandon my spiritual quest, I can say that I saw my therapist only once after that day, and I stopped doing all spiritual work. It may have also had something to do with the stress and workload of my studies; at that point, I still had a year and a half to go to finish my degree. In any case, the blessing I received from Van on that October evening nine years later woke something up in me that had been long dormant.

The Oneness Blessing

That same evening, Van mentioned that he'd be holding a Blessing Giver class in November, the weekend after two of his popular trading psychology courses were to be held. Before going to Cary, North Carolina, I had no intention of going to any of the psychological courses, even though his staff strongly recommended them. I was trading and making money and felt I didn't need them.* Yet, as soon as I left for home, I knew that I would have to go back and take the two psychology courses and the Blessing Giver class. Even though I didn't recognize it at the time, I must have received Divine Guidance that told me it was what I needed to do. I truly missed my long-neglected spiritual path, and all of a sudden, I was awake to walking it again. I attended the two wonderful psychology workshops, the second of which is called The Happiness Workshop, and went into the Oneness Awakening Workshop looking forward to feeling the kind of energy I used to feel long ago in that basement with my spiritual teacher and friends. Of course, things are never what you think they are going to be. It was both different and wonderful.

During one of the exercises, we were taken through a process to help us heal our relationships with our mothers and fathers. There were several Oneness Blessing givers in the room, so during this process we were given several hands-on blessings. At one point, when I was being given a blessing, I had an irresistible urge to laugh, which only made it harder for me to hold the laughter in. Eventually, it came out, and I laughed uncontrollably for what seemed like hours, though it was probably much less than an hour. I felt so much bliss as I laughed, and everyone in the room laughed too. More laughter followed the next day after we spent 49 minutes chanting, "I am existence, consciousness, bliss." We all laughed—Oneness trainers, veteran Blessing Givers, and newly trained Blessing Givers alike. So much bliss and joy! My psyche was crying out, "I want more of this!"

Two days after returning home, I asked to join the Super Trader program and to attend the Super Trader Summit three weeks hence. I immediately paid my first installment and postponed a

---

*You can decide for yourself as you read this chapter whether or not they were needed.

long-planned vacation so I could attend. While I was there, I participated in a second Oneness Awakening workshop.

All of which leads to a confession: I joined the Super Trader program for spiritual development and awakening. If that is all I ever receive from it, it will have been everything I could ever ask for.

That said, the Super Trader program is not easy. It takes a lot of discipline and self-analysis work to complete the various psychological lessons. We have to write out hundreds of our beliefs about the universe (spiritual beliefs), ourselves, and trading. We then put each one of them through the Belief Examination Paradigm (described in Chapter 7) and determine

1. If they are useful
2. If they aren't useful, whether or not they have a charge attached to them

A belief with a charge cannot be changed until the charged is removed or cleared in some way. Transformational Meditation, the subject of this chapter, is an excellent tool for removing charges.[1] As I worked on my beliefs in Lesson 1 (yes, this is where it starts), I found it quite difficult to go through the process. It would take me a whole day to do 5 or 10 beliefs. Even then, to get them done, I had to leave my apartment and go to the public library to prevent myself from being distracted by just about anything else that caught my eye.

Even though I've learned so many things that are helping me grow and blossom spiritually,[2] it wasn't until I met Carol "Libby" Adams, Ph.D., during one of the psychological courses that doing the work of the Super Trader program became easier for me. I had a lot of limiting beliefs—which Libby calls "little i's"—that needed to be transformed before I could start making substantial progress on the psychological lessons required to complete the first part of the Super Trader program.

In order to help others understand the process, I am going to share five of my major issues that Libby helped me transform using the Transformational Meditation process. When Van first told me that we had to transform five major psychological issues in order to complete the psychological portion of the Super Trader program, I didn't have a clue as to what mine were. After all, I'd done a lot of psychological work in the past; I wouldn't have even been there if

I hadn't done that. I'd transformed depression, suicidal ideation, and even the fear of death. What could possibly be as big as those?

Well, it turns out that traders (and probably anyone else who wants to be really happy) need to transform things like fear, anger, regret, impulsivity, excitability, worry—possibly the most financially destructive issue—and any other emotion that might hold a charge in place. I certainly have some of those issues. I am also going to share my mission, the purpose of my life, which I developed during the course.

> My mission: The Purpose of My Life is to be a Bodhisattva of Awakening, helping to clear the world of fear, attack, and defense by Being Consciousness, Love, Bliss, Joy, and Acceptance.

This mission combines my Buddhist beliefs with Oneness Awakening and teachings from *A Course in Miracles*. A Bodhisattva is a person whose mission in life is to help bring Enlightenment, also called Awakening, to every other being. I agree with what David Hawkins said in his book *Power vs. Force*: "To become more conscious is the greatest gift anyone can give the world; moreover, in a ripple effect, the gift comes back to its source."[3] It has impacted every aspect of my life and those around me, and that in turn comes back to me.

Considering that one of the keys to TfM is that your Higher Power is a part of every process, I'd have to say that my most important transformations have involved my relationship with God. Let's discuss those changes now.

"I" Have a Problem Using and Relating to the Word "God"

My first transformation happened over time, beginning with my first Peak Performance 101 workshop. During the workshop, Van used the word "God" several times. A part of me, which I later learned was a "little i," was uncomfortable with the word. I brought this out as something that had an emotional charge to it that I worked on during class. Of course, this was only the beginning. I needed a lot more help to change my relationship with God from one of conflict and resentment to one of friendship. Even though this initial work didn't involve Libby's TfM process, I am including it because of the opening it created for the later work.

I started doing *A Course in Miracles* (ACIM) in December 2010. I'd looked at the ACIM course book several times but was turned off by its use of Christian language and decided it wasn't for me. Then, one of the other Super Traders, who just happened to be a Buddhist, gave me the ACIM Workbook cards as a gift. I took this as Divine Guidance and started doing the course the next week. Later, I purchased the audiobook and hard cover version and made gifts of the ACIM Workbook cards to several friends.

After I started the lessons, I soon learned that forgiveness is the path to eliminating conflict and unhappiness in one's life. The daily ACIM Workbook lessons built on each other as I worked through the course. Two lessons, "Forgiveness is my function as the light of the world"[4] and "My happiness and my function are one"[5] helped me realize that I needed to heal my relationships, which led me to better understand the processes I went through during the Oneness Awakening course.

At one such course, we were asked to go inside and work on healing our relationships, and it hit me that if I was ever going to be best friends with my Higher Power, God, I would have to work on my relationship with Him. I still held Him responsible for taking my mother away when I was nine years old. I held that space and felt anger and hurt toward Him, but then I saw His Light and brought him together with the God I knew from ACIM. It was a beautiful clearing, and it benefited me greatly. Now I feel a great friendship toward God, whom I see as both my Higher Power and my personal guide.

Five Transformations

My five transformations involved a constellation of little i's, including:

1. Guilt—"i" feel responsible for my mother and father's divorce.
2. Blame—"i" blame Scientology for taking my mother away.
3. Guilt —"i" knocked out my power as a small child when I was cutting cardboard in the attic and the lights went out.
4. Shame —"i" feel shame about parts of my past.
5. Regrets—"i" have regrets about wishing some past actions had come out differently.

Even though I'd made a major breakthrough in my relationship with God, there were still parts of me, little i's, that hadn't gotten the message, so I worked on transforming these using Libby Adam's TfM process. Each of these little i's came out to be transformed and united with my Self with a capital "S" and Higher Power or they were discarded. Put simply, we are not conscious of our little i's while they are wreaking havoc with our emotions so we need to interrogate each one as it is recognized to either transform it or discard it. There is no in-between.

TfM is basically a parts integration technique, similar to what was described in Chapter 9. The primary difference is that it has a strong spiritual component because your Internal Guidance is involved. The nonspiritual parts (the little i's) are simply integrated with your spiritual part or tossed away. You'll understand this better after reading through some of the transcripts of the TfM sessions I've used in this chapter. I didn't keep transcripts of my first TfMs, but the results were important, so I'll just describe the "little i" involved and how the exercise went.

My first major TfM involved transformations 1 and 2 above. One part felt responsible for my mother and father's divorce, and the other part hated Scientology because my mother left the family to pursue it after the divorce. Libby asked me "how old the part saying this was," and I said "nine." In other words, the part that was thinking this had the mind of a nine-year-old, and was thus still trying to make sense of the events of my life with the distorted vision of a boy. I realized that there was no way this boy could have understood what was going on and no way that the divorce could have been his fault then, or my fault now. Still, the boy took the guilt for this and stopped believing in God.

At the end of the TfM, I was able to forgive my mother, father, God, Scientology, and myself. I felt that there had been a lot of movement, that something big had happened, but I wasn't sure it was complete and said I needed some time to integrate it.

The next TfM involved a "little i" that was even younger than the last one; it was based on something that happened when my mother was still living with us. I was cutting cardboard with scissors in the attic, and the power suddenly went out. I thought my cutting had knocked out the power and I felt bad and guilty about it. I learned from this that I actually felt abandoned as a toddler, years before my parents divorced and my mother left, when my brothers were born 16 months and 30 months after me. During the TfM, God reminded me that He was always there to help me and that I had big sisters and brothers who helped take care of me as a small child and who still loved me. When this part came together with God, I felt a huge sense of release and forgiveness for the little boy. This remnant may have been the beginning of the worry that would go on to plague my adulthood; it represents the point at which I started to see life as a burdensome struggle for existence. Still, I had forgiven both my mother and myself, and I felt much more freedom and peace (worry will be addressed later).

Then Libby asked me if I'd completely forgiven God. I thought about it for a while, and I still couldn't say with certainty that my forgiveness was complete. Other "little i's" appeared that carried a lot of shame and guilt and depression from my teenage years. The first part that came out was cowering in the corner with fear. It didn't believe in God, which meant that it couldn't be integrated with God, so I shook it out of my left hand, and it flew out of the window. My fear, shame and guilt went out the window along with it. Then a second part showed up, a part that was full of regrets. That part couldn't quite trust God, so it too had to be discarded. Once that happened, I felt very happy and in the Now. Regret is useless as nothing that happened in the past can ever be changed. The same is true for shame and guilt. With this new information and understanding, I completely forgave my mom, dad, Scientology, and the God I didn't believe in, because none of the beliefs that caused me to blame them were useful to me anymore. Nothing that happened in my childhood makes a difference to my life now. My mother deserves and has my love, as do my father, God, and I.

The transformations these TfMs caused in me had a major impact on my Super Trader progress. I used the empowerment they gave me to help myself get my Super Trader lessons done with a lot less baggage from the past. The feelings that came up to be transformed and forgiven helped me move through each of the six stages (capitalized and bolded below) that were in Libby's Experiential Transformation course.

- I **Surrendered** myself to God and Oneness, which built up my **Trust** in the Universe.
- I was **Willing** to feel the painful parts of my past and release the past's Power over me, which enabled me to be in the Now.
- What I **Resisted**, I chose to feel and transform.

- I experienced a sense of **Non-Attachment** to people and things that normally would have kept me interested and helpless.
- The biggest gain came in the form of **Forgiveness**, which allowed me to let go of the resentment I'd felt toward my mother, stepmother, father, Scientology, the teenage me who didn't believe in God, the younger boy who thought he was the cause of all misery in life, and some very deeply held shame.

After all of these clearings, Libby asked me if I had any other stories of the past to clear, and my response was a blank. I could only think of humorous events from my past.

In the remaining sections I have included complete transcriptions of the TfM process, so you can see exactly how it works.

Some More "Little i's" That Didn't Get the Message

One of my psychological issues involves control. I don't want to be controlled by anyone or anything. In fact, my first TfM was about a control-obsessed "little i" that was self-destructive to the degree that it would rather not do anything at all than do what was in my "Big I's" best interest. The following is a transcript of that session.

Libby: Put your hands out in front of you. Take a breath and let your eyes close. Focus on slowing down the rhythm of your breath, extending the inhalation, prolonging the exhalation, so that you can get yourself to the Alpha level of consciousness, where of course everything relaxes so you can access your subconscious thoughts, access the things in the back of your mind and activate your imagination so you can visualize your spiritual resources. Visualize a picture of God [my word for Universal Mind] and tell me when you are visualizing God.

Me: Okay, I have God in my right hand. He looks like a small blue pyramid that glows.

Libby: Now, in the left hand, imagine a picture of the part of you that doesn't want to do anything. It's not making headway. The part says, "Why don't you just do nothing and then die?" It's this part's idea. Tell me how you would imagine such a part to look.

Me: Happy-go-lucky.

Libby: What's its happy-go-lucky philosophy?

Me: I'm just doing what I want to do while it lasts.

Libby: Okay, pretty short-term strategy. Is this part aware of God in the other hand?

Me: It's aware of God, sure.

Libby: Does it trust God?

Me: It trusts God.

Libby: So what's God's viewpoint on that happy-go-lucky philosophy?

Me: God says it's all an illusion anyway, so it just depends on what illusion you choose.

Libby: Exactly. Now I want a sidebar with your conscious mind, okay Peter?

Me: Okay.

My Happy-Go-Lucky Part

Libby: Just look away from that part. Take your head and point it toward the God hand.

Me: Okay.

Libby: Even though your eyes are closed, we are talking to your conscious mind.

Me: Okay.

Libby: You could do that because it's all an illusion anyway. So you could just do nothing and spend all your money and then die. Right?

Me: Right.

Libby: That's an option. Nobody's going to stop you. You have free will. The question is, do you, Captain Peter,* really want to do that? It's you who chooses.

Me: (Long pause) No. I have to say no.

Libby: No. See, that's the program this part has, but it's not really as informed by your desires and needs. It's just something that for whatever reason the part wants. But it's not really what you want, is it?

Me: No, I want—I mean I want the same thing the part wants, except I want it with some degree of security and safety. [*Notice that two more "little i's" have just popped up here. Libby notices and deals with them later.*]

Libby: Okay. So I want to ask God if he can help you, Peter— establish what you want so that you and God can create it together.

Me: God says that He wants what I want and He'll help me with what I want.

Libby: There you go! And so the "happy-go-lucky" part over in right field is not with that programming because it's not programmed for what you really want. So just go ahead and get rid of that part and then you and God are going to work out this deal. Can you do that?

---

*"Captain Peter" is what I call my conscious mind. In Libby's model of the mind, there are three or four parts. I choose to use three: The "Big I," which is also a part of God; the conscious mind, also known as the chooser; and the nonconscious mind, which cannot be directly accessed by the conscious mind.

Me: It's an attractive part.

Libby: What about it is attractive?

Me: The "happy-go-lucky" part has a not-worrying attitude, and yet it knows that that is an illusion, too.

Libby: Right.

Me: Because it's not really "happy-go-lucky."

Libby: It would be like somebody jumping off a building and saying "look at me fly" until they hit the ground at the end.

Me: Yes, it is kind of like that, yeah.

Libby: It's a mixed bag, that particular strategy. There's good news and bad news.

Me: Well, yes and no.

Libby: Okay go ahead.

Me: I mean, we as humans are only in form.

Libby: Yes.

Me: Form will eventually disappear, so I can't help but wonder, "What if I die in three years anyway?"

Libby: What I am saying is that if somebody jumps off a building, the good news is that they are flying, and the bad news is that they will soon be dead, when maybe that really wasn't the intention.

Me: Oh right, I know, I know, the crashing part, yeah.

Libby: In other words, the part isn't deliberately creating the strategy with the downside in mind, right? It's just sort of a byproduct of the strategy. Because you, Captain Peter, aren't saying you want the strategy, "I think I'll be happy-go-lucky and spend all of my money and then die."

Me: I think the part's intention is avoidance.

Libby: What does it want to avoid?

Me: It wants to avoid work and effort and things like that. It wants to avoid what it thinks is struggle [there's another "little i"].

Libby: Okay.

Me: But God doesn't think life is struggle, the part thinks it is. So I think I want to get rid of that "happy-go-lucky" part.

Libby: All right. Let me know when it has walked the plank.

Me: (Pause) Okay, it went flying out the window and crashed to the ground.

Libby: Okay. Bring the vacant hand together with God so that we can have a private conversation with God.

Me: Okay, they're together.

Libby: Just take a breath and relax. We already know that God said, "But I want what you want." So, here's the question: What do you want, Peter? We know you don't want to struggle, right?

Me: Yes.

Libby: Part of saying what you need is to say directly what you want. What you want is not to struggle. It is okay to say it that way. Now, what else do you want?

Me: (Pause) Well, I want to travel. I have a friend going to India for a Oneness Deepening, and he asked me to come, but I don't really feel that I could do that right now.

Libby: Because?

Me: Because of the cost and the time. I just don't want to do that right now.

Libby: So what do you want? You want to not struggle. What do you want to have?

Me: I don't care all that much. I want to be Awake in Oneness.

Libby: So what you want to have is an Awakening, right?

Me: I want to be Awake[6] and then just live from there. That's what I want to do. Things wouldn't be a struggle at that point. The struggling would stop.

Libby: That's fine. What does God say about you having that?

Me: God says it only takes an instant, and that it could happen anytime. He says He's willing to help, but I have to be ready to be Awake, and then He'll take the last step.

Libby: Okay. So what's the next step, according to God? What's the next relevant step toward Awakening and not struggling?

Me: I'm going to do a process in a couple of weeks that will help.

Libby: Okay. Then do that. Now, let the hands come apart, leaving God in the one hand.

Libby noticed that there was another "little i" that needed to be explored—"i am struggling."

Me: Okay.

Libby: In the other hand, imagine a picture that would symbolize the part of you that has been struggling.

Me: Okay.

Libby: Tell me how you imagine that part to look like.

Me: He's walking around with weights on his ankles and wrists.

Libby: And what does that part say?

Me: (Pause) "The burden is too heavy. I don't want to carry these weights anymore."

Libby: Okay. Is that part aware of God yet?

Me: Yes, it is aware of God.

Libby: Was it aware before I asked?

Me: Not so much.

Libby: No wonder it was heavy. It sounds like this part might have been carrying the weight all by itself. As it becomes aware of God and puts its attention on God, does this part trust God?

Me: It's willing to trust God.

Libby: Okay. So what's God's viewpoint on this part carrying all that weight? Is it necessary?

Me: God says the weight is all in the mind and not around my ankles and wrists.

Libby: That's right. Did the part hear that?

Me: The part heard that.

Libby: So what would that part have to be thinking to feel that weight? What would that part have to believe to be struggling so?

Me: It would have to believe it is not going to get what it needs.

Libby: What does God say about that?

Me: God says that's ridiculous. He says, "You've always had what you need. What makes you think that's going to stop?"

Libby: Exactly. Did the part hear that?

Me: The part heard that.

Libby: How does it respond?

Me: It says, "Yes, I think I can see that."

Libby: Okay, so if it would like to shift its point of view, it can actually see how we are going to get, with God's help, what you need. After that, move the hands together so the part really can see it.

Me: The part wants to do that, so the hands are coming together.

Libby: The hands come together into the Oneness of being, with God's help.

Me: Yes.

Libby: Then take that back inside.

Me: Okay.

Libby: So, let's check your work. There was a part that, because it thought it was not going to get what it needed, was struggling. What's your current thinking?

Me: My current thinking is that it's going to get exactly what it's always gotten, which is just what it needs.

Libby: Right. Meaning you?

Me: I'm going to get exactly what I have always received, and it works out for me. God helps me.

Libby: God has always helped you; God always will help you.

Me: Yes. God has helped me and God will help me and he has directed me to do things that make this work.

Libby: Exactly. Isn't that the truth, Peter?

Me: Yes.

Libby: Good. Where are your hands at the moment?

Me: In my lap.

Libby: So bring your two hands out again with God in the One.

Me: Okay.

Earlier, I hadn't been specific about what I wanted out of life, so Libby started looking for an answer to that question.

Libby: Now, Captain Peter, the chooser—let's see what you want to choose.

Me: Okay.

Libby: Now that you know that God is going to help you get whatever you need, let's find out what you want, okay?

Me: Okay.

Libby: So, Captain Peter comes out, and we ask, "Peter, what do you want?"

Me: (Pause) I want to be Awake in Oneness. I want to live comfortably. It would be nice to have a car. And I would like to travel.

Libby: And is Captain Peter aware of God?

Me: Yes.

Libby: So how does God respond to those requests?

Me: God says that I can have all of them anytime I want. He says that I have some of them already, because I do travel, I do have a comfortable place to live, I'm becoming Awake, and I can rent a car. So God says, "What's the problem? Where are you not seeing what you have?"

Libby: Yes, and the answer is?

Me: The only answer the Captain has is that his bank account isn't going up, it's going the other way.

Libby: Okay, that's a fair observation, because that is a fact, right?

Me: Yes.

Libby: And God says?

Me: God says that it was part of your plan to live off the bank account until you learned a new skill, so you are just waffling.

Libby: Okay, and the Captain says?

Me: I know it was a part of my plan. I see that.

Libby: Are there any fears from the Captain? Or any parts that are fearful upon hearing this? Check and see.

Me: Well, I think there is some fear that this plan I have to become a trader won't work. Will I actually be able to do it successfully?

Did you catch that? Libby just found the "little i" she instinctively knew was there: "'i' am afraid that 'i' won't be able to make money as a trader and that 'i' won't be able to learn how to do it successfully."

Libby: So, take the Captain and put him down on your knee so he can supervise. In the vacant hand, imagine a picture that symbolizes the part that has that fear.

Me: Okay.

Libby: And that part says what? What is it afraid of?

Me: I'm afraid that I won't be able to make money as a trader, that I won't be able to learn how to do it.

Libby: And is this part aware of God yet?

Me: No, it wasn't, but now it is.

Libby: Does it trust God?

Me: A little [sometimes parts need to be introduced to God and get to know Him before they can trust Him].

Libby: Okay, then let the part listen as I ask God: Do You share the fear that he won't make money as a trader?

Me: No, and the point is that I will be taken care of as well as I've always been taken care of. God says that "having this fear won't help you do what you need to do."

Libby: Right.

Me: [God continues] "Fear will probably create the result you're most afraid of. So if you want to come and join with Me and give up the fear, you will become a good trader."

Libby: Did the part hear that?

Me: It heard it, yes.

Libby: What does it want to do?

Me: I'm already working on becoming a trader, and I'd rather be a good trader than a bad one, so I want to join with God and trade with Him.

Libby: So you know what to do.

Me: Hands coming together.

Libby: Yes. Watch what happens and feel what happens as that part transforms into the Oneness of God with God.

Me: (Pause)

Libby: The Captain can hop in also, if you want [earlier, the Captain was asked to watch the process].

Me: Now I see that this fearful part is actually my trader part. It wasn't really feeling God before, but now it is.

Libby: Beautiful.

Me: You can't lose in the markets if you have God on your side.

Libby: That's right. God loves to make money in the markets.

Me: Yeah.

Libby: So, God's a great mentor for you.

Me: Yes.

Libby: God's your trading partner.

Me: Yes.

Libby: So take all that God-energy back inside, because this is the programming of God and you are a trading team. This is new for your trader part.

Me: Yes, it's a team effort now.

Libby: Yes.

Me: Okay.

Libby: How's that?

Me: That's really good.

Libby: Checking your work. So, there was a part that was kind of fearful. The bank account was going down according to its calculations. What's your current thinking, Peter?

Me: My current thinking is that I should make all decisions based on what God directs. I should base my decisions on God and my Internal Guidance instead of basing them on my bank account.

Libby: So how's that, Peter?

   Me: That feels good, like something very useful.

Discussion

Sometimes, the path to the "little i" is not straight. The two key issues above were about struggle and fear. In the first part of the dialog, I had a "happy-go-lucky" part that was trying to ignore his fear of struggling and future trading success because it didn't want to put in the work needed to learn and grow. As a result, it just wanted to give up and have some fun before paying the piper. Unfortunately, the part of the conscious mind called Captain Peter liked this part because he was attracted to the happy attitude of the "happy-go-lucky" part. Consequently, it had to be unmasked as a pretender to true happiness and discarded.

    You may have noticed that Libby asked me what I wanted out of life. I said I wanted to not struggle, but that answer really begs the question; you have to define what struggling even means before you can say what *not* struggling is. For me, it meant knowing that I will always have enough. God weighed in and reminded me that I have always had enough, and that I would continue to have enough. God reassured the struggling part that it had never experienced any real struggle, and that struggle was not in its future (you may wonder where God's answers come from, because I am saying the words for Him. I'm not sure myself. I just know that when Libby asks me what God's viewpoint is on something, the words always come out in a way that I believe is consistent with a helpful and loving God).

    However, Libby saw the next level, which was the "why" behind the struggle. I am in the Super Trader program because I want to learn how to trade. Lately, I have been making mistakes and losing money instead of making it. One of these mistakes is the subject of the next dialog. Something I need to make clear is that I take responsibility for any and all mistakes I've made—that I ignored specific instructions from my coach that would have prevented me from making them in the first place. But taking responsibility doesn't mean that my mistakes have not damaged my confidence. So, the last "little i" to come out for transformation was afraid that he would not reach his goal of becoming a successful trader. We brought God into the conversation and found that He is more than willing to help me with my trading. This led to my realization that the part with the fear was actually my trader part. Going forward, God is going to be my trading partner and help me become a success. My understanding of this help is that I will use my strong connection to God and the feeling of security that it gives me to follow my trading rules and avoid impulsive trades in the future.

My goals in sharing this TfM process and the ones that follow are to give the reader some idea of how "little i's" can be transformed, and what I have learned from the process. It is amazing to me that they are transformed so directly and so quickly. I feel very lucky to have had this help in my life at this time. I am also surprised that some core themes have come up several times. I asked Libby about this and she said that this happens because these core themes are supported in my nonconscious mind by a number of "little i's" that all have slightly different agendas.

Dealing with Mistakes

Libby: Put your hands out in front of you. In one hand, imagine your image of God and tell me when you have it.

Me: I have the small, glowing blue pyramid in my right hand.

Libby: In your other hand, imagine a picture that would symbolize the part of you that feels embarrassed and doesn't want anyone to know about your mistakes.

Me: The part looks like a two-year-old who had a toilet accident.

Libby: What does that part have to say about your mistake?

Two-year-old: I don't want anybody to know I made this mess.

Libby: Now, is that part aware of God yet?

Two-year-old: Yes, I am aware of God, but I don't want God to know about me and my mistakes.

Libby: So, let the part just listen. It doesn't even need to come out, it can kind of hide in the back, just listen, okay? So what does God say to this part?

Me: God says everybody makes mistakes. I love you, mistakes or not. But when you make mistakes you can learn from them. You can get better and understand yourself and your biological needs better by making these mistakes. Once you really understand them, you won't make them anymore.

Libby: Did the part hear that?

Me: Yes, the part heard that.

Libby: Does it make that part feel any better?

Two-year-old: I feel a little better. My mistakes are not going to keep happening forever.

Libby: If we gave this part a magic wand, what would it wish for? What does it actually want?

Me: It seems like it wants to not make any mistakes, but that's kind of an impossible dream.

Libby: Sure, of course. It probably wants the mistake to have never happened ever.

Two-year-old: Yes, I want the mistake to have never happened.

Libby: "I want this mistake gone." So what does God say, very lovingly, of course, about that kind of rationale, or lack thereof?

Me: God says mistakes happen, and I'll help you clean it up.

Libby: God's going to help clean it up?

Me: God said He's going to make sure it gets cleaned up.

Libby: Did the part hear that?

Two-year-old: Yes.

Libby: Now, is that attractive?

Two-year-old: That's much better.

Libby: Does he want help?

Me: Yes, sure, he wants to clean it up so it will be gone and rectified.

Libby: So, let the hands come together, and this part is now literally bringing God in as a teammate to help with this so he doesn't have to do it on his own anymore.

Me: Yes, he got it.

Libby: And then tell me what happens.

Me: The part feels like mistakes happen and that they are correctable, they are not permanent.

Libby: That's right. So, what do you see now, visually, if anything?

Me: I see that God and the two-year-old are holding together tightly, and I see trust.

Libby: Yes.

Me: Trust and a kind of support, a hugging kind of feeling.

Libby: So take all of your energy back inside, take God back inside and come back.

Me: I'm back.

Libby: How's that?

Me: Better. I'm feeling supported now. I feel like I am supporting myself and God's supporting me, and that I can reach out and get help.

Libby: That's right. That way, you can make a mistake without compounding it.

Me: Yes, exactly.

Libby: Because there are mistakes, and there are compounded mistakes, and there are mistakes compounded over and over. So the smartest thing to do is to cut the mistake as short as possible and get some idea of what that's going to look like and how you are going to clean it up.

Me: Yes.

Libby: So, let's check your work. You had a "little i" who was embarrassed about his mistakes and didn't want anyone to know, not even himself or God. How do you feel about that now?

Me: I feel that being embarrassed about my mistakes just makes them worse and isn't supportive. Now, I can admit my mistakes and ask for help if I need it. Also, God said that He would be there for me to help clean up my mistakes, so, ultimately, I have all the help I could ever ask for.

Libby: So, you did a great, great thing psychologically for yourself in not letting that part slip anything under the radar. Can you see that that part did not have your best interest at heart?

Me: Now I can see that it didn't. The stock I shouldn't have traded went down more today.

Libby: Anything else today?

Me: That's all for me now. That was a lot.

Discussion

The biggest mistake a trader can make is to not follow his rules. What's more, if you don't have any written rules for making a trade, then everything about that trade is a mistake. I'd traded a stock that I'd traded for a profit in the past and had therefore been watching for a long time, but I had no rules and ignored my stops. I had a gut feeling that I could make some money because I believed it was in a temporary correction. I quickly paid for this mistake when the general market condition rapidly changed from bull normal to bear volatile. I lost a lot more than I'd planned to risk because my initial mental stop was so close that I was afraid to enter an order for it lest it be hit. I would have been stopped out on the same day if I'd put in the stop.

But the fact remains that the trade itself, whether it made money or not, was a mistake. In hindsight, I see it more as a payment for my trading education than a terrible loss to regret and punish myself for making. I learned so much from this trade, both about myself and trading. I finally closed the trade. That ended the bleeding, but it made the loss real. The ironic thing is that I had no trouble sleeping at night when the price was going down many points at a time with the occasional bounce to keep my hopes going, but as soon as I closed the trade and the loss became real, I started having trouble sleeping. As I continued to work on completing this transformation, normal sleep returned, and my focus moved from trading to working on the psychological portion of the Super Trader program.[7]

My feelings of embarrassment from making and sharing mistakes stemmed from childhood issues that held a charge, and that charge needed to be cleared before I could make progress. Libby's TfM process is a very direct and efficient way of getting at these charges and discharging them, either by getting rid of them or integrating them with my Higher Self, which, for me, is God. I am human, so I know I'll make some mistakes in the future. As a result of this process, I can now deal with them in real time and seek help if I need it and/or cut short the mistakes quickly. Finally, the most important lesson I learned from this mistake is how important it is to face reality. When my plan didn't work and my expectations for the trade weren't met, I should have sold my positions immediately and without hesitation. My choice was to stand there like a deer in the headlights waiting for my trade to work out as I had believed it would when I placed it. My belief was not useful, my reaction was not useful, and my embarrassment for having made the mistake was not useful. I definitely paid the tuition for getting rid of these nonuseful beliefs.

Closing Reflections

I am on a journey in this lifetime, a spiritual path to a greater connection with God, or the Divine, or Higher Power, or however you may visualize Universal Mind for yourself. My journey is ongoing. While I've made great progress on this journey through Transformational Meditation, Dr. Tharp's psychological lessons, Oneness Awakening, and *A Course in Miracles*, I can never really know what the end of the journey is going to be for me, so all I can do is continue walking the path.

I've found that the best way to walk this path is to question everything I've ever believed or done in this lifetime. Yet, even this is not important in the long run. The only moment that matters is the one I am living right now.

As I write this, I happen to be sitting at a desk in a hotel room in Cary, North Carolina. I have the window open, and the sound of highway traffic is in the distance. I like the sound of the traffic. Just above the laptop is a mirror, and I can see part of my reflection with my peripheral vision. I think the thought, *I am not crazy about looking directly at myself in the mirror.* Ah-ha! I've just discovered another "little i" that I need to work on. Since the TfM process, by definition, is always done with the help of my Higher Power, I can work on this "little i" on my own because I can never be alone when I do it; God is and always will be there with me.

My connection to my Internal Guidance and God becomes stronger every time I transform a "little i," do an ACIM workbook lesson, or attend one of Dr. Tharp's psychological courses. Still, I cannot help but feel that the Oneness Awakening process has moved me along my spiritual path at the speed of light. Giving or receiving a Oneness Blessing always reinforces and strengthens my connection to the Divine and to God. I can say that with certainty because of the joy and bliss I am continually receiving from Oneness.

Those of you who have become a Oneness Blessing giver will understand my final few words. For those of you who have never received a Oneness Blessing, I urge you to find someone near you who is a blessing giver and ask to receive one. It will change your life.

Love, peace, bliss, and joy to all.

An Addendum

My journey of transformation has greatly deepened over the past year. I no longer have dialogs where I work on "little i's" by speaking God's voice through me but rather I now have a strong and beautiful relationship with my Divine. As described in the previous chapter by Dr. Tharp, Oneness uses a process called Bhakta Paradeena to strongly encourage us to create a personal relationship with our Inner Guidance or our Inner Divine and to choose whomever we want to be that Divine. As a Buddhist, I chose the Goddess Tara, who is a female Buddha. To simplify this, for me, Tara is God and God is Tara and there is no separation. We are all at the core One with God.

While I had a relationship with Tara a year ago, I believe it has grown from level 3 to a level 8 relationship. (See Dr. Tharp's steps for establishing a relationship with a personal divine that is listed in the previous chapter under "What Does this Mean for You and for Your Trading?") To state what it is like for me now, I have absolute trust and faith in my Divine Tara and allow myself to be guided by

Her. Or as ACIM would say it, I am being led by God's Will and no longer following my own.

The changes over the past year were at times gradual and at others times parabolic. In the last chapter, Dr. Tharp talked about how he strengthened his relationship with Durga when he combined is ACIM lessons with dialogs with Durga. He also felt and expressed gratitude for Her help and guidance. Last December, Dr. Tharp requested that I do an 80-day abundance process by following John Randolph Price's book, *The Abundance Book*[8] and repeating each lesson eight times, keeping a daily gratitude diary and having a daily dialog with Tara about the day's lesson. This created a huge, major, gigantic shift forward in my personal relationship with Tara. (I'm trying to say it was big!) Sometime late in the abundance process, I started receiving "hands on" blessing from Tara whenever I asked her to "bless me." Yes, I could feel the hands of my Divine on my head just as if they were the hands of another person giving me a blessing. I still feel them every time I ask Tara for a blessing only now I say "bless us" to include everyone and everything. I could write a much longer story about the various events that preceded and followed each deepening experience since then but that story is not important. What is significant is to describe where I am now.

I have shifted into a state where I am in presence nearly 100 percent of the time and if not, presence can always be accessed in few moments. What is presence? It is our natural human state which we all experienced as babies and children in the first few months or years of life. For most of us, presence slowly became less familiar and accessible as we learned to name things, judge things, and feel like there was something lacking in us. The days of being enough in every moment simply by following our inner guidance faded away. Here is a brief dialog about how having a child's state of presence relates to transformations: (Please note that this dialog happened after the next two following dialogs.)

Tara: Presence is most important. You discovered something today.

Me: Presence is just being here. So, when I hold a baby in my arms, I don't have to say anything, just be with him or her. Two hearts beating together.

Tara: Meaning?

Me: It is the same with my thoughts. I don't need to welcome them or thank them or otherwise have another thought about them, just be in presence as they are happening. The simple shift from thought to presence is enough, and words are not required or useful.

Tara: You have it. I love you my Beloved Son and I thank you.

I love my Divine and she loves me. With Tara's help and guidance I have moved into Dr. Tharp's "Level III – Transforming Your Level of Consciousness" stage. Oneness Trainers and Blessing Givers have recently been guided by Oneness University to share our Awakening experiences to help others move into this state. I hope by sharing my experiences that it indeed helps others on their path. Still, I can only use words to describe this shift of consciousness even though they cannot fully convey its meaning. I am now seeing through my eyes in a different way. The "seer" doing the seeing is not coming from within my molecular structure. For me, it feels like it is centered a few inches behind my head and gives me a great sense of peace. This presence gets stronger and deeper every day. Your experience may be different as awakening is a very personal, yet wonderfully quantifiable, phenomenon.

And what about those pesky "little i's" that dominated, this chapter? There are hardly any left now and the few that pop up are easily transformed with Tara's help:

Tara: You are safe and secure no matter what. Trading is not the answer to your safety. Succeed or fail at trading and you are always secure.

Me: Thank you, Tara.

Tara: Be at peace because peace is your natural state just as presence is your natural state. How's the fear today?

Me: I just made the commitment to go to the retreat this weekend even if Ellie (a woman I like) does not come with me, and I am at peace about that. I feel a little nervous about being around her because I am attracted to her but I know I can be myself and whatever happens is not going to change what you just said.

Tara: Yes, you are safe and secure no matter what. How about using it as a mantra?

Me: I am safe and secure no matter what. I am safe and secure no matter what. I am safe and secure no matter what. I am safe and secure no matter what. It works!

Tara: Say it whenever you don't feel it.

Me: Thank you Tara, I will.

Tara: I love you and I thank you my Beloved Son. And it is done.

Since this dialog, presence has become my default state. However, when I wake up in the middle of the night, I don't sense it. So, I asked Tara for her guidance about a week later:

Me: How come I get stuck in thoughts during the middle of the night and can't get back to presence?

Tara: Dreams are thoughts out of control and you can never control them. In fact, don't even try to control them because your thoughts are not your thoughts.

Me: Then what should I do?

Tara: Slow down, no reason to be desperate. Welcome your thoughts, love them like a babe in arms, just like I told you to do with fear. Do you have much fear now?

Me: I haven't thought about it lately but no, I am not feeling much fear, the level is much lower, nearly nonexistent.

Tara: When you love your thoughts you bring them into presence. When you love pain, and pain is just a thought, you bring the thought about pain into presence. Love every thought and you will find they will no longer cause you anxiety. If they do, love the anxiety, like a babe in arms. Nice breath you just took.

Me: Thank you Tara. Please remind me to love my thoughts next time I ask you to bless us with presence and I am not loving them.

Tara: I will, my Beloved Son, all your wishes and requests shall be granted. Ask and you shall receive. Bless you my Beloved Son for I love you and I thank you and it is done. Amen.

As guided by Tara above, presence very clearly includes love. I am feeling a deep and abiding connection to my heart, which is indescribable as I write this. Most everything I do is now guided by Tara and done while in presence. If this does not happen, I ask for help.

I know I have received a gift and it does not make me special. In fact, I feel I am more ordinary that ever. I wake up in the morning with an idea of what I might do but if I am guided to do other things, that's what I do. I am happy, I feel loved, and I hope many others become ordinary, too.

Finally, in answer to the question "What Does this Mean for You and For Your Trading?" that Dr. Tharp presented in the last chapter, here is how having a strong personal relationship with your divine can help. Last Friday, I was paper trading the S&P Emini Futures via Skype with a friend in Germany. We are both in the state of presence described above. We were not judging the current five minute market trend correctly and my friend noted that the same thing happened the week before. So he said, why don't you ask Tara about this problem? Here is the dialog:

Me: Tara, have we missed anything in our trading today?

Tara: You missed seeing what was happening.

Me: What was that?

Tara: You want confirmation.

Me: Shouldn't I want confirmation?

Tara: Look up at the chart now and tell me what you see.

Me: A topping bar at the top of a trading range.

Tara: Short it.

Me: What target?

Tara: Three ticks less than trading range. Now wait. Be in presence, enjoy.

Me: Should I swing part of it?

Tara: You could, but why not take what is offered?

Me: What if what is offered is -1R? (Author's comment – a loss of one times risk)

Tara: Could be? That is not up to you.

Me: The stop was just hit so the trade didn't work.

Tara: You are not seeing again. Redefine work.

 Me: I am defining a trade as working when it is a win.

Tara: That is incorrect. You placed the trade, you placed the stop and target, one of them was hit, it worked.

 Me: Is trading for me?

Tara: Whatever brings you pleasure and fulfillment. It can be anything and if it changes you will know.

 Me: Will I be successful?

Tara: You are successful and in presence and with Me. Success is already yours, now and forever as you are safe and secure no matter what. I love you and I thank you my Beloved One and with fun it is done.

When the stop was hit above, we had a stop and reverse order in to switch us to long. Thus, that trade was a 2R winner.

I am so grateful and blessed to have Tara guiding me, loving me, and even thanking me just for being with Her in presence and love. I love you, Beloved Readers, and I thank you. It is in presence it is done and, in Truth. There is nothing at all to be done. I am on a journey in this lifetime, a spiritual path to a greater connection.

CHAPTER 12

Creating Your Own World

Van K. Tharp, PhD

 Before: Struggling to adopt Tharp Think principles.

 After: Clear enough to adopt Tharp Think principles and trade effortlessless and successfully.

I'm assuming that at this point you feel committed to doing the work that will make you a great trader. I'm also assuming that you now understand the key Tharp Think principles behind our modeling work. You have either mastered those principles or at least know what to do to master them and have a plan for doing so. If that's the case, your next step is to master yourself. That's what Level II transformations are all about.

In Table 12.1, I've listed all of the concepts in Tharp Think that concern mastering yourself. The table includes a blank space after each concept so that you can check it off when you feel you totally understand it. If you still don't understand it, I suggest that you reread all of the chapters in Section II of this book.

The first four concepts are general principles that were covered, to some extent, in Sections I and II. They include the idea that you are the key aspect of your trading and that you are responsible for the results you get. This point was emphasized in Section I and repeated again here. If you don't understand it, you'll never be able to correct mistakes, which means you'll never be an efficient trader.

You create your own world.

Table 12.1   Tharp Think Psychological Rules

PSychological Tharp Think Principles	Location	Check
1. You are responsible for everything that happens to you. When you understand this, you can correct your mistakes. We call this "respondability."	Sections I and II	❑
2. When you are not committed, you tend to run into obstacles and do a dance with them instead of going around them and moving on to your committed goal.	Section I	❑
3. If you are not committed to doing the necessary work on yourself and on your trading, you will not succeed.	Section I	❑
4. Do what you love. If that doesn't include trading, you should not be a trader.		❑

You must also be committed to doing the necessary work. Why? Because when you aren't committed, you end up doing a dance with the first obstacle that comes up, and that dance stops all progress toward the goal. You should be doing what you love, and if that doesn't include trading, then you probably aren't committed enough to become a successful trader.

Some people might argue that personal responsibility extends to what you do, but not to what happens to you. But it's your reaction to what happens to you that gives it meaning. Your reality is shaped by the meaning you give to things and that is always a function of your beliefs. So if you lose money, and you feel devastated, you are responsible for the meaning you give to the loss. And you are probably responsible for the loss as well because when you trade or invest, you need to accept that losses happen.

Next, if you are like most people, you have a lot of internal conflict. You frequently find yourself saying things like, "Yes, I really want to be a great trader, but I'm always wasting time," or, "I never have the time to do what it takes." This is an example of having parts of you that waste time or take time for their own desires and away from the trader part of you. You need to recognize these parts and eliminate the conflict between them. This partly involves recognizing that each of the parts will have beliefs that conflict with the beliefs of other parts. In other words, many conflicting, nonuseful beliefs control you as a whole. Let's look at these key points.

Tharp Think Principles (Continued)		Covered In	Check
5.	You are a crowd inside, and that crowd is who you think you are.	Chapter 9	❏
6.	Parts have good intentions, but they start doing their own thing and cause conflict.	Chapter 9	❏
7.	You can eliminate that conflict through parts negotiation or TfM.	Chapters 9 and 11	❏
8.	You must understand your identity and spiritual beliefs and determine whether or not they're useful.	Chapter 7	❏
9.	You can change any belief that isn't useful simply by understanding that it isn't useful—unless that belief has stored charge in it.	Chapter 7	❏
10.	If the belief has stored charge in it, you need to remove the charge through feeling release.	Chapter 8	❏

Tharp Think Principles (Continued)		Covered In	Check
11.	You need to continually monitor and work on yourself to trade well.	Section II	❏
12.	When you discover a major issue blocking you, you need to know how to solve the issue and avoid doing a dance with it.	Section II	❏
13.	Your internal guidance is your best friend. Learn to use it.	Chapters 10 and 11	❏
14.	But don't mistake "into wishing" for intuition.	Chapter 10	❏

Once you've done your part work, belief work, and feeling work, you should be quite aware of what's going on inside you and be able to continually monitor yourself and solve issues that come up before they sidetrack you.

If you want to master yourself, I strongly recommend that you go through my *Peak Performance Home Study Course.* But I want to give you everything you need in this book, so you could also take the following nine steps, which will move you a long way toward undoing your programming.

Nine Steps to Mastering Yourself

Step 1: Learn That You Are a Crowd Inside

Your parts tend to fall into several groupings. The first part might represent feelings you don't want to feel. For example, you might have a fear part that protects you from fearful things by constantly releasing stored fear. You might have a similar part for anger, fear, rejection, shame, or any number of other negative emotions.

Other parts might represent the various roles you have in life. You probably have a trader part, husband/wife part, parent part, full-time-job part, golfing part, and so on.

You might also have parts that represent various kinds of behaviors. You might have a control part, a need-to-be-right part, a perfectionist part, a procrastinator part, an excitement part, an adventurer part, and so on.

Most people also have parts representing significant people in their lives, created to make living with them easier. Most people have parts representing their mom, dad, spouse, mother-in-law, daughter, and so on.

The last kind of part is the disowned part, or shadow part. These parts are harder to find, because they only show up in your projections. What do you dislike about other people? What you see in others represents your disowned, shadow parts.

If you start thinking about it, you can probably figure out which parts are inside of you. Ask the trader part which other parts tend to be involved in trading. It'll probably tell you. When a new part comes up, don't forget to ask it about other parts it knows about. When you have a list of parts, you can go on to the next step.

Step 2: Get 25 to 30 Identity-Level Beliefs from Each Part

The result of this exercise should be a list of at least 200 identity-level beliefs, because I'm assuming you have at least 10 parts. Let's say the following parts seem to be involved in trading: (1) trader, (2) researcher, (3) excitement, (4) self-criticism, (5) don't lose money, (6) procrastinator, and (7) perfectionist. You also know about a (8) fear part, (9) a father part (representing your dad), and (10) a part that likes to play golf. Okay, that's 10 parts.

Your next job is to jump into each part (allow that part to take charge) and have it give you 20 to 30 beliefs about who it thinks you are. These would all be in the form of beliefs that start with the words "I am."

Let's say your trader part comes up with 25 beliefs. Here are a few examples:

1. I am a trader.
2. I am a trend follower.
3. I am a risk taker.
4. I am someone who takes on risk only when the reward is potentially much bigger.
5. I am careful.
6. I am a planner.
7. I am a rule follower.
8. I am lazy when it comes to doing my homework.
9. I am prone to making mistakes.
10. I am organized.

And let's say the trader gives you 15 more beliefs.

Now you ask your perfectionist part, and it comes up with 18 beliefs. Here are some examples:

1. I'm someone who likes to be right.
2. I'm never satisfied; I want better.
3. I'm critical of what is.
4. I'm very detail-oriented.
5. I'm someone who won't act until I'm sure.
6. I'm always working.
7. I'm always thinking about how to make it better.
8. I'm concerned about what others think.
9. I'm always watching the trader and the researcher because they don't like me.
10. I'm hopeless.

By the time you're done, you should have about 10 to 20 more beliefs than I've listed here for each part, but these are enough to give you an idea of what you should be looking for.

Now complete the exercise for each part until you have at least 200 beliefs about yourself written down. You'll notice that beliefs of one part can easily clash with the beliefs of another part, but when you have them all written down, you'll have a good idea of what's running your life. You'll begin to understand the matrix holding you in place, and you'll have an opportunity to move beyond it.

I usually get a lot of questions about beliefs, so let me answer a few of the more common ones here:

What's a belief? Saying that everything is a belief is a bit too vague for me.

What I can do is give you lots of examples.

You have a belief that my statement about beliefs is too vague for you. That's a belief.

I say every thought you think contains one or more beliefs. That is itself a belief. Hopefully, that makes it clearer.

I don't see how having the "right" beliefs will make me a great trader.

Well, that's a belief—that having the right beliefs aren't important. Let's say you have a belief that you are not worthwhile and that you have to continually prove it to yourself. Don't you think that belief would sabotage your trading? If you thought you were worthy of trading profits, wouldn't that be a little more useful?

Most of the Tharp Think concepts will help you succeed as a trader unless, of course, you believe they won't. When that belief becomes true, you've proved the power of beliefs to yourself.

Can you tell me what 10 or 20 beliefs I need to have to be a great trader?

Read all of the Tharp Think concepts in Chapter 6. They are all good examples.

How do I know if a belief is useful or not?

You can answer this by asking yourself some questions.

First, does the belief in any way separate you from anything? All beliefs probably separate you from something, but on a relative scale, some beliefs are more divisive than others. "When you complete the Belief Examination Paradigm" you should know if it is useful or not.

What if a negative belief comes up over and over again?

If a negative belief comes up repeatedly, you probably have a lot of charge locking it in place. You need to do feeling release until the charge is released. Then you can substitute something more useful.

Step 3: Do a Belief Examination Paradigm on Each of Your Beliefs

In Chapter 7 of this book, I describe the Belief Examination Paradigm. Give at least five answers when you get to the question, "What does it get me into?" Also give at least five answers to the question, "What does it get me out of?" Most people have trouble coming up with beliefs for that question because the parts of you that answer are the parts that have the beliefs. To make it easier, ask other parts to answer the second question.

When the perfectionist says, "I'm someone who won't act until I'm sure," don't be the perfectionist when you ask what that belief gets you out of. Be the trader. Be the researcher. Be the excitement part. Those parts probably won't like that belief and will have lots of answers.

Step 3a: Keep Your Useful Beliefs   Once you complete your list, ask yourself, Is the belief useful? If the belief is useful, then keep it. You'll find that many of them are not. It's when you start to replace nonuseful beliefs with useful ones that you really begin to see change in your life.

Step 3b: Replace Your Uncharged Nonuseful Beliefs   You'll find that nonuseful beliefs without charge on them are easy to replace once you recognize their lack of utility. For example, "Not acting until you are sure" might be replaced with "Act when the reward-to-risk ratio is heavily in your favor." It's easily done, unless the first belief has a lot of fear associated with it.

Step 3c: Find the Charge on the Remaining Beliefs   You'll probably find that at least half of your nonuseful beliefs have a powerful emotion attached to them. When that's the case, list it and the associated emotion and move on. You'll be releasing the charge in step 5.

Step 4: Learn about Projection and Your Shadow Self

Once you've completed step 3, find your shadow parts. A shadow part is a part of you that you've disowned because you find it so hateful or repulsive. It's still a part of you, though, and will show up when you least expect it. How do you find it? Think about all the types of people you dislike and why you dislike them. Those people represent your shadow parts.

For example, suppose you hate people who are bigots. You absolutely detest them. Now think about it. Aren't you being a bigot yourself to those people? Suppose you abhor violence and you do everything you can to avoid it. Don't you have a lot of violence going on inside you when it comes to violence? These are your shadow parts.

Find at least five shadow parts and identify 20 to 30 beliefs from each of them. Chances are that most of the beliefs of these parts will have charge that you need to release.

Step 5: Work on the Charge through Feeling-Release Exercises

The next step is to list the stored charges attached to your nonuseful beliefs and apply one of the feeling release methods discussed in Chapter 8. These methods include:

1. The Park Bench Technique discussed in Chapter 8.
2. The Sedona Method techniques given in Hale Dwoskin's *Sedona Method* course.
3. The quick-release method we teach in the Peak Performance 101 workshop.

Start using one or more of these methods regularly, and you'll be amazed at the result.

I also usually get a lot of questions about releasing the charge in negative beliefs, so let me answer some of those here:

How do you discover the amount of charge attached to a belief or what your most charged beliefs are?

The nine-step program that you are reading about will help you with this. In addition, if you're simply aware, you'll be alert to the feelings as they arise. If you aren't aware, you resist and run away from negative feelings instead of fully experiencing them.

To release an emotional charge, is it necessary to identify the core belief, or can you just work with the feeling/emotion?

If you release negative feelings as they arise to the point where those feelings disappear, then all the nonuseful beliefs that were held in place by that charge will tend to just dissolve.

If I release a feeling, does it mean I can't experience it again? Will I lose something?

Let's say you have fear in a particular situation, and you do a feeling release exercise. When you do, any of the following could occur:

1. The same situation comes up and you're simply neutral about it. Have you lost anything? Well, you've lost a negative emotion that comes up in certain situations, and you might have lost the charge that keeps certain non useful beliefs in place. Is this a loss? Do you want to claim to own that because that's the only way you can lose something?
2. The same situation comes up and you have less fear than you did. This just means you need to do the feeling release some

more. It might mean you have several parts that bring up fear in this situation and you've only gotten rid of one of them.

3. A different situation comes up, and you have fear. This could easily be a different version of the same feeling. You need to treat this as another feeling release.

What if I experience resistance?

What you resist tends to persist. My finding is that when I resist a feeling, it just makes the feeling seem stronger. Without resistance, a feeling might be like a gentle breeze. With resistance, the same feeling might seem like a Category 5 hurricane. When you experience resistance, work on the resistance as a feeling, and then work on the resisted feeling.

Step 6: Do a Life Review and List the Beliefs That Come Up

The next step you might consider will take 20 to 30 minutes for each year of your life, so if you're 40 years old, plan on setting aside about 14 to 20 hours for the exercise.

Here's what you do. For each year of your life, write down everything you can remember about what happened. Write down all your memories. It's okay to check with people who were around when you were very young to refresh your memories.

As you complete each year of memories, write down any significant beliefs you think you might have formed at that age. When you finish, run each belief through the various steps listed above:

1. Repeat the Belief Examination Paradigm for each belief.
2. Replace non useful beliefs.
3. Release stored charge.

The Life Review exercise is one of the key exercises that I have my Super Trader candidates do. I'm willing to share this one with you for no charge. If you contact us at www.matrix.vantharp.com, we'll send it to you for free.

Step 7: Make a List of Your Problems and Find the Root Cause (Beliefs and Feelings)

Perhaps by now you might believe you've done enough. But have you? Do you still have problems in your life? Do you still have behavior patterns you'd like to change? If so, then you are not finished.

List each of your problems. Notice the feelings at the root of each problem and the beliefs behind them. Then repeat the same steps.

For example, suppose you decide that you waste too much time watching television. It's a form of escape. Next time you decide to watch television, don't—at least not at first. Instead, notice the feeling going on inside that is telling you to watch television. You might call it boredom. You might find that you are anxious and want to escape. You might be lonely. Or you might notice some feeling in your body for which you have no label at all. What are the beliefs behind that feeling? What would happen if you did a feeling release on that feeling? Notice, too, your reaction to even doing that. Perhaps that's something you need to work on as well.

Now you are really beginning to see the matrix that controls you and your behavior.

Step 8: Get in Touch with Your Internal Guidance

When you read Chapters 10, 11, and later Chapter 13, notice your reactions. What are they? If you're not sure, then review them now. What beliefs do you have about talking to your Internal Guidance? Run each of those beliefs through the Belief Examination Paradigm and the steps given.

Here's what *A Course in Miracles* has to say about avoiding this topic.

> The oneness of the Creator and creation is your wholeness, your sanity, and your limitless power. This limitless power is God's gift to you, because it is what you are. If you dissociate from it, you are perceiving the most powerful force in the universe as if it were weak, because you do not believe you are a part of it.[1]

Notice any problems you have with trusting your Higher Power, and work to solve those. Again, these are just beliefs, feelings, or parts of you that don't trust. We've been talking about how to deal with each of those.

Start having a daily written conversation with your Inner Guidance. Ask your Higher Self a question, and wait for an answer.

When something comes, write it down. Keep doing this every day, and notice any issues that come up. Work on the issues as they appear. When your internal guidance is well established, it will lead you through this process.

Here are some of the common questions people usually ask about finding and strengthening their internal guidance.

How can believing in God help me be a better trader?

I can only give you several examples, and then you have to decide for yourself. First, David Hawkins says that if you're an atheist, your level of consciousness calibrates at about 190. I've already made the point that people don't trade well from a low level of consciousness. If you don't believe in God, then to increase your level of consciousness decide what type of God you don't believe in and then *find something else that fits you and that you can believe in now.*

Second, when you believe in God, you can start to establish an Inner Guidance, which is critical to helping you make transformations. Over and over again, the authors who wrote the Level III chapters stress the importance of trusting their Inner Guidance.

Finally, if it's important to you, your Inner Guidance can help you trade well. All you need to do is trust it.

I think God is only here to threaten/punish us. I'd rather just make a lot of money and do my own thing.

You don't have to believe in that sort of God. It's not useful at all. Why don't you find a more useful God and use that? If you believe in a threatening, punishing God and try to just do your own thing and make money, that same God will impact everything you do in life. It's much better to find one with whom you can have a great relationship and trust the guidance you get from it.

What is my Inner Guidance? Is it "me" or something outside me?

If you're willing to buy into the assumption that we are all One, then your Inner Guidance is your internal representation of that. Your Inner Guidance loves you unconditionally and is always available to help you, no matter what. That should be a test for you. If you're willing to believe that God is everything, then it's your internal way of connecting with God. In either case, it is definitely inside you. It is not outside of you. And if God is everything, wouldn't that include you?

However, it is not you, because as you transform yourself, your parts disappear, and soon there is no thinker—there is no you. What's left is your Inner Guidance.

I don't believe in any religion. How do I find my Inner Guidance?

Perhaps what you mean is that you don't believe in God. That's also fine. In fact, I had that belief, too. What you need to determine is what sort of God you don't believe in and what kind of God would be useful to you. You need a God you can relate to as your Internal Guidance. The first thing you have to do is get rid of the belief that your Internal Guidance comes from some religious belief.

Step 9: Work to Eliminate Parts, or to at Least Get Them to Work Together with You

We talked about conflict resolution in Chapter 9 and its spiritual form (TfM) in Chapter 11.

Use these methods to deal with conflicting parts of you. You've been told how to do each of them in this book.

Working on yourself can be frightening, and most people don't do it. But if you're willing to undertake the task, it will probably be the most rewarding thing you can do. If you need help, get it because the results will be amazing.

The conflict resolution exercise described in Chapter 9 usually requires that you visualize each part of you, but some people can't do that. If that happens to be your problem, I suggest that you simply make up what it looks like. Even if it comes from your imagination, it still comes from you, and that works. If you can't visualize at all, then you probably have some kind of blockage that will be solved as you work on various issues. Until you solve that problem, just use your feelings and auditory senses.

Finally, when you do these sorts of exercises enough, you'll start making significant transformations. For example:

- A nonuseful belief suddenly disappears.
- A negative feeling that used to come up frequently in a particular situation no longer comes up when you're in the same situation now.
- A part that was often in conflict other parts becomes a team player or disappears.
- You become happier for no particular reason.

At first, when you transform yourself, you'll be able to take control of the Matrix. This means you can transform nonuseful beliefs into useful ones. This will allow you to program yourself to become very efficient at almost anything you do, including trading well.

As you transform yourself more and more, you will lose parts of yourself and have less internal conflict. You might call this losing your personality, but what would you rather have—lots of conflicting parts or more peace and happiness?

As your consciousness increases, you will attract things into your life that correspond to your level of consciousness. If you have friends who are very negative, you might lose them, but you will probably replace them with friends who are closer to your own level of consciousness.

MOVING BEYOND THE MATRIX BY TRANSFORMING YOUR LEVEL OF CONSCIOUSNESS

Van K. Tharp, PhD

Dr. David Hawkins was one of the most successful psychiatrists in the world. He had a very high level of consciousness and performed miracle cures on his patients. He eventually closed his practice to pursue a PhD in psychology, and his thesis was on levels of consciousness.

What exactly is consciousness? Consciousness might be considered awareness, or self-awareness, or the mental state out of which you operate. For example, a trader would be much better off trading out of "acceptance" (much higher level of consciousness) than "fear" or "greed" (both low levels of consciousness). In one sense, the level of consciousness, actually measures the Truth of something. Low levels of consciousness are steeped in illusion whereas higher levels of consciousness tend to move out of illusion toward the Truth.

In the preface to this book, I mentioned the log scale Hawkins uses in his book *Power vs. Force* to measure human consciousness levels, but I'd like to go over it again, because I think it's useful. The scale goes from 1 to 1,000, with 1,000 being the highest level of consciousness achievable by a human being. Only a few very enlightened individuals have ever reached 1,000—people like Jesus and Buddha. Hawkins says that 200 is the level that separates the positive from the negative; levels below 200 are self-destructive and lead to war and suicide.

There are other, similar consciousness scales. The Sedona Method has one, as does a series of coaching programs I went through called Dynamism. I've reproduced all three of them in the table below, in which a particular state of consciousness, such as inner peace, is given a specific number.

Perhaps you don't believe that human consciousness can be measured on a log scale that goes from 1 to 1,000. If you believe that, you are right, at least within your personal reality. However, think about the various levels of emotions. Wouldn't you agree that the feeling of peace is a much lighter and expansive (i.e., higher vibration) than the feeling of, say, reason? What about "acceptance?" Isn't that a higher and more expansive vibration than, say, "neutrality?" When you get down to the negative emotions like grief, apathy, shame, and guilt, it should be clear that when you experience them, you feel quite heavy and constricted.

Think about these different levels and how you might trade at each level. How do you think you'd perform as a trader if you were feeling "guilt," "shame," "fear," "grief," "anger," or any of the other lower emotions? It should be clear that you wouldn't do that well. You need to be at a minimum level of "acceptance" to expect to have much chance of successfully trading the markets. You can also think about levels of consciousness from this perspective. Do you want to know your level of consciousness? Then ask yourself, "Where do I spend most of my time?" Can you elevate your consciousness so that you are at least at a level of acceptance, which would allow you to accept both wins and losses?

Three Measurements of Levels of Consciousness			
Hawkins Scale		Sedona Method Scale	Dynamism Scale
Enlightenment	700+		
Peace	600	Peace	
Joy	540		Joy
Love	500		Amusement
Satisfaction			
Reason	400		Enthusiasm
Acceptance	350	Acceptance	Interest
Willingness	310		Hopeful
Neutrality	250		
Courage	200	Courage	Boredom
Pride	175	Pride	Bitter/Contempt
Anger	150	Anger	Anger/Hate
Desire	125	Lust	Envy/Hostility
Fear	100	Fear	Fear
Grief	75	Grief	Despair
Apathy	50	Apathy	Depression
Guilt	30		Apathy
Shame	20		Insanity/Depravity

Our goal is to help traders take large leaps forward in consciousness. Think about the simple Level II transformation of making a belief change. Now, imagine again the impact of getting rid of around 5,000 nonuseful beliefs in a year, especially if half of them were charged beliefs and the charge is now gone. That probably would raise your consciousness several hundred points.

Similarly, think about the impact of merging two parts into one—whether through conflict resolution or TfM. This too can have a major impact on your life. Now think about getting rid of perhaps 500 parts. Depending on how many parts you're composed of, you'd be very close to whole. Imagine the impact that would have on your level of consciousness.

Our Most Powerful Tool

My belief is that the stories given in this book are only the beginning of what is possible. Let me give you an example. I once had dreams of forming a company with a few other like-minded people and changing the world; however, those dreams faded quickly. At some point, I realized that nothing would change until I changed.

This is the basic idea of performing well in the Matrix and going beyond it.

Over much of my adult life, I've pursued many directions and methods of personal development, but when I became a Oneness Blessing Giver and trainer a few years ago, everything changed. Nothing I've done in my 30 years of personal transformation has been as powerful as my experiences with the Oneness Blessing (or Deeksha) over the last few years. Now, most of my staff members are Blessing Givers, and the business has grown in success. Chapter 12 and all the Level III chapters illustrate the power of this process to change lives.

I first started giving blessings in some of my psychological workshops. What I noticed, especially from those getting blessings all the time, were the huge transformations and jumps in consciousness that they experienced as a result. It was what I'd been searching for most of my career.

I originally had no intention of making Oneness part of the Van Tharp Institute curriculum. It all seemed very "far out" to me when I started, but for some reason, I was drawn to it. I'm constantly looking for what works and helps people. And as I've watched the transformations that have occurred as a result of the process, I've been amazed. All of the Level III transformations detailed in the next section, in my opinion, would not have been possible without the influence of Oneness Blessings. Without going into too much detail, I'd like to share some of those experiences with you through the stories given in Section III.

Super Trader Journeys through Transformation

One of our Super Trader candidates entered the program after taking the Oneness training. It turned out that she thought it was the cheapest, quickest way to get into the program, but it was difficult for her because she wasn't sure if she believed in God. And if she did, she certainly didn't *trust* God. However, part of the program involves doing the 28-day TfM course, in which you are constantly bringing up issues that are blocking your path to your Internal Guidance. It's hard to complete that journey if you don't trust your internal guidance. Chapter 13 is all about her journey moving toward trust. It's been a major journey that has certainly raised her level of consciousness dramatically.

Many of my Super Trader candidates have strong engineering backgrounds, which means that, for most of them, everything needs to be logical and make sense and work. One of them has gone on an amazing journey, transforming himself from someone who was just existing into a spiritual warrior who now seems to be constantly happy for no reason. His story is given in Chapter 14.

Another one of my Super Trader candidates started his trading journey as a professional "employee" trader working for various large banks. He soon realized that you were just expected to pick up the craft of trading by being around other traders. Many of them were good market- makers, but they knew little about making money in the markets. His journey through his personal issues to become a happy, grounded person, and be able to gain a base from trading well, is given in Chapter 15.

Finally, one Super Trader candidate, after being given a Oneness Blessing in one of our workshops, reached a deep, profound state of inner silence. When she told me about it, I suggested that she trade through that state. She had a background in Buddhist training and asked to take off six months to further that journey. When she finished it, she was able to constantly enter into and trade in that state. In November 2010, when I asked her to monitor her trades on a system for which she was working on getting approval, she was able to make 134R. During that month, she made money on 86 percent of her trades and didn't make a single mistake—100 percent efficiency. I watched her trade for one day, but she was in such a focused state during her trading that she couldn't talk about what she was doing. Her story is given in Chapter 16.

David Hawkins says that there is a correlation of one between one's level of consciousness and one's level of happiness. We now have a scale that measures happiness, and people can monitor it on an ongoing basis. As a result, each of the authors in Section III present graphs that clearly show their changes in happiness (i.e., consciousness) as a function of the transformations they make. You can take this test for free at matrix.vantharp.com.

Finally, in Chapters 17 and 18, I explore a little of what's next for you, including how to change your level of consciousness and, once you succeed, do more advanced things to help you in your trading such as develop a great plan. While I'm not expecting you to jump into the Super Trader program, which, as of this writing, is almost full, I can give you some critical steps that might aid you on

13

How I Turbocharged My Transformational Journey

Kim Andersson

Kim Andersson grew up in rural Manitoba, Canada. After graduating from the Royal Military College of Canada in 1995 with a bachelor of engineering degree, she worked as a Satellite Communications Engineer at the Canadian National Defence Headquarters in Ottawa, where she also earned a master of engineering degree in engineering management. In 2000, she was posted to the U.S. Air Force Headquarters at the Pentagon as an exchange officer, working in Information Technology and Enterprise Architecture. She "retired" from the Canadian Air Force in 2004, but stayed in the Washington, DC, area. She currently works full-time for Lockheed Martin on a government consulting contract as an Information Security Analyst. Kim is currently enrolled in the Super Trader II program at the Van Tharp Institute and plans to become a professional day trader within the next year.

 Before: Unsuccessful swing trader with a lack of trust and an innate ability for self-sabotage, including an unconscious fear of becoming a millionaire.

 After: Made 45R during a week of day trading at a recent live trading class at the Van Tharp Institute.

Y ou may be wondering what unique qualifications I have to contribute to a book on transformations. Well, I'm an expert on self-sabotage. I have 15 years—if not more—of experience in sabotaging myself. Once I overcame one seemingly small obstacle, however, most of the self-sabotage began to magically disappear.

I'll reveal my secret for doing that a little later on, but first I'd like to touch on the topic of self-sabotage. Dr. Tharp defines it as a lack of discipline to act in one's own best interest or repeating the same mistakes over and over again. For me, self-sabotage was like being trapped in the Matrix. The Matrix was my mind running on unconscious, faulty programs ("little i's") that lead to self-sabotaging behavior. Theoretically, once I realized I was in the Matrix, I could start trying to get out, but until then, I was stuck.

I now understand that my self-sabotage was mainly due to a lack of self-knowledge (it's hard to know whether or not you're in the Matrix when you're actually in it). This is what makes self-sabotage so difficult to cure—the cause is often hidden from your conscious mind. You may realize that you are sabotaging yourself, but you just can't figure out why (i.e., you're trying to lose weight, but you just can't resist the five-layer chocolate cake on the menu). In some cases, like mine, you may not even realize you're sabotaging yourself—you simply manifest bad things in your life but can't explain why. The text of *A Course in Miracles* (ACIM) says it very well when it says:

> And yet it is only the hidden that can terrify, not for what it is, but for its hiddenness.

> —*A Course in Miracles*[1]

Before I started doing self-work in the Super Trader program, I figured most of the problems I had were simply due to causes external to me. I only found out after several months of self-work that I had two major subconscious sabotage issues: (1) I based most of my decisions and actions on fear—particularly the fear of failure—and (2) I had a very strong need for control.

As you can probably imagine, both of these issues manifested themselves in poor trading decisions, which I often repeated (i.e., self-sabotage). For example, I was afraid of losing, so I would cut my profits short, or I would hold onto mediocre positions longer than I should in hopes that they would turn around so I wouldn't have to take a loss.

My need for control also manifested itself in several insidious ways. I wanted to control the way I looked, so I resisted aging. I wanted to control my two-year-old son's behavior, but the more

You just can't resist the five-layer chocolate cake.

I tried to control him, the less control I had. I also developed an unconscious fear of becoming a millionaire (sounds ridiculous, I know), because, subconsciously, I felt it would change my personal relationships in a way that I couldn't control. My need for control was so strong that I wanted to control the future. Going with the flow and trusting a "Divine Plan" were, obviously, not in my vocabulary.

Because of my extreme need for control, which was mostly subconscious, I became easily frustrated when things didn't go the way I felt they should. These feelings of frustration created a vicious circle: When something didn't go my way, I'd feel frustrated, so I'd try something else in another futile attempt to control the situation, which would lead to further frustration, and further attempts to gain more control. You can certainly see how this could have a negative impact on my trading and on my happiness in general.

Figure 13.1 is a graph of my annual happiness levels before I began the Super Trader program (as measured using the same scale Dr. Tharp uses to measure individual happiness levels in his Peak 203 workshop). From this graph, you will notice that my early childhood was a genuinely happy time in my life. My happiness levels took their first nosedive when I entered school and a second when I entered university. These were times when my control issues and frustration really began to surface. The downward spike at age 23 occurred after my mother passed away.

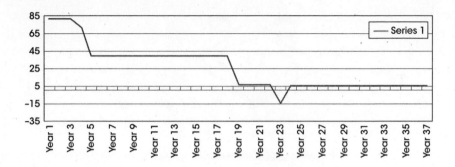

Figure 13.1 Kim's Annual Happiness Ratings before the Super Trader Program

I was determined to stop the cycle, so I began to slowly dismantle my fear and control issues using techniques that you've already learned in this book. However, I had one seemingly insignificant obstacle that was standing in my way of completely curing these self-sabotage issues. I believe it would have been very difficult, if not impossible, for me to solve these issues if I hadn't first surmounted that obstacle.

That obstacle was a distrust of my Higher Power. Seems completely unrelated to my other problems, right? But it wasn't. It was the linchpin that was holding all the other issues in place. Why, you might ask? I was trying to control it all myself. I think lesson 47 of ACIM is very appropriate when it says:

> If you are trusting in your own strength, you have every reason
> to be apprehensive, anxious, and fearful.
> —*A Course in Miracles, Lesson 47*[2]

What could I control? What could give me the ability to be aware of all aspects of a problem, find an appropriate solution, and guarantee that it would be accomplished? I finally understood that, by myself, I couldn't possibly accomplish any of these things. Trusting in myself (i.e., my own ego) to figure out how to resolve my issues practically guaranteed that I would continually experience fear and anxiety. I needed to trust and have faith in something greater than myself. In *Think & Grow Rich*, Napoleon Hill sums up the importance of having faith: "FAITH is the only known antidote for FAILURE!... FAITH is the only agency through which the cosmic force of Infinite Intelligence can be harnessed and used by man."[3]

For those of you who get queasy at the mention of the words "God," "Higher Power," or "Faith," I completely understand where you're coming from. I was the same way not that long ago (more on that later). For now, I would just ask that you contemplate the following question: Although nobody knows the truth about whether God or some other Higher Power exists, if it's useful to believe in an Infinite Intelligence that can lend you a helping hand and provide guidance when needed, then why not believe in It? What if miraculous things start to happen when you actually believe it (i.e., have faith)? Wouldn't that be useful?

Looking at it from a different perspective, you could say that when it came to problem solving, I was only using my conscious mind to come up with solutions. According to popular science, the conscious mind only makes up 10 percent of your brain capacity, so, basically, I was failing to take full advantage of the other 90 percent of my brain to solve problems! I didn't trust my gut feel—or my sixth sense, if you will—which is the conduit to the nonconscious mind.

However, here's the kicker: I wasn't even consciously aware that I didn't trust my Higher Power. Mistrust was wreaking havoc in my life, but because I hadn't been able to see it, I couldn't fix it. As ACIM says:

> A problem cannot be solved if you do not know what it is. Even if it is really solved already, you will have the problem, because you will not recognize that it has been solved.
>
> —*A Course in Miracles*, Lesson 79[4]

Because most self-sabotage is created by faulty programming of the nonconscious mind by the conscious mind, my mistrust and lack of faith also ensured that it would be virtually impossible to solve any sabotage issues that had been programmed nonconsciously. As Einstein pointed out, "We can't solve problems by using the same kind of thinking we used when we created them."[5]

So, here's the story of how I overcame that obstacle to complete four other major transformations in a span of four short months. I'll also provide you with a model you can use to turbocharge your own transformational journey.

Discovering the Linchpin

Rewind to January 2011. My New Year's resolution was to become a professional day trader by my fortieth birthday (within two years). I had been reading Dr. Van Tharp's books and eNewsletter since 2002 and attempted to swing trade back in 2004 to 2005, with little success (mainly due to self-sabotage issues). This time, I decided I would do things right and follow the advice that Van provides in his books. I figured the only way I could learn to do that effectively and efficiently would be to take all of Van's courses and workshops, which meant I might as well join the Super Trader program.

At that time, one of the prerequisites to get into the Super Trader program was to either take the Peak Performance 101 workshop or the Oneness Awakening[6] workshop. Since the Oneness Awakening workshop was much less expensive than Peak 101, I decided to take it. However, having never done any spiritual or self-work before the Oneness workshop, I was a bit apprehensive. The syllabus talked about stuff that, at the time, coming from an IT and engineering background, I categorized as pretty far-out stuff. Actually, it seemed "woo-woo" (i.e., kundalini, chakras, etc.) to me. It also made reference to the word "God" several times, which made me a little skittish, since I was a devout agnostic—practically atheist—who saw religion as the main cause of most major conflicts on Earth since the beginning of civilization. I remember saying to myself, *Hey, it's only going to be two days. Don't lose sight of the end goal, which is to be accepted into the Super Trader program.* Before I left for Cary, North Carolina, I briefly explained the workshop syllabus to my husband, who promptly said, "If they offer you Kool-Aid, don't drink it."[7]

So, you could say that I walked into this workshop with a relatively closed mind. But, after two days of meditating, chanting, dancing, receiving "blessings," forgiving, and "evoking my Divine Presence," I walked out of the Van Tharp Institute with what could only be described as a new lease on life. I know that sounds trite, but it's true. On the five-hour drive back home to Washington, DC, I felt incredibly peaceful, as well as grateful. It was a feeling I had rarely, if ever, experienced. If that could happen to someone like me, perhaps there was something useful in it after all.

Of course, the feeling subsided after about two days, but I yearned to revive that post-workshop bliss, so I found a local Unity church that offered ongoing meditations and Oneness Blessings. During the Oneness Awakening workshop, I'd become a Oneness Blessing giver, and every week for months thereafter, I readily *received* them, but I discovered that, for some reason, I couldn't *give* any. I knew it was some sort of mental block; I just couldn't put my finger on what it was.

Meanwhile, I was accepted into the Super Trader program in February 2011, whereupon I started working on the 20 lessons in the psychological portion[8] of the program and doing daily 15-minute meditation sessions. One of the prerequisites to completing the psychological portion of the Super Trader program is documenting five major life transformations. I was a tad stressed over this requirement. I'd already spent two months in the program and hadn't yet completed one major transformation—other than having somewhat rediscovered the virtues of spirituality.

Here is the original list of things I wanted to work on (exactly as I worded them in March 2011):

Issue #1: Self-confidence: I lack confidence in my trading abilities. A tiny voice makes me question my ability to become a successful trader.

Issue #2: Relationship with son: I sometimes feel inadequate as a mother because my son appears to prefer my husband to me. Since my son is only two years old, it seems silly for me to be bothered by this; however, I still am a bit.

Issue #3: Afraid of failure: This is a big one. Whenever I think of past failures (e.g., failing college exams), I get a real feeling of dread and tightness in my chest. Also, I really try to do anything to avoid having those feelings. I am afraid this may sabotage my trading.

Issue #4: Ambiguity about spirituality: On the surface I believe in the importance of spirituality and am trying to work on developing my relationship with God. However, I sometimes feel embarrassed about doing this, because I'm afraid that people I care about (i.e., my husband and my sister) will think I'm nuts.

Issue #5: Relationship with money: I never thought I had an issue with money until very recently. Last year, my father passed away and left what I thought would be a small amount of money to my sister and me. I figured it would be enough money to open a trading account and have a chance to make a living off it using a good system with proper position sizing but not enough that I would be considered an instant millionaire. My father had his assets spread across several different banks and investment brokerages. One of the investment brokerages recently sent an account statement, which stated the account was worth approximately $5.6 million. However, instead of feeling euphoria at the prospect of becoming an instant millionaire, I got a feeling of panic and anxiety. Before then, I never thought that I might have an unhealthy relationship with money. I believe this will sabotage my trading (a week later the brokerage company sent a revised statement that there was really only $35,000 in the account).

At the time I wrote this list of "things to work on," I felt that issue #1 (lack of self-confidence) was the most debilitating of the five issues in terms of its ability to affect my trading. However, I later discovered that this one was entirely based on a trapped feeling. It dissolved almost completely when I released that trapped feeling. We'll talk more about that later.

Issue #2 (relationship with son) and issue #5 (relationship with money) were actually both related to my need for control; at that time, however, I was not consciously aware of that need. I was simply aware of two of the manifestations of the self-sabotage related to my need for control. I didn't think these (especially #2) would have much of an impact on my trading.

As you can see from #4, I still had a major issue with spirituality, but I hadn't quite been able to pinpoint the precise cause or effect. At Van's suggestion, I started doing the lessons in A Course in Miracles. Van claimed it was one of the most important things he'd ever done in terms of self-work, so I thought it would help me gain clarity on my spiritual issues.

I felt that issue #4 would just somehow work itself out eventually, but that issue #3 (fear of failure) would definitely sabotage my trading results, so I decided to tackle issue #3 next in my psychological work. Here, I was introduced to Transformational Mediation (TfM) as described in Chapter 11.

During my first "little i" clearing exercise, when I was attempting to clear my fear of failure, I had my Higher Power in my right hand, which looked like a miniature sun,[9] and my "fear of failure" in my left hand, which I imagined to look like a bowling ball. At the point where Libby asked, "Does the fear part trust your Higher Power?" To my surprise, the bowling ball said, "No, I don't trust that dude, and neither should you!" Because this was my first-ever TfM session, it surprised the heck out of me that (1) I imagined a bowling ball talking to me and (2) that I sided with the bowling ball instead of the sun (i.e., my Higher Power). When Libby suggested that we toss or get rid of any parts that didn't trust the Higher Power, the bowling ball refused to leave my hand! To top it all off, I started feeling affection toward the bowling ball and felt like tossing my Higher Power instead.

I don't trust that dude, and neither should you!

At the end of the TfM session, I suddenly understood what my nonconscious mind was trying to tell me—that there was a part of me that did not trust my Higher Power. Because of that, I was unable to clear the fear of failure issue. In fact, it would have probably been impossible to solve any self-sabotage issues with that big trust issue standing in the way.

I mentioned this to Van and Libby after the exercise, and Van suggested that I receive a Oneness Blessing to clear the trust issue. Libby had just become a Oneness Blessing giver, and this was a perfect opportunity for her to give her first blessing. During that blessing, my Higher Power repeated over and over again that He had been and always would be there for me. My Higher Power also showed me a picture of my mother and stated that she had never really left me, although she had passed away 15 years ago. Suddenly, it felt like a light bulb turned on above my head—like in a cartoon! I finally realized that my mistrust of God stemmed from my belief that God had taken my mother away from me.

This was a very emotional and revealing time for me. I suddenly realized why I did, or was not able to do, certain things. In particular, it explained why I had been spiritually ambivalent for so long.

After the Oneness Blessing, we did another TfM session to help me clear the trust issue. This time I established a dialog between the untrusting part (which appeared as a fuzzy, eggplant-colored sphere in my left hand) and my Higher Power (which again appeared as a miniature sun in my right hand). My Higher Power reaffirmed that He was and would always be there to support me in everything I do. He also stated that everyone's physical life must eventually come to an end, but that the person lives on inside you in spirit—hence the picture of my mother. The fuzzy eggplant seemed okay with that explanation, and they came together as one when I put my hands together. I felt such a tremendous amount of relief after that experience, as if a huge weight had been lifted from my shoulders.

In the two remaining days of the Peak 202 workshop, I was able to clear several other issues with relative ease. For example, I cleared away a part of me that didn't like to perform self-work because it didn't like to pop the hood of my subconscious mind and reveal all the junk in there. What's more, the Wednesday after I returned, I was able to readily receive and give seven Oneness Blessings in one day. I felt a tremendous amount of gratitude after giving the blessings, which I believe confirms that I was able to reestablish trust in my Higher Power.

Transformations Turbocharged!

Transformational Pillar #1: Getting Rid of Fear

Although I hadn't realized it at the time, my newfound trust and faith in my Higher Power suddenly cleared up the communication path between my conscious and subconscious mind, which, according to Libby Adams, acts as a conduit to one's Higher Power. This meant that I could begin to trust the signals I was receiving from my Higher Power. *Once I finally figured that out, it really put the turbo-boost into my transformations.*

In the meantime, I was still working my way through the Super Trader psychology lessons. During these lessons, Van requires that you keep an "emotion diary" to help determine negative emotions that come up so that you can release them using the techniques described in Chapter 8. If you don't release them, you'll project them out into the world and potentially create self-sabotage.

I have to admit that I hated keeping an emotion diary because I tend to pride myself on being emotionally in control (yet another control issue!). By putting my emotions in a diary, it blew my cover. However, looking back, I found the emotion diary to be the most useful tool to help me determine a major subconscious emotion that had been basically running my life for years and causing inordinate amounts of self-sabotage.

That emotion was fear. I believe the biggest problem with fear is that it often masquerades as other, seemingly positive mechanisms—a guarantor of survival, for example, or a motivator to action—so it's difficult to see the fear-related projections for what they really are: self-sabotage. Van says that if you project fear in the market, you'll get what you're looking for—losses and further stress to justify your projected fear, which is certainly what I got when I was trading.

I decided to work on fear using the park bench exercise described in Chapter 8. In doing so, I suddenly became consciously aware that fear was running my life. On the first day of the exercise, I was able to spend 40 minutes solely focused on fear, without reaching boredom. I realized that I was afraid of a whole range of different things, including death, unemployment, homelessness, losing family members, not being a good mother, getting old, looking old, feeling old, not living up to my own expectations, not reaching my goals in life, not being happy, and so on, and so on, and so on.

During my next psychological workshop, I decided to make diminishing my fear my primary objective. However, I was a little apprehensive about getting rid of my fear completely because it was actually a very strong motivator for me. For example, it was fear that drove me to complete my bachelor and master's degrees in engineering. It was fear that helped me gain my current employment (fear of poverty). I also felt that fear motivated my survival. I felt that if I suddenly became fearless, I might also become careless.

I might stop looking both ways before crossing the street or stop taking my vitamins and get cancer.

I mentioned my "fear of getting rid of fear" to Van, and he said that I should just try to completely release it, work on my issues related to survival, and remember what I learned in Oneness. After some thought, I realized that Van was right. The fear had gotten me to where I was, but it probably wouldn't be useful in getting me where I really wanted to go (i.e., profitable trading). I also realized that I should completely hand over the task of ensuring my survival to my Higher Power, because that's what it helps me do—no use duplicating effort.

So, at the workshop in May 2011, guided by Van and using the "intense feeling release" technique he teaches, I was able to successfully release fear. I believe that all other fear-based beliefs (i.e., fear of failure, fear of dying, fear of criticism) have since dramatically diminished, if not disappeared completely. Along with the fear went worry, anxiety, and a major amount of stress that I had been carrying around for years. In fact, shortly after releasing the fear, I gave a Oneness Blessing, and people said they could feel a difference between that one and the one I'd given the day before.

With two major transformations down, I still had another three to go. I still didn't have a good understanding of what the issues were. Remember, I knew the results of the self-sabotage, but I still didn't know the cause. I knew I'd have to get to the cause in order to find the solution, which meant I needed to tap into my Higher Power to help me deal with the remaining three subconscious issues. The problem, however, was that I'd spent such a long time ignoring the constant signals from my Higher Power (because I didn't trust it), that I didn't know the signs or, more likely, I no longer even recognized them.

Transformational Pillar #2: Tapping into a Higher Power

> The part of your mind in which truth abides is in constant com-
> munications with God, whether you are aware of it or not.
> —*A Course in Miracles*, Lesson 49 [10]

Even though ACIM says a part of you in is constant communication with God, how does one go about tapping into one's Higher

Power? Until very recently, I really had no clue, but Libby Adams had suggested that it was through using your sixth sense. Sounds like it would require special mystical powers, right? Not so. What I learned while working with Libby really helped turboboost my transformation journey. You see, the sixth sense is simply the gateway between your conscious mind and your nonconscious mind. Since your Higher Power operates in the same realm and uses the same language (i.e., pictures) as your nonconscious mind, the sixth sense is also the gateway to your Higher Power.

This might still sound a little far out, but it's really not. There are clear differences between the messages from your Higher Power and those from your ego. You simply have to learn to distinguish the differences. Here's what I learned about my signals: *The signals from my sixth sense often come in flashes of images accompanied by a feeling like a light bulb turning on above my head—like in cartoons. Also, my sixth sense usually sends only positive messages (unless I'm in some sort of physical danger), whereas my ego generally sends me negative internal dialog like, "Are you crazy?"*

Messages from my sixth sense are very subtle, whereas "little i's" like to harp and nag. I learned how to recognize the difference between these two types of messages simply by paying very close attention to all my thoughts, emotions, and actions. I'm sure everybody has major, but subtle, differences between the messages from these two sources. Your job is to figure out what they are.

So, armed with this new information, I became very vigilant about looking and listening for signals from my sixth sense. One of the most powerful tools I used to tap into my sixth sense and communicate with my Higher Power was TfM and meditation. During all the TfM sessions with Libby, I paid close attention to what my Higher Power was telling me through my sixth sense. This really helped lay the foundation for subsequent transformations.

However, communication with the sixth sense is not the only ingredient required for major transformations. I would argue that knowing one's purpose in life is also an essential structural element required to support a strong transformational platform. Consequently, one of the first things I did in Libby's 28-day course was to clarify my purpose in life. Not only was this paramount to laying a strong transformational platform, it practically guaranteed my future happiness. So, what does one's life purpose have to do with happiness? Everything. Just think about it for a second. Are you happy doing anything for which the purpose is nebulous or questionable? It's not likely.

Transformational Pillar #3: My Purpose in Life

Before working with Libby, I had only a vague sense of my purpose in life—nothing concrete, which is probably why I wasn't ecstatic about where I was going in life. You see, I had a pretty good idea of what I didn't want in life and a pretty good sense of what I wanted my day-to-day life to look like, but I hadn't put it all together in a nice neat little package that made sense. So, after a short TfM session guided by Libby, I came up with the following life purpose: *To achieve my highest potential, so that I can help others achieve theirs.* Seems pretty simple, right? But this simple, little sentence is what I needed to get that spark back into my life. In fact, I now feel energized when I wake up in the mornings. I no longer dread having to face another day at the office.

Once I got clarity on my life purpose, my Higher Power (now a voice) kept reminding me that I hadn't finished the eBook I'd started writing two years before. I'd let the eBook idea slide because I didn't believe it was in line with becoming a professional day trader. Once I got clarity, my Higher Power knew that I needed to complete it and sent me subtle messages the entire day after the "Purpose" session. However, there was still a "little i" in me that was not convinced that finishing the eBook was a good use of my time. The conflicting internal messages I was receiving were bothering me so much that I talked to Libby about it. We did a TfM on the "little i" that was "feeling lazy" about getting my eBook done. Once I had clarity, I realized that the eBook was in line with my purpose and my goal to become a trader because it would generate revenue, so I decided to complete it. And I haven't had any regrets about the decision. My eBook is now complete.

Transformational Pillar #4: Finally Getting Rid of My Need for Control

During Libby's 28-day course, we did many TfM sessions to get to the bottom of my self-sabotage issues. During each session, my Inner Guidance or Higher Power would leave me little clues as to the root cause of the sabotage. For example, it often flashed images for me to indicate that the resulting self-sabotage was caused by my need for control. With this information, I was finally able to pinpoint the source and get to the root of the problem, which was what Libby called "a need-for-control cluster." It's like a cluster of grapes, with each grape being part of the control cluster.

Over several weeks, using TfM, I slowly dismantled the control cluster.

- The first "grape" in the cluster to go was my desire to control the aging process.
- The second was my unconscious fear of becoming a millionaire (more on that later), which was based on resistance to change and wanting to control relationships with others.
- The third grape to fall was the part that didn't want to go with the flow. Again, this was a part of me that wanted to control the future.
- The fourth was the part that wanted control over my unconscious thoughts. This one was important, because once I got rid of it I could more effectively work on the control cluster as a whole.

During TfM, this control cluster looked like me wearing a cowboy hat, carrying a whip, riding a horse, corralling little cotton balls (oh, the power of the imagination!). The part, we'll call her Cowgirl Kim, said, "I just don't like the thought of not having control over something, because I like to control what happens in my own future."

My Higher Power (the sun in my right hand) responded, "You [Cowgirl Kim] can't control the future, because you do not have Kim's 100 percent best interest at heart; I do. I have a plan, which is for her to follow her purpose in life. I will provide the road map for her to follow that purpose. Hence, there is no need to predict the future; we know it already. We know that the future entails Kim achieving her purpose in life."

That made a whole lot of sense to me. I knew it was my Higher Power's job to provide me with guidance, and I didn't need a separate part trying to control all the details of my life and giving me potentially conflicting guidance. I finally realized that I may not know all the details of what the future holds, but I do know the end result. I can take different paths in life, but I will get there in the end, and I am happy with that. This adds a tremendous amount of flexibility and really helps me relax and go more with the flow.

Taming My Unconscious Fear
of Becoming a Millionaire

As I previously mentioned, I recently discovered that I had an unconscious fear of becoming a millionaire. During the 28-day course, I wanted to get to the bottom of this issue, because I knew it would sabotage my trading, so Libby guided me through a TfM session to attempt to clear this very limiting "little i." The part manifested itself in my left hand as a picture of me looking at a brokerage statement. The part said, "Whoa! $5.6 million is a lot of money. This might change my relationships with people I care about. Will they expect more from me than what I provide now? Are they going to start asking me for money?" I realized the part was simply resistant to change. With the control cluster out of the way, it was very easy to negotiate with the part, allay its concerns, and bring it into alignment with my Higher Power.

Are they going to start asking me for money?

Doing a parts negotiation with a part that my conscious mind didn't agree with and was ready to veto might sound silly, but it's important to remember that self-sabotage is caused by the subconscious mind and will continue to wreak havoc until you reprogram it; it won't reprogram itself or let the conscious mind reprogram it. Anyway, I'm glad I did it. I'm sure my trading account will thank me, too.

A Snapshot of Before and After

Table 13.1 provides a before-and-after snapshot of the impact my four-month transformation journey has had on my life so far (and I've just begun!).

Also, you can see from the graph in Figure 13.2 that my happiness scores have improved dramatically within the last three years.

Table 13.1   My Life Before and After

My Life Before	My Life Now
Constantly frustrated by life's little challenges.	Much better at going with the flow.
Fear was a dominant emotion that factored into most life decisions.	Fear no longer present. I now use my life purpose to weigh major decisions.
Feared becoming a millionaire.	Being a millionaire would be great!
Feared failure so did not venture out of comfort zone.	Fear of failure is no longer an issue. I just finished writing an eBook, which would have been way out of my comfort zone before.
Alienated son because of extreme need to control his behavior.	Much improved relationship with son. Now he runs to me when I pick him up at daycare, whereas before he would only run to his Daddy.
Held onto losing trades because I didn't like to lose.	At a recent live trading class I was one of the top traders in the class. I made 45R in a week of day trading (note from Ken Long).
Traded a system that didn't fit me and that I hated because I didn't know myself or my beliefs.	Have a much better idea of my beliefs and will spend more time designing a trading system that fits me. The one we traded in the class seemed to work pretty well but not while I have a full-time job.
Hated my job because I felt that all the problems I faced were outside of me (i.e., excessively bureaucratic rules, incompetent co-workers, micromanaging boss, etc.).	Enjoying my job much more now that I finally realized I create my own reality through my thoughts, emotions, and actions.

(continued)

Table 13.1 My Life Before and After (Continued)

My Life Before	My Life Now
Never happy with the status quo.	Daily happiness greatly increased since determining my life purpose (see Figure 13.2).
Lacked focus and clarity, which showed in my lack of ability to complete long-term goals.	Since gaining clarity on my life purpose, I feel energized when I wake up every morning. I finished writing an eBook that is in line with my purpose, will generate revenues for my trading account, and bring me one step closer to financial freedom.

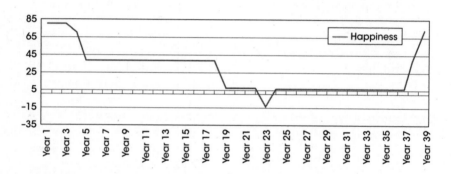

Figure 13.2 Kim's Annual Happiness Ratings—before and after Starting the Super Trader Program

The Turbocharged Transformational Model

I believe that anyone who follows a similar path and employs tools similar to those I used can achieve the same results, if not better. I also believe that the model I used is practically guaranteed to give anyone's transformation journey a turboboost. In fact, I believe it has put me on a solid platform to achieve even greater transformations in the future. This is because it addresses the basics required to achieve a sabotage-free subconscious. I strongly believe that only a sabotage-free subconscious can go on to attain greater levels of consciousness like the ones described in my chapter and the other chapters in this section of the book.

The transformational model that I described in this case study consists of three major components as shown in Figure 13.3:

1. Transformational Foundation: Trust in a Higher Power. Without this solid foundation, I believe that significant transformation would be next to impossible.
2. Transformational Pillars: The following pillars provide important structural support for achieving a sabotage-free mind, but would be difficult to achieve without a strong foundation:
   - Pillar #1: Get rid of nonuseful emotions (like fear, guilt, and anger).
   - Pillar #2: Learn to communicate with your Higher Power.
   - Pillar #3: Determine life purpose.
   - Pillar #4: Surrender to a Higher Power (i.e., give up need for control).

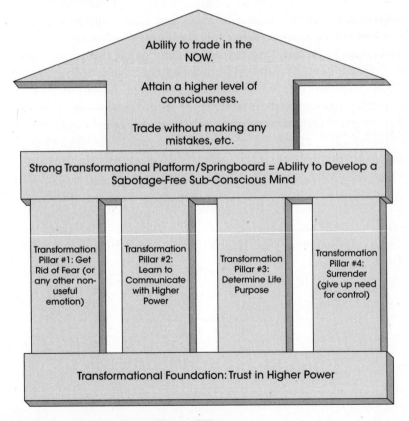

Figure 13.3   My Transformational Pillars

3. Transformational Platform/Springboard: Ability to achieve a sabotage-free mind. This platform is supported by the pillars. Most, if not all, of these pillars need to be firmly in place before you can spring up to a higher level of consciousness.

Right now, I believe I've got my feet firmly planted on the platform; I just need to use the springboard to catapult myself onto a higher level of consciousness, which should make it much easier to achieve my trading goals.

Conclusion

The important take-away from my transformational experience so far is that I wouldn't have been able to make so many important transformations in such a short amount of time if it hadn't been for the strong transformational foundation I laid in the beginning of my journey. I would argue that that foundation—trusting in a Higher Power—is absolutely paramount to making any significant changes. Without that trust, I don't think the transformations would have been as quick, deep, or lasting.

But trusting in my Higher Power was just the beginning. I then used that newfound trust to help me figure a way out of the Matrix (i.e., begin reprogramming my subconscious mind to get rid of self-sabotage). Of course, all of these transformations were dependent on my consciously recognizing my unconscious programming and reprogramming my nonconscious mind (i.e., recognizing that I was in the Matrix). I believe it would have been almost impossible to do that without trust in a Higher Power. Although it takes some serious soul-searching and willingness to lift up the hood of your nonconscious mind to clear out the junk, I definitely believe it's worth the effort.

14

From Engineer to Spiritual Warrior

A TRADING JOURNEY

Anonymous

Biography: The author of this chapter has spent most of 2012 in an awakened state and said that in that state he could no longer have written this chapter. He prefers to remain anonymous.

 Before: Cynical and depressed over-thinker who is unhappy most of the time.

 After: Constructive and effective business professional who is happy for no reason.

I am a 45-year-old engineer from Germany. I work as a consultant in the IT industry, helping my clients structure their challenges and simplify their businesses. My background in beauty-care manufacturing, corporate cost-cutting, and business process reengineering gave me a broad base of experience when it came to structuring and implementing change in organizations. Some might say that I am the proverbial management consultant who knows a little bit about everything but nothing in full depth (this may well be true).

This engineering and consulting profile is mirrored by my INTJ Myers-Briggs profile. Like so many other engineers, I am introverted, pragmatic, and fact-oriented. Another aspect that will make the following easier to grasp is that more than 50 percent of all IT projects fail in any given organization.[1] Thus, I have extensive experience in observing and participating in failure, as well as a strong appreciation for anything that works. This separates me from a typical scientist: scientists tend to want to understand why things happen; I just concentrate on whether I can reproduce or improve it.

Timeline 1: Downhill Accelerating

With the benefit of hindsight, I can say that I had a happy and well-protected childhood in a small German town, where everyone knew everyone. Until early adolescence, I was an average child with average interests and no hobbies. Regardless, I was always able to find fun things to do beyond the scope of organized recreation. I just took what appeared, and neither I nor my friends saw this as a problem. That changed when my friends entered adolescence and decided to be in grown-up mode. All of a sudden, they wanted to preplan recreational activities multiple days in advance to sync it with their hobbies. This was way beyond my interests at the time. With my friends now out of reach most of the time, I turned inside and continued to live my one-day-at-a-time approach on my own.

I was different from the other kids, and though I thought this might become a problem, I didn't have time to worry about it. I had a more pressing issue to deal with: my grades in school had fallen from an A/B to B/C average. It was a wakeup call for me. I decided to put more effort into my schoolwork, and after one year, my grades were back in B+ territory.

At that point, my only contacts were school-related because I didn't see much sense in organized and scheduled recreation. My parents started dropping hints that it was "nice" that my grades were good, but that I should also be part of a social environment. I ignored these hints, though, because I believed they would likely change their minds if my grades were to go down.

When I left school, I'd pretty much forgotten how to enjoy life. I was aware that I had, but I thought it would be temporary. After my compulsory military service (which was actually enjoyable because there were always comrades around to have fun with), I decided to become an engineer. I always loved inventing, I was good in math (at least that's what I thought before I started university), and there were good job prospects for engineers at the time.

Within the first month of my studies, the professors did all they could to recalibrate my self-esteem and instill in me the perception that to succeed in this curriculum I would have to work hard (about 50 percent of students would eventually drop out of this particular field). Consequently, I gave up the idea of relearning how to enjoy life during my university years. I was instead consumed by a fear of failure and subsequently focused all of my efforts on just getting the degree.

I would have to work hard.

Of course, I didn't study all the time. Instead, I spent hours analyzing why I was unhappy and tense. I was trapped in a self-created prison, a downward spiral that became so strong that I was no longer able to work on my studies. Luckily, this was at a time when private television channels were allowed in Germany; having the TV on in the background while I was studying helped to quiet my negative, overanalyzing mind.

Once I completed university, I entered the corporate world, only to find out that I was re-creating the same situation again: I faced a steep learning challenge and gave up all ideas of having a more pleasurable emotional life. My fear did not disappear. It merely changed its focus from getting a degree to keeping a job.

Everywhere I went, I was taking my problems with me! I'd create an outside expectation that would be difficult enough to keep me fully occupied with work and sedating enough to not think about my approach to life. In my few leisure hours, I would use TV, radio, or lots of food to keep my mind occupied.

The internal pressure to face my joy-of-life problem eventually became so strong that I was no longer able to ignore it. Looking at my life, I saw a reasonably successful professional who was unable to translate his external success into internally felt happiness. Because I wasn't able to experience happiness, my life had degraded to a mere consumption of resources. If I'd viewed my life like any business I'd ever worked for, I would have considered it a loss-making business and recommended that it be shut down. I was living proof of the second law of thermodynamics: simply put, it is easier to create untidiness than tidiness (e.g., to create lukewarm water by mixing hot and cold water than to do the opposite). The realization was so devastating that it actually led to ongoing suicidal thoughts.

I used the score of Van Tharp's Happiness Test to plot the evolution of my emotional state. The Happiness Test consists of 35 questions about your view of self, spirituality, life, and the world around you. I created a lifelong timeline and noted the key events of each stage with just a few words (e.g., end of military service, first year in university, move to city of Aachen, survive studies; see Table 14.1). This allowed me to reenter the mindset of those years and answer the questions for that mindset.

The happiness test score through starting the Super Trader program is given in Table 14.1 and graphed in Figure 14.1.

My suicidal tendencies were not very emotional. There was just the realization that if I continued to analyze my life, I would arrive at the conclusion that suicide would be the only rational next step. Then, two good things happened:

1. My nonconscious mind made sure that I always had enough sedation (work, TV, food) to never finalize that thought.
2. A good friend argued that if I wanted to kill myself anyway, it would not be necessary to do it right away. I could attend psychotherapy first and then—if it really didn't work—kill myself afterward.

Table 14.1 My Happiness Scores Prior to the Super Trader Program

	Key Timeline Elements and Drivers for Emotions
Early Childhood 1965–1972	• Happy, protected childhood without big problems. • Sets the baseline for my happiness.
School— Lazy Time 1972–1982	• Society gradually puts more constraints on me. • I learn that my intelligence may be high but not high enough to give me good grades forever without studying.
School— Being Busy 1983–1985	• Based on the school problems of some classmates, I become fearful of failure and start studying with high intensity. • Grades pick up quickly, but happiness deteriorates as I start to feel trapped in the hamster wheel. • I lose the ability to enjoy life because "I should study instead."
Army— 1985–1986	• At the time, Germany has compulsory military service, which means that the military contains people from all walks of life. • The only objective is to get through it with as little pain as possible. • I realize (afterward) that, because I was distracted from my feelings of guilt, my time in the Army was relatively happy, even though it didn't feel like much fun at the time.
University— 1986–1991	• Overwhelmed by the intellectual challenge of engineering classes, higher math, and thermodynamics, I decide to give up on having a life and just surrender to getting the degree. • I end up making a few attempts to enjoy life, but not enough to make a true change.
First Jobs— 1991–1997	• Working hard to make it in professional life, realizing more and more that my ability to enjoy life is gone. • Suicidal thoughts. • Decision to start psychotherapy.
Therapy— 1997–1999	• Psychotherapy gets me off the immediate suicidal thoughts. • Hope comes back that there could be a path out my low state.
Breathing Classes— 2000–2002	• Combination of rebirthing breathing, Neuro-Linguistic Programming, and coaching helps me to learn to let go of old limiting beliefs and allow myself to enjoy life. • Feeling positive again.
Spiritual Journey— as of 2002	• Starting a journey to find my own calling and slowly making peace with the world around me.
Stable Relationship— as of 2004	• Start of happy relationship with my wife brings in a role model for enjoyment of life and acceptance. • Certain issues just melt and disappear.

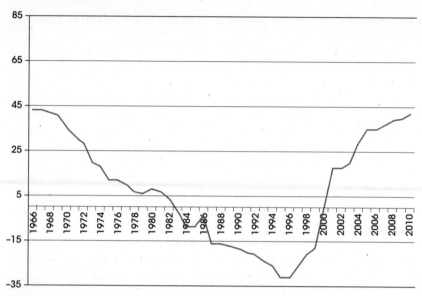

Figure 14.1 My happiness scores just before starting the Super Trader Program

That made sense to me at the time, so I went into psychotherapy.

Timeline 2: Crawling Out of the Pit

It was hard for me to align my beliefs with the approach taken in psychotherapy (which I considered talk therapy). I wanted to see results, and the therapist wanted to just talk! Still, she found the right approach to reduce my immediate desire to kill myself and create hope that I would eventually find a way to enjoy happiness again. This process took about two years and ended when I realized that the therapist could get me out of the fire, but wouldn't be the right person to get me into happiness-positive territory (I am, however, still very thankful to the therapist for getting me out of the fire). I exited this episode of my life with the hope of moving on, but, again, with no clue how to do it.

By sheer luck, I was introduced to Wolfgang Malik Wöss, an Austrian therapist who offers a 15-month part-time course that focuses on feelings released by breathing (rebirthing) and Neuro-Linguistic Programming (NLP). At the time (about the year 2000), this was really outside of my comfort zone. Rebirthing? NLP? Even *more* talking? Fortunately, I had the privilege of observing the transformation of a colleague who participated in this course and completely changed from an incredibly abrasive and negative person to a wonderful team player and friend within just a year. When I was invited to her wedding, I met more participants of the program. Seeing their relaxed friendliness and acceptance, I decided that, whatever it was, I wanted to have what they had!

The Malik Wöss program is primarily a train-the-trainer program for breathing therapists, but many people participate in order to achieve the personal transformation that typically happens during the course. There are nine four-day weekend seminars and one longer seven-day seminar over the course of the program, each about six weeks apart—enough time to let the experiences sink in, yet frequent enough to maintain a high momentum. Each seminar contains physical experience elements, meditations, and theoretical training.

I cannot pinpoint a single element that created the change,[2] but the overall program consistently put me into emotionally positive territory for the first time since I was about 16. I was able to enjoy life without needing to have a particular reason for it. This was a huge improvement, with only one little caveat: Now that I had the freedom to master my life, what would I do next?

A Message from Somewhere

Following Malik Wöss's program, I had the opportunity to vacation in the United States for a few days and decided that the wide open spaces would be a good setting in which to use my newly acquired meditation skills and really listen for a clear message from inside (from God?) on what to do with my life.

After about a day of driving, I found a nice place to roll out my meditation mat and started addressing an imaginary counterpart in the skies: "I am here! What do you want me to do?" My question was answered with another question about 20 minutes later: "Are you really ready to hear the truth?" Was I ready? I didn't know, so I jumped back in the car and drove off. After a full day's drive, contemplating my willingness to face the truth while reading billboards in New Mexico along the highway, I was finally ready. I wanted to get over this. How bad could it be?

The same procedure was repeated: I sat outside and spoke to an imaginary counterpart in the sky: "Okay, I've thought about it," I said. "Yes, I am ready!"

To my big surprise, I received a response in just about 15 minutes: "If I tell you the truth, you must accept it and implement it. Listening but not acting upon it is not an option. Are you ready to act?"

How many more questions would I get? I was frustrated. This was not the answer I'd hoped for. Again, I was not sure if I could wholeheartedly agree. So, once more, I hopped back in the car and drove off to chew on the message for a while. It took me another two days of driving through the countryside to accept that if it was truly the voice of a higher entity, it wouldn't make much sense to run away from its message. It would get me sooner or later anyway, so it might as well be right now.

For what I hoped was the final time, I sat down, turned to the entity[3] and said, "Okay, I am ready. This is the last round, and I will sit here until I get clear feedback! Tell me what you want me to do. Should I have a family? A corporate career? Become a monk? What is it? I am ready!" This time it didn't even take five minutes to get a simple answer: "Be yourself."

What is *that?* I thought. I could be myself in any of these roles! All that meditation for this cryptic answer? I was furious. The answer was so far off from any of my expectations or previous models. Apparently, there was no mission for me to do anything special. On the other hand, I would be able to do anything I wanted and still comply with the source that gave me the message, so there was no hardship involved. Shouldn't I at least be a little grateful for this freedom?

Okay, so I got an answer that was somewhat useful. It was not asking for big sacrifices. I decided to be grateful and make peace with my ambitions and the voice that had spoken to me. But again, I still had no direction for my life and no workable plan.

Finding Out That I Would Be a Professional Investor as Soon as I Retire

In 2001, I became interested in trading. The prospect of easy profits and, moreover, the fractal beauty of bar chart patterns was alluring. I started to randomly read books about trading, and when I heard about the Elliott Wave concept, both my engineering and my artistic mind were hooked by its seeming simplicity and frustrated by the difficulty of deducting robust trading signals from it.[4] Too bad it didn't work for me, because now I was obsessed with the markets.

While searching for interesting trading systems, I accidentally stumbled upon Van Tharp's book *Safe Strategies for Financial Freedom.* With its concept of *financial freedom,* which was completely new to me at the time, I experienced my first true paradigm shift in how I saw making and consuming money. Moreover, with the structural risk of Social Security,[5] I realized that I would have to take care of my retirement by myself. Private retirement insurance products were delivering in the range of 5 percent interest. I would have to do a lot of saving to get a decent pension, and, on top of that, I had to trust that there would not be any significant inflation over the next 50 years. Even a high-level look at German history showed me that Germans had not been too successful in protecting their currency.

There is a common memory among German people that inflationary risk is real. When we were young, the kids in my generation were shown 500 billion* marks by our grandparents and older family members. Each grandparent had their personal story of experiencing hyperinflation in the 1920s. When inflation struck, many people were wiped out because their funds were in long-term assets or pensions. For the little that was liquid, people bought gold coins. Growing up, I remember many old ladies wearing jewelry made of gold coins on a daily basis because this was the only thing left that they could carry over from those times.[6]

500 Billion (Trillion) Deutsche Marks

---

* The German term for billion is "milliarde," whereas the German term "billion" is 1,000,000,000,000, which we'd call a trillion.

With the inflation risk in mind, I decided that the insurance option would not fit me. I would have to learn to manage my money on my own to be able to successfully navigate through the coming decades. Even if I delegated the management to an investment fund, as soon as I stopped working in a paid job, I would become a professional investor—where the term *professional* was to be interpreted as "person who lives off the return of this occupation."

What followed was a short period of nonsystematic intuitive trading ("Whoops, where did the money go?") and the quick realization that (a) I had no clue about trading or investing, and (b) I would have to find a systematic approach to financial freedom. Only with a systematic approach could I hope to get reproducible results and gradually learn from mistakes. I assumed that I would need a set of successful trading systems to run my personal "pension fund." To get these systems, I participated in several seminars, bought a number of open and black-box systems and read more books. At first, when I found something that sounded reasonable, I immediately traded it at a small position size, only to find out that my losses would pile up over time.

I then dabbled in mechanical systems, newsletters, and one managed futures account. Overall, the results were lackluster, and I realized that I'd made some systematic mistakes in my trading:

- Psychologically, I was not ready to be successful in trading: My self-worth was so low that I was only comfortable in a losing position. I was not aware of this at the time, however, so I continued trying.
- I tried to get out of doing the homework. I did not put in enough thought of my own because my issues with self-worth made me trust others more than myself.
- I gave systems too little time to achieve their statistical edge. I found reasons to sabotage myself; every failed system lessened my already low self-esteem ("See? I told you that you're too stupid to trade").

In hindsight, the low self-esteem was the key driver. I didn't understand this at the time, though. I just felt bad but didn't know why.

Do I Have a Real Problem, or Do I Just See Monsters in the Closet?

Once I realized that my investing/trading was a net-losing exercise, I decided to focus on skill building. I was busy in my day job as a consultant, so there wasn't much time for systematic learning, and the idea of financial freedom was slowly crawling off my radar.

Overall, I was very happy with my job and had a comfortable cash flow, but there was still a nagging feeling that I was not doing enough to prepare for retirement. Moreover, in my particular job, there was an additional complication: to deliver peak performance, I could only work for one client at a time so as to give them my full attention, if needed, seven days a week. This meant that my entire business model depended on a single customer. As long as that was working, it was really great, but as soon as my client no longer needed my services, I had no preestablished second option.

I was oscillating between comfortable sedation with work, food, and TV on the one hand and the nagging feeling that I was missing a key risk on the other. On top of that, every now and then, the universal question of my life popped up: What is my purpose? What am I finally going to do with my life? Am I just hiding from life?

Over time, I became less emotional about my inability to answer these questions. I had, more or less, put these thoughts aside and accepted that, for the time being, there was no answer. In the area of financial freedom, I continued to gradually add trading systems to my ever-growing library, just in case. But mainly I was busy working for my client: go to work, come home, watch some TV, go to bed ("*metro, boulot, dodo*").[7]

Meeting Super Trader Program Students: I'll Have What They're Having

During my relatively systematic effort to collect trading systems, I read about the workshop offerings of the Van Tharp Institute. Dr. Ken Long was presenting his mechanical long-term and mechanical swing/day trading systems. I decided to participate because I was told I would "get a lot of good systems in Ken's workshop." That was all I needed to know.

While I originally attended for the systems, I wound up discovering, in my opinion, a much more interesting side to the workshop: Among the participants were several of Van's Super Traders. We chatted during the breaks, and, in spite of their broad spectrum of individual personalities, they commonly demonstrated a distinct quality of serenity, a detached focus, and a sense of humor. Obviously, they had found an approach to trading that I was still lacking. I wanted to have what they had.[8]

This was a déjà vu experience; it reminded me of my friend's wedding, where I met a number of people who had participated in Malik Woess's rebirthing training and had the same gut feeling. I took the fact that the Woess training had already dramatically improved my quality of life as a good sign and decided to join the Super Trader program. Had I not been admitted for whatever reason, I still would have attended all the workshops and continued to try to get admitted at a later time.

My first step was to find out the program's entry criteria and how I could operationally participate. After all, I was living in Europe, and my day job could be quite demanding. I consoled myself with one of my survival beliefs: "The operational side has never been the bottleneck."

I figured that the admission process would take some time, so in the meantime, I registered for the upcoming Peak Performance 101 and Peak Performance 203 workshops, scheduled two months later.

Over the course of the next eight months, I went through many significant transformations. I tend to look for structure in my life, so I've segmented the description of each transformation into three parts: the original situation, what I did to achieve the transformation, and a description of the transformed state.

Transformation 1: Dropping the Pain of Past Projections

Original Situation

Negative thinking was a constant struggle for me. With the attitude that "a good joke must be worth a good friend," I was continuously searching for opportunities to see the deficits in others and to make "witty," cynical remarks about said deficits. I really didn't understand why the other people were so dumb, uncooperative, and slow to get the joke. I had heard about the psychological concept of projections, but I never associated it with myself. Besides, when I decided that someone was stupid, I felt I had a justifiable reason to make fun of him. Every time I got in a car and drove, I was provided with new proof that something was wrong with this world.

Deep down in my heart, I felt that there was a correlation between how I perceived the world and how the world would react to me, but I never consciously worked on it. Overall, I just followed Janis Joplin's approach: "Wait for delivery each day until three."[9]

Actions to Achieve Transformation

My participation in the Peak Performance 203 Workshop, which is rightly called the Happiness Workshop, helped me overcome this stuck state. While there are many different elements in the workshop, three particular aspects really made a difference for me:

1. The workshop's activities loosened my emotional structures so that I was more willing to work on changing my attitudes and moving outside of my comfort zone. This was critical for me because it removed many of the negative distortions I projected on the world.

2. The workshop introduced me to Byron Katie's process in *The Work*® in which you answer four questions about your neighbor and then three turnaround questions about the first four questions to investigate whether these thoughts are not just your own projections.[10]

   Normally, I would have just held my breath, blinked, and waited for the next topic in the workshop. However, there is an extensive six-week homework assignment after the workshop for which you are teamed with different participants to share your answers. I couldn't just pretend that I'd overlooked the concept and move on. I would have had to tell six different people every day for seven days that I "accidentally overlooked the task," and that wouldn't have worked for me. So I bit the bullet and completed the worksheets.

   The *Judge Your Neighbor* worksheets had a particularly dramatic impact on me. As part of the process, you take a person that pushes your buttons and go through a written, self-directed process (this approach matched my INTJ personality nicely).[11] Without a single exception, I was in a neutral state toward all people that I believed had treated me badly. I went through them all: my parents, my siblings, the whole set of relatives, friends, colleagues, and foes. In each case, I looked at them after the analysis with a stunned face and realized that I could not recall my original problem with any of them.

3. The third element for my transformation, which was also introduced to me during the Peak 203 course, was the *Sedona Method* by Hale Dwoskin. The method uses different strategies for the release of feelings; all of them are very simple and do not require you to go through extensive emotional periods to make them work. They seemed so easy that I was unsure whether they would actually work. In the weeks following the workshop, I had the chance to listen to the 20 (!) audio CDs several times so it could really sink in.

The *Sedona Method* helped me clear out any negative feelings that still remained after working through the Byron Katie worksheets. Every now and then, the *Judge Your Neighbor* worksheet could resolve the issue with the other person, but it left me with a feeling of inadequacy (e.g., "I am so stupid/ unworthy/slow"). The *Sedona Method* helped me to release this feeling, or at least to rattle it loose so that it would disappear within hours.

The vanilla ice cream solution: You can never have too much of it.

I like to describe this as a vanilla ice cream solution: It's nothing extraordinary, but everyone loves it, and you can never have too much of it.

Transformed State

After dropping my projections, I had an increased sense of peace toward other people and myself. I realized that most of the time I was just projecting my own internal problems onto other people. When I acknowledged that, I was able to stop it immediately. My relationships have improved significantly since this change.

A second change was an increased willingness to work on myself. The process of realizing that most problems are just projections shifted my focus inward—an area where I have full control and that actually drives the change process.

Based on my newly found peace and the resolution of internal problems, I started to consciously forgive myself for all of the many negative projections I imposed on people. Now, when people do something objectively wrong, I am much quicker to forgive: I just believe that they would have acted much more constructively had they been able to. This is what I experience with my own actions, so why shouldn't I give the other person the same benefit of the doubt and forgive?

However, I would like to point out that this doesn't mean I accept or condone negative actions. If the other person insists on stepping on my toes, I just increase the protective distance.[12] As soon as they wake up, I am willing to let them get closer. Table 14.2 shows the whole process.

Table 14.2 Dropping the Pain of Past Projections

Original Situation	• Other people are seen in a negative light.
	• Although I am now aware that I project my problems onto other people, I have not forgiven anybody, because I believe my position is justified.
Approach	• Participate in Peak Performance 203 workshop.
	• Work through all of the homework assignments given in the workshop.
	• Continue to release negative feelings as they are observed.
	• Continue to complete *Judge Your Neighbor* worksheets whenever I observe someone pushing my buttons (there were fewer than five!).
Methods	• *The Work.*
	• *Sedona Method.*

(continued)

Table 14.2 *(Continued)*

Work Aids	• Peak 203 workshop notes.
	• Self-created Excel sheet to speed up *Judge Your Neighbor* process.
	• *Sedona Method* Course (especially the audio CDs).
Timeline	• Peak 203 workshop, plus homework: Week 1–7.
	• Additional clean-up: Week 8–15.
	• Forgive 95 percent of all people, including myself: Week 15
	• Release negative feelings as they come up: Ongoing.
Key Success Factors	• Persistence in doing *Judge Your Neighbor* worksheets and Sedona feelings release. Didn't seem to work at first, but after three weeks, I experienced amazing results.
	• Third-party accountability from workshop participants. I would never have put in all the work without the moral support and supervision of my peers.
Transformed State	• I no longer fight *my* problems with *other* people.
	• I have forgiven 95 percent of all people, including myself.[13]

Interlude: There's Money for Everyone

Shortly after the Peak Performance 203 workshop, I was admitted to the Super Trader program and was able to participate in the Super Trader Summit. The summit is a three-day annual meeting of all the active Super Traders, and it is used to share the best practices and experiences that have been gathered by the students over the past 12 months.

When I participated, I was brand-new to the program and not too familiar with Tharp Think or specific modules of workshops that were frequently mentioned. However, I was able to observe about 15 presentations from different Super Traders, and I could see the common patterns among a very diverse group of people. While I did not have the background knowledge to understand the details of the presentations, I realized that all of these people found an approach to making money in the markets that fit *their* personalities. In essence, there was apparently money for everyone (good). More specifically, there was money for everyone who did

Table 14.3 There's Money for Everyone

Original Situation	• I am not sure if there are particular characteristics that would be required for being a successful trader, or if I can develop these characteristics.
Approach	• Participate in Super Trader Summit.
	• Listen to presentations from 15 different Super Traders.
	• Observe the commonalities and differences.
Methods	• Analyze and compare the key messages from the other Super Trader candidates.
	• Follow-up during the breaks if I did not understand the message.
Work Aids	• An open mind.
Timeline	• Super Trader Summit (three days).
Key Success Factors	• Willingness of presenting Super Trader candidates to share their best insights (which they all had).
	• General understanding of all participants that they are not in competition with each other. The other person will most likely never trade another one's systems because the personalities are different. There is no risk in sharing.
Transformed State	• There is money for everyone.
	• It requires diligent work (but not more).

the homework, mastered themselves and the trade, and applied skills in a highly disciplined and continuously improving manner (still good, but a lot of work).

I was surprised to find out that there was no standard personality pattern that would be indicative of success in the market. I knew then that if I could do the homework, I could be a successful trader. With that prospect in mind, I was all too ready to do the required work and more. Table 14.3 gives a summary of my realizations.

Transformation 2: Firsthand Experience of a Benign Universe

Original Situation

Before I entered the Super Trader program, my spiritual beliefs focused on a monotheistic view of the world where everything, good or bad, comes from the same God. Depending on my state of mind in a given situation, I would sometimes think that there would actually be a counterpart that I could have a dialogue with. Other times, I would just assume that the entire universe is one big machine that evolves around a divine plan, and that I was just a little gear in the big gearbox of life.

The older I got, the more I liked the idea of being a little gear in a larger machine that would start to want to have a life of its own: "I do not want to spin all day long!" "I want to have different teeth!" "The other gears are not nice to me . . . can I go play outside?" And like any driver who faces reluctant gears while driving, I envisioned a grumpy God who was driving the yellow school bus of life, cursing and hammering any reluctant gear back into its God-given position to keep things moving along.

I never could make sense of what I wanted to do in my life and whether there was a free will or not, so I just tried not to think about it, which kept me from slipping into depression. Life was lukewarm with a few ups and downs, but at least I had overcome the deep valleys of pain. What reason would I have to believe that there was more? Looking around, the average person on the street didn't seem to be too happy either. And from an engineering point of view, I accepted this as a statistically valid assumption: Life is more or less a frustrating adventure. Maybe you can cherish some happy moments, but ultimately it will remain a struggle. If you could learn to love the struggle, you had it made.

Actions to Achieve Transformation

After the Super Trader Summit in December 2010, Dr. Tharp held a Oneness Awakening Workshop. I had no clue what to expect, but since I had already made a lot of progress with the transformation of my projections and the release of negative feelings, I was eager to move on.

The Oneness Movement[14] originated in India and, in summary, states that certain techniques can affect physiological change in your brain, which will then allow you to see the world as it is. This goes hand in hand with dropping nonuseful beliefs and negative ego parts and will ultimately allow the practitioner to "awaken into Oneness," where he will be in a permanent state of bliss.

Having had my own little experiences with consciousness-improving techniques during my rebirthing training, I was open to the exercise, but I didn't expect too much. I was ready to have three days of joint meditation, completely open and willing to accept whatever.

The days were structured as a set of consecutive steps. Each step was designed to overcome the resistance and habitual patterns of the brain in small increments. I felt good, but nothing more—until we started a 49-minute session of chanting ("I am love") and dancing. During this process, I could suddenly detach myself from my body. I felt as if I were standing behind myself and observing the chanting and moving. From this detached position, I observed that my body was "doing talking" and "doing moving"—but it wasn't me! Having already had some weird moments in my life, I remembered that I was still an engineer and decided to do a test. Maybe, if I retested, I could prove that I was just a little carried away from the meditation and everything would go back to normal.

Well, it didn't. I continued to observe myself for some time. Every 10 to 20 seconds, I made the same observation that my body was moving, but was not me. There was speaking, but it was merely my physical body making funny noises. The mind that perceived itself behind and outside of my body decided to accept this strange experience, grab a proverbial bag of popcorn, sit back, and just watch with utmost curiosity what would happen next.

Nothing happened. The meditation was over, and what was separated went back into the body. I was stunned and needed a break.

The night after the meditation, my engineering, analytical mind took a second, more rational look at the situation: The detached observer part was immensely peaceful and happy when it was detached. There was no sweating, no catching breath. The drops of sweat that were running down my glasses and obstructing my vision were observable, but they did not disturb me. In that detached state, I was just a happy blob of mind, no longer linked to a physical body. I reckoned that this must have been a short glimpse of the state that everyone had been talking about.

When I analyzed further, I found more interesting implications. If the detached mind was purely in a state of happiness and peace without reason or need, then any emotion of unhappiness, scarcity, stress, and lack of peace would have to be separate from this detached mind. The identity of the detached mind was not defined by body, emotions, goals, actions, or physical sensations. These were all external.

If I applied my "I am just a little gear in the big gearbox of life" metaphor and assumed that I was no different from anybody else, then I just experienced the fact that every creature in the world had a happy, peaceful, benign core. The only reason it couldn't be experienced in daily life was that everyone was carrying around a physical body, beliefs, and emotional patterns, which filtered the perception from the outside and distorted the signals that the "pure mind" could give to any other creature. And the icing on the cake was that the experience of the projections and the belief that "people would be nicer if they could" matched perfectly with this new experience.

Transformed State

After these experiences, I realized that *there was a conscious mind that was not linked to my physical body*. Moreover, this detached conscious mind was genuinely happy, peaceful, and without any desires or needs. It existed in a state of completeness, even beyond abundance, as abundance includes the potential of scarcity.

The second part of the transformation was a new belief: The true core of the universe is benign. If anything in the material world was not benign, it was just a nonuseful outside add-on to a benign core. Releasing nonuseful parts would not risk anybody's true identity; it would be more like taking out the trash. Nothing additional was needed to be happy; I would just have to get rid of the ballast.

It didn't take much to access this state of detachment. *By following a sequence of meditations and exercises, I could go back into that state whenever I wanted*. But for the time being, I had a clear target: get rid of the ballast. This would make the connection to this happy and peaceful core easier to achieve and maintain. The transformation is illustrated in Table 14.4.

Transformation 3: Realizing My Purpose

Original Situation

Even though I managed to overcome or even master many of the psychological challenges, the question, "Why am I here?" remained unanswered. Over the previous 10 years, I'd managed to reduce the emotional charge of this open question and just accepted that I would not know. Maybe I wasn't wired to have a clear, attractive purpose in

Table 14.4   Firsthand Experience of a Benign Universe

Original Situation	• I am my body. • Everything is God, and everything comes from God (good and bad). • I am open to new experiences. • Spiritual but nevertheless very down to earth (hey, I am an engineer!).
Approach	• Oneness Awakening Workshop. • Structured sequence of meditations and exercises.
Methods	• As above. • The particular transformation happened during an exercise of dancing and chanting.
Work Aides	• None for the participant.
Timeline	• Just one seminar: 3 days.
Key Success Factors	• Effectiveness of the Oneness processes. • Participant's openness to new experiences.
Transformed State	• In its core, the universe is benign. • I am not my body. • I can easily achieve a detached state by meditation. • Releasing the ballast of negative emotions/patterns allows the benign core to shine through.

my life. The message from "somewhere" that told me to just be myself was still present, but it was too indifferent to guide my efforts.

I have a very simple requirement for a good purpose statement: It needs to help me make decisions and eliminate options. When I'm in the grocery store and stand in front of the milk cartons, a good purpose statement should be able to tell me whether I should buy whole milk or skim milk. I believe general statements for prosperity and progress (in my case, "be yourself") are a waste of time.

Actions to Achieve Transformation

My first move in the right direction happened about seven years ago when I met my wife. Aglow with the joy of finally having found a soul mate, I asked her if she had any wish that I could satisfy. I was thinking along the lines of a ring or other jewelry, but, after about 30 seconds, she answered: *"I want to have 50 years of love, joy, and bliss!"* That definitely caught me off guard, but when I looked at it from a management consultant perspective, it was really a very wise wish that met all criteria for goal-setting:

- It was process-oriented (i.e., it asked for action every day and didn't put a limit on the upside).
- It was linked to a specific date (i.e., 50 years).
- The goal was both an individual and team goal; both sides would have to contribute and appreciate the other's contributions to make it work.
- Even though it wasn't technically specified, both of us would immediately be able to assess any given situation and check whether it contributed to "love, joy, and bliss."[15]

This gave me the first indication of my purpose. When applied to the milk carton scenario from above, there was a simple answer: Skim milk does not add joy to my life; thus, it can be eliminated from the list of alternatives. On a broader scale, there were still undefined areas that were almost like the "be yourself" message. The new purpose statement would be achievable in any professional setting, be it as a manager, consultant, trader, or artisan. I was already in positive territory, but I was still on the lookout for more. I had already spent enough time brooding over it. If the brooding got out of control, the negative thoughts would come up again and have to be suppressed with TV, food, and work to keep me going.

The next evolutionary step happened during the Oneness Awakening workshop, which I have already mentioned in the second transformation section. During the three days of meditations and exercises, I was just listening inside and waiting for messages or insights. As soon as I realized that I apparently had access to parts that I normally could not reach, I pulled out the long list of open questions that had bothered me for so many years and tried to get them resolved here and now. I entered into an internal dialogue with the nonconscious part inside of me that was willing to give me answers and checked if we could clarify my purpose statement. Over the course of several minutes, I was able to craft a new purpose statement that covered all new impressions, but that became quite cumbersome over the different iterations. It was almost like a design-by-committee process:

- Initial hypothesis: *Love, joy, and bliss*
  → The experience of detachment from the physical body and connection to the universe needs to be included!

- Iteration 1: *Love, joy, and bliss AND connection to the universe*
  → This is just a collection of nouns, I need to put in a verb!
- Iteration 2: *To have love, joy, and bliss AND connection to the universe*
  → This is too selfish, and it is not process-oriented!
- Iteration 3: To have/increase love, joy, and bliss AND connection to the universe for myself and others
  → This is acceptable for the time being. But why is it so complicated?

Initially, I was happy with this statement, but over the course of the next months I heard other Super Traders talk about their mission statements that were also complicated and difficult to grasp. I doubted that a mission statement is truly workable and inspiring if you need to explain it after you have said it. Truly visionary statements (e.g., "life, liberty, and the pursuit of happiness") did not care about process orientation, balance, and time aspects, yet they inspire generations. With that in mind, I felt a bit like my mission statement was spinning its wheels but not touching the ground.

The latest step of further evolution was completed during Libby Adams' 28-day program, which is also part of the Super Trader curriculum. During one of the coaching sessions with Libby, I told her about my struggle to find an inspiring, attractive mission statement that would allow me to decide "which milk to buy." With Libby's help, I was able to distill the essence of the long journey: *to be happy and grateful.* The happiness would address the immediate wish to be in a good mood, sparkling with positive energy, and loving the world as it is. The gratitude part would serve as the balance to the extrovert happiness because it would ensure that I could see the gift of every little experience and would allow me to develop a deep sense of peace and joy over time. I no longer bothered with complicated phrases; I felt they would limit me more than they would help me.

Transformed State

I felt a deep sense of relief after finding my super-simple mission statement. Could it really be that simple? My conscious mind checked all the previous roadblocks and found that they had all been removed.

In particular, the purpose statement released me from the pressure to define a target in the future. Instead, I would be able to

Table 14.5   Realizing My Purpose

Original Situation	• I have overcome depression. . .
	• . . . but I do not know what to do with my life.
	• General mission statements do not stand the test of time.
Approach	• Listen inside.
	• Establish working hypothesis.
	• Continuously improve until done.
Methods	• Meditation.
	• Awakening Workshop (more meditation and exercises).
	• Libby Adams' 28-day program.
Work Aids	• None for the participant.
Timeline	• 2001+: Ten years of occasional self-work.
	• As of Q4 2010: Systematic self-work.
Key Success Factors	• Persistence to keep trying.
	• Openness to new experiences.
Transformed State	• Simple mission statement: To be happy and grateful.
	• Living the mission 9 days out of 10.
	• Deep sense of relief from past overthinking.

live my purpose in the here and now. I would not have to wait for some outside parameter to align to be "on target." Testing it with the milk carton scenario, I found that it also worked: buying good-tasting food would make me happy, and the ability to do so would instill gratitude. If I ever had to go on a diet, other food items would improve my health, which again would make me happy. I actually found a robust rule set that could be used to navigate through everyday decision processes. Table 14.5 shows a summary of this process:

Transformation 4: Finding a Vehicle That Suits Me

Original Situation

With all that gratitude and happiness, I felt like I really had it now. It took a while until the next layer of unanswered questions popped up like the buoys in *Jaws*.

I was now in a position to optimize my daily life and was freed from decades of brooding about how to approach my life. But with all that freedom, in which direction would I go?

I decided to use my engineering mind to look at the facts without any emotional bias:

- I have a simple mission statement, "happy and grateful," that helps me be exactly that in everyday life.
- I do not have a single attractive external target picture (e.g., start a manufacturing company and build spaceships).
- The past six months of going through VTI workshops and Super Trader self-work have shown that I am still rapidly evolving. Any target picture that I may choose today could well be outdated in a few weeks when I potentially go through the next evolutionary step.
- Any useful target needs to be flexible enough to cover potential dramatic changes in the way I look at the world (e.g., it would not be wise to take out a big loan to buy a car dealership down the road).
- The insights I gained during VTI workshops, in my interactions with other Super Traders and through meditation followed a common theme: I like simple solutions, and there is evidence that simple solutions work.[16] If you look at alternatives with a total-cost-of-ownership view, the simple solution is mostly the one that has the highest likelihood of making you happy in the long run.

Actions to Achieve Transformation

Based on these observations, I was not in a position to create a single attractive business model that would meet my current or potential future requirements. I reverted to a guideline that I had heard years ago when working with business strategy consultants: If you do not know where to go with your business, the mind-set of a "holding company" is the default option. The holding company does not care what business it is in holding or its core capabilities; it is just company focused on short-term and long-term profit. That sounded boring but effective. And, as boring would imply, it is simple, which covers one of my basic requirements.

I decided to use a scenario-analysis approach to define different business models and to create a business case model for each of them. These are illustrated in Table 14.6.

The different business models would then be subdivisions in my holding company and would be divested or frozen when they were no

Table 14.6   Simple Business Scenario Model

Trading Timeframe	End-of-day trading	Consultant[17] and EOD trader	Inventor, coach,[18] and EOD trader
	Day trading		Day trader
		Frequent travel	Single location
		Travel Frequency	

longer viable. Based on the analysis, I would be able to define commonly needed capabilities and infrastructure and implement these *nonregret moves* regardless of the particular scenario selection. Overall, I would optimize the business model of a nimble businessman who flexibly navigates his subdivisions through the economic waters.

While I was already quite happy with the approach, I was still able to take another step forward, again with help from Libby Adams as part of her 28-day program. We worked through the topic of desire and my limited ability to create a truly attractive target picture (the holding model was just a workable default). I jokingly remarked that the only nonconscious guidance was the wishy-washy statement, "Be yourself." Libby transformed this indifferent message into an eye-opener: "Be your SELF," where the SELF would represent my true core, the one that I had briefly observed when I realized that I was not my body. Apparently, whoever had given me this message about 10 years earlier was not trying to make me look stupid after all.

Transformed State

At first glance, a change in capitalization and the insertion of a space between "my" and "self" should not make a big difference, but I immediately saw two benefits:

1. I had already glanced at my inner SELF and knew that it would not ask for complicated worldly targets. The inner SELF was happy as a default; it was the conscious mind and the negative nonconscious patterns that could potentially limit my happiness.

   → Thus, the first target for the holding company would be to create an environment where the existing negative nonconscious patterns would not be disturbed. Example: If I had a pattern that was afraid to take a leadership position, I would have to create a business model that I could run as an individual.

2. All of a sudden, the self-work of releasing negative emotional patterns was becoming a key driver for my business model success. My ability to be my SELF was limited by the boundaries that my negative patterns would set. If I managed to move the boundaries of these patterns (e.g., by letting go of a negative belief), I would have a larger comfort zone for my SELF.

Ultimately, letting go of all negative patterns creates an infinite comfort zone!

→ This mechanism would allow me to create a quantified financial model of self-work.

If I had a pattern in which I would only be worthwhile if I had a new Porsche and I could let go of this pattern, I would have an immediate financial savings of one Porsche. It would not mean that I would never have one, but I would not need to have one to meet my objectives.

Ultimately, I didn't just find a way to manage my target vehicle: by finally making sense of the "be your SELF" statement, I had a clear business case and intention to work on my negative patterns. My fourth transformation is summarized in Table 14.7.

Table 14.7   Finding a Vehicle That Suits Me

Original Situation	• I have found a simple mission statement . . .
	• . . . but I do not know how to translate this into a business model.
	• I understand that simple solutions suit me.
Approach	• Two-fold approach:
	♦ Part 1: Pure rational logic: Scenario analysis
	♦ Part 2: Get coaching as part of Libby Adams' 28-day program
Methods	• Requirements analysis
	• Business scenario analysis with two varied parameters: trading timeframe and travel frequency
	• Libby Adams' 28-day program
Work Aids	• Simple MS Word document (paper and pencil would do it, too)
Timeline	• Six months of occasional work
	• Total spent time: Less than 40 hours
Key Success Factors	• Rational, single-direction approach (no endless loops)
	• Persistence
	• Willingness to accept guidance from outside

(continued)

Table 14.7 (*Continued*)

Transformed State	• Key target to be a nimble businessman, acting as a holding company.
	• Multiple business submodels, none of them believed to last forever
	• Goal to be my SELF (true inner self)
	• Operational target 1: Create setting where current negative patterns are at peace and the SELF can flourish.
	• Operational target 2: Release negative patterns to increase the comfort zone for the SELF to flourish.
	• Letting go of all negative patterns creates an infinite comfort zone.

Transformation 5: Become an Active Manager of Emotional States

Original Situation

During most of my life, starting with late adolescence, I was dominated by my thoughts and emotions. Whenever I was not active, my internal chatter would start. Depending on the mood of the day, this would vary from "I am bored" to "I am not worthy to live." I developed the habit of drowning out my mind with work, food, and TV. When I tried to work at home, there was hardly a time when I didn't have TV or radio on in the background to cover up the negative internal chatter.

Every now and then, my emotions would become so strong that even food and TV would not be enough to keep me sedated, and an emotional downward spiral was triggered. Usually, this was only stopped when enough outside pressure (e.g., from work backlog) built up and the fear of failure kicked in and got me going again. Whenever I was emotionally stable enough to look at the situation from a detached perspective, I observed myself as a victim of my emotions and thoughts. The sedation mechanism and the fear-of-failure-triggered recovery would normally work, but this was neither sustainable nor fun.

The more I learned about the mechanism of employed labor and the carrot and stick that organizations tend to give their employees to get them going, the more I found that it was time to get out of the victim mode and become a master of my emotions and thoughts. But whenever I started to work on it, sooner or later, the daily routine would kick in. The self-doubt would whisper in my ear, "Just give up; you won't make it anyway," and I would find myself sitting in front of a TV with junk food on my lap, complaining about the difficulties of life and my inability to succeed. I truly felt like a victim.

Actions to Achieve Transformation

The first systematic approaches to overcoming my victim patterns began in the Malik Woess's rebirthing program. I learned to identify my victim patterns and how to theoretically overcome them. Over time, I realized that communicating my victim feelings would make me look incompetent in a business context, so I stopped complaining. I just kept my problems to myself and got feedback from other people about how much I'd changed for the better. So, even if it didn't remove the root causes, it simplified my interactions with other people. That was a good enough first step for me.

A true shift in my approach to emotions was triggered in the first Peak Performance 101 Workshop, where the task was to tell victim stories and then turn each story around to see how you create the situation that leads to the problem. Suddenly, I realized that the victim role is much more of a choice than I had ever thought, and that it is much more effective to be in a resourceful controlling role. This triggered a new perspective when thinking about my negative emotions and thoughts. I decided to no longer accept them as given. Whenever any negative item showed up, it was immediately a target for release. I had exploited my victim role for so long, I just couldn't stand it anymore—and I was determined to take any action that would help me get it sorted out.

The work I did in the Super Trader program was useful in resolving the first layers of negative thoughts and feelings, especially the transformational meditations in the Peak Performance 202 Workshop and the self-work of the *Sedona Method*.

Next, I had to document on a timeline how much time I spent at different levels of consciousness,[19] with shame, agony, and grief on the lower end and love, bliss, and enlightenment on the higher end. I was surprised to find that I still spent a lot of time in a negative state. Based on a three-year look-back period, I reckoned that I wasted about a quarter of my time staring at my computer screen not getting any work done as my internal voice kept giving me negative messages. When Van received my homework, he asked me to analyze why I spent so much time in negative territory and how I planned to resolve this.

I decided to apply the strategy of going into the feeling to solve this. I reserved a long weekend and locked myself in my private office, and for the first day, I just experienced the feeling of agony in front of a computer: trying to concentrate but not being able to and hearing all of the distracting negative messages from my internal voices. After several hours, I managed to get into a dissociated position and look at myself from a distance. Whenever a negative statement popped up, I questioned where it had come from. At the end of the first day in solitude, I had traced all my negative feelings back to a single feeling of general guilt. As I felt guilty, I would deserve negative experiences and at the same time *not* deserve good things. Both led to self-sabotage that manifested the punishment and scarcity in the material world. I tried to release the guilt feeling with the *Sedona Method*, but I couldn't access it; I had to find another way around it.

On the second day, I inquired further and went into the guilt feeling again to analyze what drove it. I found out that there were four rules from my childhood that ensured that almost any wish I had or action I took would qualify for guilt feelings:

1. Do not make other people sad.
2. Do not be a burden to other people.
3. Do not take anything away from other people.
4. Do not betray other people.

While each statement sounded reasonable, I could easily see the implied limitations:

1. Do not make other people sad.
   → I give full control of my feelings to a third party.
2. Do not be a burden to other people.
   → I limit my ability to collaborate with other people. Collaboration means give and take!
3. Do not take anything away from other people.
   → No surprise that I hadn't succeeded in trading yet.
4. Do not betray other people.
   → This would stop me from being truly cheerful. Deep down, I would have a general guilt feeling that would not allow me to be cheerful, but I'd pretend to be happy!

Unlike the general guilt feeling I couldn't access with any of my releasing methods, I had immediate access to the childhood rules. The emotional charge was gone in the instant that I could really get at them. On the second day of analysis, I replaced these limiting beliefs with more useful ones that would put me in the position of being a resourceful driver instead of a passive victim.

On the third day, I tested the impact of the root cause belief transformation. I found that the feelings of guilt were immediately gone. I then checked each resulting negative behavior and all of the key problems that I had documented as part of the Super Trader curriculum. The emotional charge on the negative behavior was gone and the key problems in my life and my trading were addressed. I could already see that they had been partly released as well. My ideas on how to transform myself are summarized in Table 14.8.

Transformed State

After I let go of the guilt, I felt like a new person. I was able to listen to my internal voice without fear of negative feedback. In turn, I became more willing to listen to my internal voice. This completely eliminated the need to have background noise (TV, radio) to keep my mind at rest.

Table 14.8 Logical Sequence of Analysis and Belief Transformation

- I observe that I spend a lot of time in a negative state of consciousness (i.e., constant negative self-talk sedated with TV, food, work, not being able to work).
  → Why?
- I feel that I do not deserve good things. I feel that I deserve bad things.
  → Why?
- I feel that I am guilty of past bad actions and inappropriate wishes.
  → Why?
- I violated fundamental rules.
  → Which rules?
- Four childhood rules (e.g., "Do not make other people sad").
  → Are these rules still valid?
- No, they are not. They debilitate me.
  → What are better rules?

Four better rules were defined.

Immediate effect 1: Guilt feeling was immediately gone and never came back.

Immediate effect 2: Key problems in my trading and my life were addressed, if not already resolved.

Overall, I am now a much happier person, and I feel that I no longer have a tendency to play victim games. My key life and trading problems, which had been dominated by the victim pattern, have already disappeared. If new patterns arise, they slowly dissolve like a snowman in the sun.

Whenever negative thoughts or emotions arise, I no longer have the reflex to stay passive. I've slowly developed the opposite reflex and can now tackle them on the spot. I've created a list of thoughts and emotions to work on, and I'm resolving them one by one with the multiple methods I've learned over the past months. Transformation 5 is summarized in Table 14.9. And the changes in my happiness score are shown in the shaded part of Figure 14.2.

Table 14.9   Become an Active Manager of Emotional States

Snapshot Transformation 5: Become an Active Manager of Emotional States	
Original Situation	• Victim of my negative thoughts and emotions • Constant negative internal chatter compensated by TV, radio • Difficulty to concentrate on work due to chatter (about 25 percent loss of productivity)
Approach	• Trigger from Van to dive deeper • Three days alone in my office going into the feeling • Day 1: Understanding that there is a guilt issue • Day 2: Tracing it back to childhood rules • Day 3: Finding replacement beliefs for childhood rules • Connected beliefs automatically "popped"
Methods	• Going into the feeling • Tracing problems back to their root causes • Find root cause and replace with useful belief
Work Aids	• Create an issue tree with MS Excel (paper and pencil work, too)
Timeline	• Three days with about 10 hours of each day spent in solitude
Key Success Factors	• Outside accountability (I wanted to give Van a reasonable answer)
Transformed state	• Active creator of my thoughts and emotions • Increased happiness and sense of peace • Increase of productivity due to better ability to concentrate

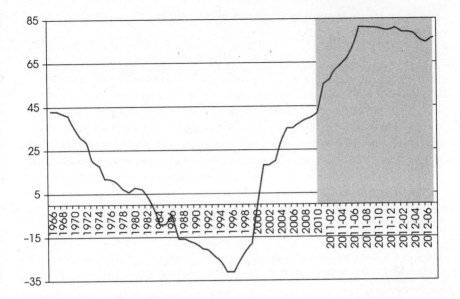

Figure 14.2 Happiness before and after My First Year in the Super Trader Program

Bottom Line: Net Winner in Life

Looking back at the past seven months in the Super Trader program, I can report that it has truly transformed my life. My happiness score improved dramatically, my work productivity has increased by about 20 percent;[20] and I have every reason to believe that there will be further improvements.*

For an engineer like me, such a story is hard to grasp. Maybe I am just fooling myself.

In order to address these concerns, you will find a list in Table 14.10 of the experienced "real world" changes so you can judge for yourself.

Thanks for pushing, Van!

---

*The scale only goes from minus 35 to plus 85, so there isn't much room for improvement.

Table 14.10   Measurable Changes in My Life as Result of Transformation

Before	After
Spend about 25 percent of my intended work time trying to concentrate on work but not getting anything done.	Less than 10 minutes per day (less than 2 percent).
Baseline productivity = 100.	Improvement of 20 percent; this means that my week has effectively gained an additional workday!
Watch more than 15 hours of TV per week.	I gave away my two TV sets and my radios.
Have the radio on while driving my car.	Car radio is mute.
Score in Van's happiness questionnaire: 60 to 65, depending on daily mood.	Score is regularly above 80 and the highest possible score is 85.

15

A Professional Trader's Journey beyond the Matrix

Curtis Wee

Curtis grew up in Toronto, Canada. His interest in trading began when he was in high school. Although he graduated from the University of Toronto with a degree in human biology, his interest in trading continued, which led him to study for the securities licenses as well as the CFA and CMT while working client orders for a major Canadian bank. Upon completing all levels for the CFA and CMT, he worked for a wealth management firm in Toronto where he filled orders, performed market analysis for portfolio managers, and traded a proprietary account. He learned that the key to successful trading is knowing yourself, something that was never emphasized in any of his previous work and studies. Now he realizes that trading is a metaphor to help him achieve a higher level of consciousness. He has completed Super Trader I and is now working through Super Trader II.

 Before: Trading professionally but unconvinced of his abilities, trading mostly out of fear.

 After: Has not lost money and is able to work out his many trading related issues with improving results while trading out of a state of being happy for no reason.

My father is a firm believer in the traditional idea that, in order to succeed, you must be better than the people around you. You must work hard to distinguish yourself, or those who are hungrier than you will push you aside and take what could have been yours. He was denied a promotion even though he thought he'd done a good job because he didn't have a required professional designation. Undaunted, he went on to earn the designation, and his career continued to grow. As far as I know, he never realized that he was playing someone else's game. In fact, he probably still believes that he has no option but to play it. He allowed others to invent and define the rules he used to run his life. He spent years fighting his way up the corporate ladder, and his example shaped my view of what it meant to be successful.

According to that view, the world was not abundant. Others had to fail so that I could succeed. I had to keep secrets and lie to gain advantages. If I did what was asked of me without also getting what I wanted, I was a victim. The outcome was all that mattered, and I should do whatever I needed to do in order to win.

But there was also another side to me, a side that, from a young age, struggled to understand reality and spirituality. We were told to go to church when we were young, and one of the questions I always thought was, "Why do we *have* to go to church?" After all, wasn't God omnipotent and omnipresent? I didn't want to go; I thought it was boring, and I thought the only reason my parents went was because the rest of the family expected them to.

My father is normally on time for everything; he loathes people who are not on time. Yet, for some reason, we were frequently late for church. At the time, I concluded that people only went to church because they were afraid of what God might do if they didn't. I saw it as hypocritical, at best. I didn't understand the church's interpretation of sacrifice and suffering in a world where God was supposed to be a loving Being. I mistook the institution of religion for spirituality in general and decided that religion was for ignorant and pretentious people. There was nothing more to the universe, I believed, than those phenomena that science could study. The cosmos was mostly random, here and there punctuated by an order that only scientific theories had the power to explain.

In high school, I was a cynical and sarcastic student. I mocked others and developed a deep disdain for "positive thinkers." I decided that things like nationalism, school spirit, or any other activity that encouraged a collective mentality was for inferior people who didn't believe they could be better than others. At the time, I could afford to think this way. I was the best swimmer in my school and ranked among the top few in my province. I was getting good grades without even trying. In fact, the school administrators wanted to take me out of the public system and put me into a gifted program.

I thought church was boring.

And yet, for some reason I couldn't understand, I was miserable. Whatever joy I felt from getting a good grade or winning a race was always temporary. I sometimes felt a little dirty from it, because for me to feel good, somebody else had to lose. One time I took pity on a boy from another high school who was deaf. I actually let him win what he thought was his best race. He was happy, of course, and that was certainly a good thing, but I felt like a fraud who had betrayed my team. No matter what I seemed to do, guilt and fear followed me.

When I got to the university level, my problem set changed. Now, the academic and athletic competition was much tougher. In high school, I'd been a star, but here, I barely qualified for the team. Once I did, I rarely won races. Meanwhile, I was doing poorly in my classes. I was always distracted, tired, and afraid—afraid that I'd flunk out, afraid that I'd get cut from the swim team, afraid of being average. Finally, after deciding that I wouldn't graduate unless I dropped swimming altogether, I quit the team.

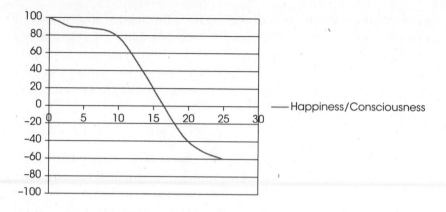

Figure 15.1   Happiness/Consciousness

That was definitely a low point for me, and I fell into a deep depression. You can see in Figure 15.1 how my happiness level started to decline when I reached adolescence and fell to its lowest point during my college years.*

My Early Trading Experiences

Fortunately, though, there was still one activity that brought me joy: trading. I'd started trading as a hobby in high school when I bought my first stock at the age of 16. By the time I was in college, the 1990s bull market was in full swing, and I was trading large-cap NASDAQ stocks. I believed that, in order to succeed, I needed to pick the right stocks, and the risk was in the instruments themselves. I looked at the fluctuations (which I thought was volatility at the time) and knew that I wouldn't be able to handle the wild swings of some of the more speculative stocks, so I just stuck to stocks like Apple Computer (NASDQ:AAPL) and Intel Corp. (NASDAQ:INTC). The only thing I looked at was the fundamentals of the companies, even though nothing changes on a day-to-day basis and the fluctuations of the prices have little to do with fundamentals. I'd grown my margin account from about $6,000 to $100,000 in about seven years, which was close to a 50 percent

---

*Curtis has changed the scale from the test so that it goes from −100 to +100.

annual compounded return, but I'd made most of that money in 1999 during the extremes of the bull market. I knew nothing about what it took to trade for a living. I didn't understand risk or position sizing strategies, and I knew little about the impact personal psychology has on trading. I was making money at the time, so I thought I was pretty awesome.

But then, when I started to encounter difficulties, the fact that I'd simply transferred all of my psychological issues into trading came back to bite me. Suddenly, I wasn't so sure of myself anymore. I questioned my ability to trade on a professional level, the same way I'd questioned whether I could compete in college. I feared losing money, and I feared that I'd never be able to trade professionally, which is what I really wanted to do.

But I didn't realize that it was me at the time. Like most people, I was looking for the Holy Grail. I thought I just needed to learn more about the secrets of the professionals. Trading was something that I really wanted to do, and I thought I was good at it.

I have a rather low opinion of brokers and investment advisors. I believe their only goal is to make commissions. They have little incentive to make sure your money grows because they can always add new clients. I'd had some discussions with my parents' investment advisors, and what they said always sounded just like what I was hearing on CNBC. I figured they just watched it and then fed us some story they'd seen. I had no intention of letting people like that take care of my life savings for me, so, after graduation, I decided to join the trading profession.

I got a job at a major Canadian bank, executing client orders, but I wanted a trading job for a large investment bank. To my surprise, large investment banks only wanted people from Ivy League graduate schools with 4.0 GPAs. I didn't have that, so I tried to get my foot in the door in other ways. I encountered a number of people who didn't strike me as particularly bright and who didn't know much about investing but still managed to get good jobs as traders, investment bankers, and portfolio managers. Their secret seemed to be that they'd become Chartered Financial Analysts (CFA) and/or Chartered Market Technicians (CMT), so I decided to earn a CFA and a CMT.

After that, I went back to job-hunting. I got several interviews with a few well-respected banks, buy-side firms, and the like, but none panned out. I felt like a victim: I'd jumped through all the hoops they told me to jump through, but I still wasn't good enough, so I continued on executing client orders, waiting for something better.

Working at the bank was bad for my trading education. The atmosphere was competitive, everyone who worked there was obsessed with choosing the next Big Thing, and most decisions were based on emotions. Nonuseful beliefs were rampant. Many claims were either not tested or applied incorrectly. There was a real need to be right.

Later, I worked at a wealth management firm and encountered the same kind of dysfunctional environment. The people I worked with didn't know what they were doing; they had a poor understanding of charts and had no idea how to use or test indicators to see if they were providing any measurable trading edge. I also found it interesting how they often claimed to have picked the exact top or bottom in their trading even though it's likely that there was only very small volume trading at those prices. So instead of learning how to trade well, I learned what didn't work.

In any case, my studies didn't help me return to being the successful trader I thought I was early on. I was frustrated, and I had the same doubts I felt when I was in university. It was like all of a sudden I was no longer able to compete in things that I was good at on a different level. I believed that trading professionally was as high a level as one could get in the trading world, and that there were no other factors needed to be successful at it except to be brilliant. I wanted to avoid the corporate game and not have to depend on somebody hiring me. These seemed like useful beliefs at the time, but, of course, they limited me.

Without knowing it, I had transferred my issues once again. I worried that I might not be good enough, that I might never be good enough. I desperately wanted to strike out on my own, to leave behind this job that wasn't doing anything for me and become an independent full-time trader, but I was afraid of taking the plunge. I still didn't really know what I was doing.

Stumbling on the Van Tharp Institute

I don't remember exactly how I came across Dr. Van Tharp. It could have been while I was studying for the CMT. I do remember reading the chapter Van wrote for the book *Market Wizards* and feeling as though I'd been exposed to something revolution-ary. His ideas resonated with me in a way nothing else had before. I borrowed Van's books and courses from friends and read through Van's archived newsletters on the Van Tharp Institute website, and what I learned only made me hungry for more, so I decided to take the next logical step, which was to attend the Peak Performance 101 and Blueprint for Trading Success workshops. It was there that I really started engaging with the ideas that would change both my trading and my life.

The workshops showed me just how ill-prepared I was to follow my dream of trading full time. I lacked discipline. I had little under-standing of how or why I was making my decisions. I was completely unaware of my beliefs. I was making tons of mistakes and routinely changing my rules after one or two unprofitable trades. I had no business plan. I realized that I had a lot of work ahead of me, and I wanted to have someone who could coach me through it and keep me on track, so I decided to join the Super Trader program.

As part of the Super Trader process, I attended a number of workshops, both psychological and technical. I also completed Libby Adams' 28-day course, which got me into a routine of con-stant self-analysis and started me on the path to self-awareness. All of these resources really helped me understand where I was, where I needed to be, and what I needed to do to get there.

But perhaps the step that made the most difference for me was completing the *Peak Performance Course for Investors and Traders*. From it, I learned what it takes to be successful in whatever I do. For those candidates in the Super Trader program, the five vol-umes of the Peak Performance course are broken into 20 lessons, and it took me about 10 months to finish them all. It was probably one of the most challenging things I have ever done, but it was well worth it. In fact, I still refer to the course when I see that I need to work on specific issues. One of the exercises I do regularly is the Beliefs Examination Paradigm, explained in Chapter 7, in which I log beliefs that happen to come up over the course of my day. This helps me stay alert to any nonuseful beliefs that might be creeping into and influencing my daily thinking.

I also read a number of books that were discussed by Van Tharp and others in the Super Trader program. Those books are listed in my reference note section.[1] Not all of the books listed will work with every-body's belief system, but I can say that they did help and teach me.

Key Lesson 1: Taking Personal Responsibility

As I worked through the courses and workshops, I learned a number of concepts that transformed, not only my trading, but the way I see the universe and my place in it. One of the first was that *I am responsible for everything that happens to me.* As it turned out, I'd learned to play the victim over the years, and I'd learned to do it because it had been a great strategy for me, especially when I was a child. I was the younger of two children, and I could get away with murder as long as I played the victim. Many of the negative issues I was trying to work through as an adult had grown out of that strategy. There was no question: I'd created the problem, and I was responsible for dealing with it.

I'd learned to play the victim over the years.

But I had trouble accepting the idea that I was somehow responsible for events over which I had no control. How could that be? Terrible things sometimes happen to people, things they can't help. Why are they responsible? Dr. Tharp suggested that I complete the 365 exercises in *A Course in Miracles,* and when I did, I finally understood.

In and of themselves, events have no meaning; they only have the meaning I give them. If I decide that an experience is frightening,

I feel "fear," with all of that word's associations and connotations—even though what I initially felt was nothing more than a physical sensation. In other words, I define my experiences. I decide what they mean, or whether they even mean anything at all.

Learning this concept triggered a real paradigm shift in my whole outlook on things. I realized that I can feel my feelings without being consumed by them. It doesn't mean that I no longer experience sensations of anger or fear; it means that I can simply observe them as mere physical sensations without attaching to them. I can distance myself from them because I don't name them.

Key Lesson 2: Able To Deal with Thoughts, Emotions, and Actions

Dr. Libby Adams[2] teaches that *thoughts, emotions, and actions (TEA) are interrelated,* and that *you should monitor and assess them on a regular basis.* Consciously monitoring TEA is essential to achieving self-awareness.

When I listen to a thought and make that thought real, emotions follow. If the thought is negative, I'm liable to do something destructive. It only takes a split second to lose control; before I know it, I could find myself doing something rash that ends up destroying my account. Many traders look for the Holy Grail, and there is a Holy Grail, but it isn't what they might think it is. It has nothing to do with having the best indicators, stops, exits, entries, or position-sizing™ strategies. Rather, the Holy Grail is knowing your "Self" and seeing the reality of things instead of living in an illusion you've created. It is being able to trade from a space where you have a quiet and peaceful mind, and where there is truth.

That capital on the "Self" wasn't a typo but a way to distinguish between the true Self and the false self.[3] My true Self is the one that acknowledges that I am a spiritual being. As Wayne Dyer said, "We are not human-beings having a spiritual experience, we are a spiritual being having a human experience."[4] When I listen to a thought and make that thought real, emotions follow. I create suffering as if it were real. By training myself to regularly monitor my thoughts, emotions, and actions (TEA), I bring myself back to awareness and away from the issues and feelings I've often named and made real—feelings like loss, anger, and inadequacy. As Eckhart Tolle said, "you are not your thoughts. You are the awareness behind the thoughts."[5]

Now, the following things generally are true of me:*

- I no longer believe thoughts that once brought me suffering.
- I am no longer preoccupied by my emotions, which helps me perform/trade better.
- I see the lessons in what happens.
- I take emotions as signals for me to return to the present.
- I return to peace.

When I monitor my TEA, I realize that I am grateful for the strong emotional signals I receive because they get me to look within and remind me that there is something for me to learn. At first, I sometimes forgot to look at my TEAs. As time went on, though, I improved, but I noticed something incredible starting to occur: When I discovered a negative thought, emotion, or action, I found that I didn't want to let it go of it! I had to come up with a method for doing this, and these were my options:

1. Ignore the feeling.
2. Believe that the feeling is real and hold on to it so that I can be "right."
3. Feel the feeling completely and be the awareness of that feeling so that I can learn the lessons in it and still be completely detached from it.

Ironically, the better I dealt with my thoughts, emotions, and actions, the fewer signals I got, and with fewer signals to alert me, I fell back into being unconscious. This is why I've developed a rule to remind myself to go back to the present on an hourly basis. I am also working on lessons from *A Course in Miracles* (ACIM), many of which require me to spend a few minutes throughout the day thinking about the lesson; doing this helps me return to the Now.[6]

I also discovered that when it slipped my mind to routinely check in with my awareness, the universe, being perfect, had a way of reminding me with negative emotions. Now that I'm consistently checking in every hour and during the ACIM lessons, I find that I can

---

*Sometimes nonuseful thoughts or beliefs might just slip by without me realizing it, but, as I'll explain, it doesn't happen too often.

increase that awareness by setting an intention for the hour. In whatever I'm doing, I am completely in the present and totally devote it to the awareness. I find that my mind has a lot less chatter, and I am not serially multitasking. I am a lot more productive, and my work and trading seem to require a lot less effort.

Key Lesson 3: Knowing My Thoughts Are Not Mine

I first encountered this idea in the Oneness Awakening workshop, which, I must admit, was somewhat confusing to me at first. I didn't really understand the concepts; they seemed strange and esoteric to me. It wasn't until I took it a third time that I felt something inside me click—something that finally unchained my mind and freed my spirit. I discovered that *my thoughts come from the one ancient mind, and that they flow through me but do not originate with me.* When I attach to them, I make them real and create an illusion. When I am my true Self, which is the awareness behind the thoughts, I am able to quiet my mind.

After I understood this, being "in the now" became easy. Thoughts disappeared as gently and easily as they had appeared. I felt no attachments. I was able to tune into a divine inner being that continues to amaze me. I could see that everything in the universe is done for me, and that everything is a miracle.

I also realized that it is within the instant of the now that the world is created. Here is how it happens.

1. I notice a thought.
2. I believe that it is mine exclusively and that it is true.
3. I attach meaning to it.
4. I create a complex story around it with me as the central character.
5. It becomes my identity, my past.

And, thus, my entire world is born in that moment.

Oneness essentially taught me the 12 teachings that are given in the conclusion to Section III and repeated in the reference notes for this chapter.[7] All of these teachings are really just one teaching. They are all ways of saying that we are not who or what we think we are—that we are, in fact, pure awareness and love. This belief really empowers me because through it, I discovered the true meaning of being totally responsible for myself. If I want to, I can change everything.

Key Lesson 4: Trusting My Inner Guidance

Van teaches that in order to know your true Self, you must *follow your Inner Guidance*. Putting that teaching into practice, however, proved difficult for me. There were too many questions. How do I follow my Inner Guidance? How do I know it's not just another thought? How can I trust what it says?

It turns out that what was really troubling me was my deep-seated distrust of God. I mentioned earlier that I went to church when I was little, and that the experience led me to reject spirituality as a whole. I considered myself agnostic, but the probability I gave to the existence of God was so low that I might as well have been an atheist.

The problem was that I didn't want to give up control to some inner voice. I wanted to rely on my own judgment. I wanted control of the wheel.

Gradually, though, I started to let go. I practiced meditating upon, listening to, and even conversing with my Inner Guidance directly. Sometimes there'd be nothing but quiet, but I kept trying. I started to write whatever questions I had in a journal and then listen for answers for about 15 minutes a day. I had no expectations and believed that whatever is best would be what I'd want. Eventually, I ended up receiving some very interesting insights and answers, and I have no idea where they came from. When they arrived, they did so without effort. There was no doing involved—only being.

I am now able to ask for guidance many times a day without effort, and I am able to keep the mind quiet so that I can be in the present. I am still doing the same things, but everything is different because I am *doing* from the place of *being*.

Key Lesson 5: Understanding That the World Is Perfect

When I call myself a "perfectionist," I don't mean that I'm obsessed with achieving some desired result 100 percent of the time. That kind of perfectionism is a self-made hell in which whatever you reach for remains just outside your grasp forever. If you see the world as imperfect, you can fall into that trap. I know I had. Before I discovered Dr. Tharp, I was intent on becoming a perfect trader—one who never suffered a losing trade. I was too focused on each result, so I changed my own rules constantly.

All that changed when I was exposed to Byron Katie and The Work®. Before she awakened in 1986, Byron Katie was chronically depressed and living in a halfway house, but one day she suddenly awakened to who she really was. All the concepts of Oneness made perfect sense to her. And from that state she learned a procedure to question her thoughts. She calls it The Work, and it consists of four questions and some turnarounds. Now she shares what she's learned with others and you can download her worksheets for free through her website[8].

Her basic premise, like that of many other enlightened people, is that the world is perfect, and that it is our belief in our thoughts about the world that causes suffering. When the thoughts are questioned and exposed, suffering disappears. She believes that there is no such thing as enlightenment—that it is really an ongoing process that constantly requires one to ask, "Am I enlightened to this thought?"

In one workshop, we worked through a number of Katie's *Judge Your Neighbor* worksheets as a writing meditation. The main lesson I learned from them is that I am constantly projecting and that the world is only what I believe it to be. I project parts of myself that I don't like onto somebody or something else so that I can escape responsibility for them.

The worksheets have two main sections. The first section asks you to question whether a particular belief of yours is true and asks what happens when you believe it and who you would be if you didn't have it. My ego loves this part of the worksheet. It's where I get to vent and be as petty and childish as I want.

The second half of the worksheet is where I think I get the most benefit. It asks you to turn your beliefs around in various ways and then observe how these new, altered versions are also true. You end up seeing one issue from many different angles and realizing that every angle, including the original belief, is imagined. You are merely projecting your beliefs onto the world. You are making the world a reflection of what you already believe is true.

Regularly doing the worksheet has trained me to be in the present because it directs me to use whatever stressful emotion

I experience as a point of inquiry. At first, I couldn't do this without the worksheet; I had to be able to physically write everything down, or else I couldn't see the projection. Now, I can use the knowledge of the worksheet questions as a psychological anchor to automatically bring myself back into the present, even when I don't have the worksheet handy.

Even so, I still write out my answers whenever I can. I do this because it's important for me to regularly examine my beliefs in full and complete whatever feeling I was experiencing, even when I realize that it was nothing but a projection. Otherwise, the projected feeling just comes back with a different disguise.

I read one of Byron Katie's books, *A Thousand Names for Joy*, along with *A Course in Miracles* as part of my daily routine, and what I see is that truth is all the same, and that all is really just one. There are no beginnings and no ends; what I get out of it just depends on my level of consciousness.[9]

Now, I'm a perfectionist in a different sense. *I see the world as it already is: perfect.* During my transformational process, the need I felt to make sure that everything turned out "perfectly" slowly disappeared. Without that need, I suddenly had the courage to do things without worrying about the results, and it actually improved my performance. I've accepted the fact that I can never know everything, and that if my trading systems work—that is, if they make enough money without too much drawdown—I'm fine with it. Even a loss is perfect. All outcomes simply are what they are—results that happen. There are always lessons in them for me.

Key Lesson 6: Knowing My Purpose

I know that trading is an activity that is joyful to me. I also know that my purpose is to be the consciousness or awareness of my Higher Self. David Hawkins's scale of human consciousness was introduced at the beginning of Section III. To recap, it's a logarithmic scale from 0 to 1000 that defines the lower levels at and below 200 as "Force." The "force" levels include, in ascending order, shame, guilt, apathy, grief, fear, desire, anger, and pride. All levels from 201 to 700 are called "power" levels and include, in ascending order, courage, neutrality, willingness, acceptance, reason, love, joy, and peace. "Enlightenment" occupies the top of the scale from 701 to 1,000.

Hawkins' model helped me understand where I would like to spend my time—as high as possible in the "Power" section. How could I do that? I asked this of my Inner Guidance in one of my meditations, and I was shown a different kind of scale in which my personal purpose is a state of being at the top; everything below it is just a tool to help me reach that state of being.

My purpose: *Increase my consciousness as much as possible.* I estimate my level of consciousness by my day-to-day level of happiness.

I also wanted to know how I could function on the illusory level of reality and reconcile what I do on a day-to-day basis to my life's purpose. Once again, I turned to my Inner Guidance for the answer, and the reply was simple: I can achieve my purpose regardless of what I do or have because purpose is not a state of doing, it is a state of being. There is nothing I can do for it, and it is not something for me to have. The path, the journey and how I walk the journey are all that is up to me. There are no other rules.

Whatever occurs in my life is part of my path. If I fully understand that, I can live effortlessly. I can be at peace with everything that happens because everything that happens moves me on my path. Trading is a spiritual exercise for me; through it, I learn about my inner voice and practice being in the awareness of my Self. It isn't the only spiritual exercise possible; it is simply a metaphor for my path. Maybe in a different universe I would be chopping wood and feeding cows. What I do doesn't really matter; the important part is "being" while I do anything.

Now, I can accept and welcome whatever may happen and focus more on my spiritual path. I see challenges as lessons that I have yet to learn, and that only appear to me because I am viewing them from a different consciousness. With purpose, there are no excuses and no victims; I know that the present is all that I have and that it lasts eternally. I'm not trying to imply that I don't make plans or have any goals. I just mean that I have the perfect contingency plan. If something doesn't go according to plan, it's because I've been given an opportunity to go within and discover some lesson.

Key Lesson 7: Reinventing Myself

One of the most important transformations I've experienced is my increased ability to recognize my continuous transformation. I seem to constantly reinvent myself now in a number of ways. The more I transform, the more I continue to move forward and allow my consciousness to catch up. This happened the first time I experienced the Oneness Blessing®, and it was nothing short of a miracle. When I became a blessing giver, a shift occurred in me without my understanding and without my doing. There was definitely resistance to the change from my ego, but something in me definitely changed nonetheless, something for which I had no explanation. At the time, it didn't feel very dramatic; I only realized the next morning and in the following months how much my world had changed.

The lessons I learned in Oneness gave me the courage to feel what comes up. When I confront, embrace, and accept those feelings, the suffering miraculously disappears. Suffering actually occurs when one runs away from those feelings. Sometimes, the only way to get around something is to burn through it. Carl Jung explained it well when he said that "all neurosis is a substitute for legitimate suffering.[10]" Embracing suffering allowed me to move away from suffering and toward truth, love, and contentedness.

Oneness has also taught me to be content with my journey rather than to seek an end result, and that has done wonders for my life situations[11] as well as for my trading results. When I let go and simply follow my path, I stop being concerned with the outcome of every trade; I just have faith that it will work out. Byron Katie wrote in *A Thousand Names for Joy* that "seeking is the movement away from the awareness that your life is already complete, just as it is. Even at moments of apparent pain, there's never anything working or lacking."[12] This doesn't mean, however, that I never look at the results overall to see if any trading strategies are no longer working, and I still change some rules based on good evidence, experiences, or insights. My trading results show the benefit of adopting that belief.

So Where Am I Now?

I've tried hard to apply what I've learned over the last two years, and the result is a happier, more conscious me. Enlightenment is

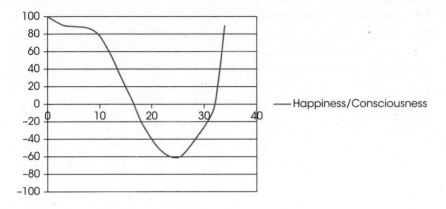

Figure 15.2 Happiness/Consciousness

beyond me, because it resides in a different realm that cannot be described with words or charts; it means there's no longer any need to inquire, and I am certainly not there yet. But I have reached the point where I am at peace and feel contentment most of the time, and I am much closer to living as my true Self than ever before.

Here, you can see how in Figure 15.2 the concepts I've learned and applied have changed my life. The happiness curve that found its lowest point in my mid-twenties has since rebounded and continues to climb. The y-axis is a measure of happiness/consciousness, and the x-axis is age.

In the realm of enlightenment, all spiritual teachings are limiting in some way. When it comes to linear thinking, I am closer to being awake than not, but when it comes to consciousness, the metaphorical distance is immeasurable. It can be as wide as the Grand Canyon or as narrow as the width of a subatomic particle. The width of the gap is the measure of how much fear one has. It is not a physical distance; perhaps that's why it's called a leap of faith. I believe a leap of faith into enlightenment can be taken by anyone, no matter where they are on the consciousness scale.

I urge you not to take my word for it, but to experience it for yourself. I can only talk about my own experiences, which may be very different from someone else's. All I can say is that the knowledge and experience I've have gained helped me.

Describing the difference between knowledge and perception, *A Course in Miracles* states, "to know in part is to know entirely because of the fundamental difference between knowledge and perception. In perception the whole is built up of parts that can separate and reassemble in different constellations."[13] In other words, knowledge is absolute and changeless because it is truth, and perception is relative because it is based on observations that change. What I have written here is a mixture of perception and Truth, because to gain knowledge, one must experience it.

16

My Journey to Trading in the Now

Thanh Nguyen

Thanh Nguyen is a Vietnamese-born entrepreneur who now resides in Canada. She joined the Super Trader program at The Van Tharp Institute in 2008 and completed the psychological portion in 2011 and graduated in 2012. She's been a full-time day trader in U.S. equities for the past several years. Thanh applies a unique meditative technique to various swing and day trading systems, a simple technique that could aptly be called an "empty-state" or "Oneness" trading style.

 Before: Stressed, unprofitable, and could not make money in the market no matter how hard she tried.

 After: Serene and could seem to just sense what the market will do and thus was able to pay for her entire training program in just a few months of trading

I grew up in Vietnam during and after the war. When I was a little girl, I always asked my mother, "Why I am here in this world instead of somewhere else?" and, "Why are you my mom?" She'd laugh and continue about her business. Mom worked 13 hours a day to support the family because my father was arrested for supporting the Americans after the war ended. I didn't like the life my mom lived; I remember telling myself that my life was going to be different when I grew up.

I am now 37 years old. I am a businesswoman, married with no children; I live in Canada. I acquired a business degree and have opened many businesses—some have made a lot of money, and some have failed. I've managed three beauty salons, an export furniture business, and a wholesale chemical supplies business. My husband and I used to work long hours every day. We hardly had time to eat! Our typical day ended at 11 P.M., and every night we would go to bed exhausted. The only free time my husband and I had was spent visiting the Buddhist temple for 20 minutes every Sunday. Doing so helped me relax and quiet my mind. This was our life for 10 years until one day I realized that I was just doing exactly what my mom did. I'd been focusing on my career instead of my family.

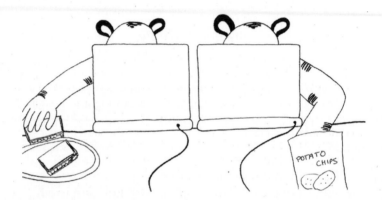

We hardly had time to eat!

I knew that I wanted to have more time to go to the temple and study, so we decided to close two of our five businesses (we kept the three spas). My husband started learning about investing in real estate, and I started to participate in spiritual activities at the temple.

My goal was to achieve Nirvana, the enlightened state of mind. I was meditating once each day, but I thought I needed to give up my goal. I thought Nirvana was unattainable unless I became a nun and devoted all of my time to my spiritual practice.

I was not going to become a nun, but I still wanted more free time to practice my beliefs. I thought I would find this time through changing my career from business owner to trader, an occupation in which I believed I could make more money in less time.

Initially, I believed that there was a magic system out there that I could learn and apply to my trading in order to be successful (i.e., make money), so I took an expensive day trading course that taught me other people's systems and techniques, all of which were quite mechanical (e.g., enter on the green arrow and exit on the red arrow). While I was able to follow those systems, my trading equity didn't grow. I'd have some winning days and some losing days. I wanted to know why I was losing. What was I missing—something in my methodology, or something else?

One day, my husband came home and told me that I needed to stop trading and start reading *Trade Your Way to Financial Freedom*. I read the entire book that night. The next day I decided to join the Van Tharp Institute Super Trader program.

Most people think making money from trading is easy, but I knew that I needed to devote a substantial amount of time and work to it to truly be successful. Consequently, I sold all of my businesses and kept the real estate for generating my passive income so that I could have time to do the work necessary to become a profitable trader.

My Transformation Journey

> There are only two mistakes one can make along the road to truth; not going all the way, and not starting.
>
> —*The Buddha*

While I had yet to realize the importance of beliefs and trading psychology fully, I was initially attracted to Van Tharp's teachings because of one of his more famous quotes: "People do not trade the market; they only trade their beliefs about the market." I wanted to find out the right beliefs, and once I joined the Super Trader program, I was on my way.

The Super Trader program has five phases: learning Tharp Think,[1] personal psychology, developing a complete business plan, developing three noncorrelated systems that work in different market types, and trading them with at least 95 percent efficiency.

When I started the program, I actually presented Dr. Tharp with what I thought was my complete business plan. It was about five pages long. He laughed and handed it back to me, saying that my finished plan would be well over 100 pages in length. After going through the necessary workshops and other information that

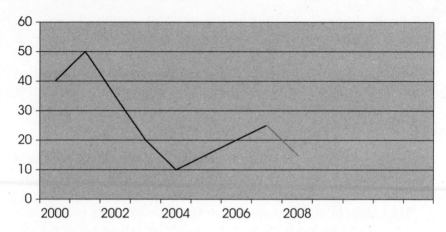

Figure 16.1   My Happiness Score in the Years Prior to my Super Trader Program

I received as a part of the program, I was able to give Dr. Tharp that full-length plan.

Out of the five phases of the Super Trader program, the psychological section was where I found the most benefit. My personal happiness, according to Dr. Tharp, is a good way to measure my life, both psychologically and spiritually. I joined the Super Trader program in late 2008, and I've graphed my happiness level for the eight years prior to that in the graph in Figure 16.1.

Although I wasn't at my lowest point, I definitely wasn't at my highest, and I was far from where I wanted to be. I knew I had work to do. There were six areas in which I felt I had to make major changes in order to be happy and successful. In this chapter, I'll talk about each of those six areas, and then I'll talk about my transformation journey and how I made it happen.

Area 1: My Anxiety or Worry

I have a strong accent, and I always used to worry about what others would think of me when I spoke in front of large groups. I was afraid that people would laugh at me. Now, things are different; I can control my mental state quite easily. When I talk in front of a group, I put myself in a neutral state. I focus on what I want to say instead of what others might think.

But that was only one part of my worry. Upon entering a trade, I'd typically worry that the market might go against me. I wanted security and certainty, but I didn't have it. I was anxious about losing. As I went through the psychological workshops, I began to understand how, with that mentality, I would lose, because I create what I think about.

I also realized that when I was really attuned to the universe, feelings of worry might actually be a message, and that I could perhaps listen to them instead of denying them. Nowadays, when I feel "worry" well up inside me, I understand that it may be an important message. I often ask myself, *What am I missing?* or *Why am I feeling this?*

Dealing with Anxiety

Now before I trade, I run through the Top Tasks of Trading. The first task is self-analysis, and if I notice any parts ("little i's") coming up that might interfere with my trading, I solve that issue before I trade. Another task is mental rehearsal: *What can I do to be prepared for anything that comes up?* This helps me avoid the mistake of not following my rules, and the worry just seems to disappear.

Area 2: My Impatience

I lacked patience with the markets. I didn't want to wait for the market to give me the just-right signal to enter. In addition, I would jump to conclusions too quickly at times. Both of these traits have caused me to have small wins and big losses.

Part of my solution to solving this area again involves the Top Tasks of Trading. Through these tasks, I am able to be in a state of mindfulness where there are no distractions. If I just follow my system with no chatter, the profit tends to take care of itself.

Area 3: My Fear of Failure or Being Wrong

I used to have a belief that failure was bad. That belief was combined with a belief that runs deep in Asian culture: the fear of losing face. It was a useful belief in that I always made sure I could do something to avoid failure. Nevertheless, I've missed many business opportunities because of this belief.

When I trade, I'm looking for concrete data. And I get information back, through asking questions, but that was not always enough to convince me of a particular course of action. Why? Because of my fear of failure, I was afraid that I would be wrong about the trade.

Now I believe that there is no right or wrong. There is only feedback from my thoughts and actions. Everything happens for a reason and each experience is an opportunity for learning.

One of the more advanced workshops that I attended has helped me realize that I'm always projecting my beliefs. My beliefs are really only in my head, but I see them as outside of myself. When I meditate, I reach a state of wordless awareness, and from this state, I don't project. As a result, I'm in control of my trading. My thoughts do not interfere, and the market just does what it is going to do.

Area 4: Being Overwhelmed

When I take on a new task, like trading, I'm always afraid that I won't have enough time to master everything. I'm very hungry for information and absorb knowledge the way a sponge absorbs water. Although I desire to comprehend a lot of information quickly, I always think that I am slower than other people—my action and thinking tend to slow me down. I'm competitive, and I think I should be fast, but very quickly during my studies I learned that I just have to slow down.

There were numerous psychological lessons to work though in the Super Trader program, and for some reason, I was usually required to redo each lesson—either because I didn't actually understand it or because I wasn't expressing my understanding adequately.

I've now learned to adjust my time so that I'm doing only one thing, but doing it well. When I finish one major chunk of a larger project, I go out and treat myself. This makes me feel great and gives me the energy to do more.

Area 5: Tendency to Believe That I'm Always Right

In trading, this bias to be right once led me to a big drawdown. I thought I was right, and I wanted the market to prove me right. It didn't. When I finally admitted I was wrong, the lesson was quite expensive.

Now I do a daily debriefing to review my performance, especially any mistakes. What caused the mistake? Wanting to be right! What can I do to prevent that from happening? Learn my lessons, meditate, and make sure I only trade from a state of mindfulness.

Because I now focus directly on a single task and the steps needed to complete it, I can see what might go wrong and take the necessary preventive action. This helps me avoid the need to be right and the desire to prove I'm right. When I trade mistake-free, that's my new way of being correct 100 percent of the time— and that way is in perfect alignment with good trading skills.

Area 6: Trading with No Plan or System

Before I began the Super Trader program, I knew nothing of what I have now come to know as Tharp Think: R-multiples, the importance of objectives, position sizing strategies, a worst-case contingency plan, a thorough business plan, and so on. I thought all that was involved was trading some black box system that would make a lot of money. I was very wrong.

I especially didn't realize how much my beliefs affected trading. I have hundreds of beliefs about myself, the markets, and my systems, and I needed to examine each one.

Here are a few of my beliefs about myself:

- I am a logical person, not a feeling person; this helps me make better trading decisions.
- I am organized, and I think it is important to be prepared to trade.
- I only care about the bottom line, which sometime makes me impatient.
- I jump to conclusions quickly.
- To trade successfully, I have to have a set of rules to follow.

Here are a few of my beliefs about the markets:

- Short-term trading naturally fits with my personality.
- I have an edge in the market that sets me apart from other traders.
- I only trade systems that fit my beliefs.

I also have numerous beliefs about my systems:

- I decide whether to go long or short based on where the first bar opens.
- When price is below the open, I go short.
- When price is above the open, I go long.
- My stops are at previous bars to prevent big losses.
- Bottoming and topping tails can present great trading opportunities.
- I only trade in the direction of the daily bar.

Now that I am fully immersed in Tharp Think, I can trade at a low-risk level that will allow me to survive the worst-case scenarios. I know how to collect R-multiples and determine the qualities of my R-multiple distribution. As a result, I'm always thinking in terms of reward-to-risk in my trading. I understand how my systems work, and I can adjust them to fit in the current market's condition. I now have a great position-sizing algorithm to ensure that my system will meet my objectives. I am not worried about blowing up my account.

I now trade my system in the market with confidence. I always look at my journal to see the lessons I've learned as well as the mistakes I've made. I want to make sure not to repeat them again.

Every month I see if my system is still working for the current market. I am grateful for what I have today.

How It Happened

I worked on examining my beliefs extensively. When I discovered a nonuseful belief that had charge on it, I released the charge. I did a lot of transformational meditation.[2] And my biggest transformation was a spiritual one.

At one of the workshops during the Super Trader program, I received a Oneness Blessing®. That blessing put me in a very deep and profound state. I mentioned this state to Dr. Tharp, and his response was, "Why don't you trade in that state?" I thought this was a great piece of advice, but the question was "How do I do that?"

When I returned home, I decided to sign up for a one-month Buddhism course. I did very well in the course, and my Zen Master suggested that I spend six months meditating in India. During my six months in India, my Zen Master taught me the knowledge of dharma, the meditation concept, some neurological science, and some meditation techniques so that I could succeed in the development of body, mind, and spirit. In order to attain the mindfulness state, I practiced 9 to 12 hours a day. We'd typically meditate from 9 P.M. until 6 A.M. We were not allowed to sleep during that time, but because of the meditation, we'd typically only need a few hours of sleep in the afternoon. I think that without passion and a mission, no one could go through that process.

The three methods I learned—contemplation meditation, stabilization meditation, and mental tranquilization meditation—can be easily applied to everything in life. I have also trained in silence in five postures (standing, walking, lying, seating, and eating) to always observe my thoughts and feelings and keep a state of mindfulness even when I am sleeping. This has created in my mind a new habit of *emptiness* instead of the normal chatter.

One of the more interesting ideas I learned was the *impermanence law* (Anupassana). I know that this life is temporary, but I wondered how to make that relevant in the present. I realized that living in India and Vietnam was very different. Impermanence causes all suffering, and all suffering comes from impermanence. It is the universal law of this world, and it is applicable to everything.

For example, after birth comes old age, sickness, and death—all because of impermanence. The market is up and down all the time, never staying at one price because of impermanence.

The illusionary mind pursues impermanence, and that causes suffering. Being enlightened is to return to true essential nature. It is the path to freedom from death and birth.

When I trade, I go into the mindfulness state. It is a full awareness state without any attachment to objectives. I am an observer in an empty space. I feel light, and I can actually experience a chain of biological activities in my body such as blood flowing toward the extremities of my limbs, my blood pressure lowering, my blood sugar level lowering, and my body temperature rising. My mind becomes serene and peaceful without attachment to underlying prejudices and biases toward others and the outside world. My mind becomes stable and tranquil, while my intellect becomes brilliant and transformed. That's my trading in the *now* state.

By the time I returned from my six-month meditational experience, I'd anchored that state so that I could get into it at will. Most importantly, I could trade from that state. The state, as I mentioned, is characterized by a complete lack of internal chatter, so I cannot talk about my trading when I'm in it—but I can trade from it, and I can trade well.

Where Am I Now?

One of the tasks in the Super Trader program is to develop a trading system and then prove that you can trade it at 95 percent efficiency or better (i.e., you can't make more than one mistake in 20 trades).

I have a day trading system that trades one stock that I know very well (although there are other stocks I can use). This system usually gives me five or more trades per hour. In November 2010, I made 152 trades to meet Dr. Tharp's 95 percent efficiency requirement for my system. I usually didn't trade for longer than two hours, making between four and 11 trades each day. For the month of November, I was up 132.5R. That gave me an expectancy of 0.87R per trade and an SQN score of 7.34 for my system for that month. I made money on 81.58 percent of my trades, and I didn't make any mistakes (except to wake up late one day, which I didn't count). So my trading efficiency was 100 percent.

Even though I was trading with a very small position size, this kind of trading made it very easy for me to (1) pay for the Super Trader program quickly and (2) achieve the kind of income I was looking for while just trading for a few hours each day.

I have a swing trading system for silver futures, but it still needs some work. It's difficult for me to trade a swing trading system from the mindfulness state because of the time period involved, but I'm pleased with my progress at this point in time.

Now, I have more control over my life than ever before in that I know that I must assume total responsibility for whatever I do and for whatever happens to me. In trading, I know exactly what I want from my system based on my beliefs. I also have clear objectives and a detailed plan to meet my objectives.

Trading is a journey toward self-mastery, and money is the measuring stick. I consider my trading success to be the concrete proof of my spiritual development, and that's exciting. Trading is probably the most difficult profession you can learn, because you have to learn how to master yourself first.

I know there is still more that I need to learn, but the transformations I've made have helped me become a better person. I'm now living my dream life. It required a combination of commitment, passion to trade, and purpose (i.e., "Why do I need to do this?").

I started the Super Trader program in late 2008 and finished the program in early 2011. The graph in Figure 16.2 measures my spiritual state during the course of the program. Notice the impact that these transformations have had. I think they are permanent.

I want to thank the Van Tharp Institute for pushing me out of my comfort zone; without you, I don't think I would have had a clear vision and mission. You helped me awaken my edge, which had been sleeping for a long time. You helped me find a vehicle through which to balance the spiritual and material worlds by applying Oneness to trading, and it's helped me grow my capital consistently.

These changes will help me to be a great model for my family. I also plan on using my trading skills as a vehicle to help Vietnamese nun communities learn about the money game. They already know how to get into the appropriate state, so teaching them basic Tharp Think will be easy.

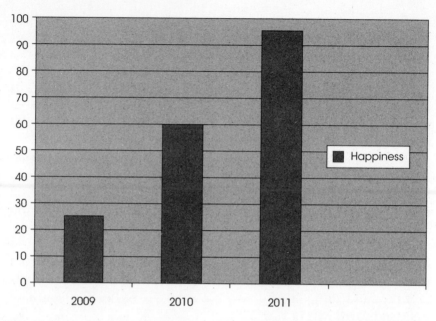

Figure 16.2   How My Happiness Scores Changed During the Program

My trading transformation has given me time to travel anywhere in the world, work freely anywhere, and spend quality time with my family, plus improve my spiritual life. I am now in complete control of my time and my life without any imposed limits. I am able to pursue my potential to its fullest, which gives me ultimate joy and happiness.

Editor's Note

Dr. Ken Long watched Thanh trade during one of his five-day live trading events. He said, "She just seems to know where the market is going to go and is 'right' on most trades. She's a trading goddess." Over those five days, she made 53R, outperforming Ken himself.

Thanh graduated from the full Super Trader program in June 2012 and is our first female graduate.

CHAPTER

17

Thoughts on Raising Your Level of Consciousness

Van K. Tharp, PhD

 Before: Traded from low levels of consciousness such as fear and greed.

 After: Trading from higher states of consciousness such as acceptance, peace, and enlightenment.

In the first two application sections, you've learned the principles of successful trading and how to apply them. Chapter 6 contains the basic Tharp Think trading principles. In addition, we've given you the basic psychological elements of Tharp Think plus nine steps to undo your programming in Chapter 12.

Your next step is to continue the process long enough to raise your level of consciousness to the point where you can see what's happening without a lot of internal interference, at which point trading will become easy for you. All of the following should help you do that:

- What would happen if you transformed or eliminated 5,000 major beliefs? You can do that through the belief examination paradigm.
- What would happen if you gradually eliminated the crowd inside you until the internal chatter in your head actually

stopped? You can do that through conflict resolution or TfM as given in earlier chapters.

- What would happen if you could actually observe what the market is doing right now with no interference of any kind?

The result would be amazing trading, and you could actually measure your spiritual progress by your trading success. As you reach the level of consciousness that David Hawkins calls acceptance (i.e., 350 on his scale), you should be capable of successful trading and be able to work your way through the remaining three areas.

Some Exercises for Trading in the Now

Let's go through a series of exercises on getting to know yourself. First, close your eyes and just watch your thoughts for about a minute. Notice each thought that comes up. Notice what happens to it, and notice what happens after it disappears. When one thought goes, you might even observe where the next thought seems to come from if you can. Do it now for a minute.

So what happened when you did that? Did your thoughts tend to slow down? Did you at any time notice the silence between the thoughts? Did you feel a little more relaxed at the end of the exercise? Write down your observations in the space below.

_____

_____

_____

_____

Most people think that they *are* their thoughts, but if you do this exercise long enough, you might begin to notice that each thought isn't you. Those thoughts merely pass through you. As Eckhart Tolle generally says, through such meditations you begin to realize that you are not your thoughts, but the awareness of your thoughts.

Now, let's do the same exercise for a little longer, for three minutes. Pay close attention to the thoughts that seem to flow through you. Be very focused, and really watch them. Again, at the end of the three minutes, write down what happened. Did your thoughts stop or slow down? Did you go into a state of no-thought or silence?

Did you fall asleep? Did you feel peaceful? Did you feel joyful? What did you feel? Again, write down your observations.

_____

_____

_____

_____

Perhaps you felt something like peace, joy, profound awareness, or even just silence. When you do the exercise again, notice any such feeling that might arise. Again, it could be something as simple as silence or nothingness.

Let's do the same exercise again, but this time for five minutes. Throughout the exercise, notice your thoughts and where they seem to come from and go to. Notice any silence that might occur. Notice any feelings that might come up, while you're doing the exercise, even if it's just a feeling of silence or awareness. Just watch and notice whatever is there. You don't have to do anything. There is nothing for you to do. You don't have to control anything. There is nothing to control. Just notice what happens and watch it. When a feeling comes up, observe it and nothing else. Again, do this for five minutes. At the end of the five minutes, open your eyes and notice that the feeling is probably still there. Write down your observations.

_____

_____

_____

_____

The awareness, the silence or the feeling that you feel is who you really are. In Chapter 10, I talked about my own journey toward finding my higher Self. Well, welcome to your Higher Self. Chances are that it didn't take you years to find. You are that Awareness. You are that feeling of peace, joy, or bliss.

Okay, this time let's repeat the same exercise for about 10 minutes. Notice when you become aware of a feeling. When it occurs—whether it's a sense of deep silence, awareness, or whatever—just focus on it. Observe it and appreciate it, because it's You. Who else could it be?

At the end of 10 minutes, open your eyes and look at something while staying aware of this feeling. Look slowly about the room, noticing what is there. Look at each object you see, one at a time, keeping your awareness on this feeling.

Now walk around the room. Notice what you experience. Notice that you can keep the feeling with you. It might transform itself—people have been known to spontaneously laugh, for example—but just notice the feeling as you actively walk around the room. When you finish, write down what you observed.

_____

_____

_____

_____

If you feel lighter, more peaceful, more joyful, or even more aware, congratulate yourself. You've achieved what some people take years to achieve in meditation. In the process, you've become more aware of who you really are—more aware of your Self.[1]

Now ask yourself, what do you think would happen if you were to trade from this state? I'm not giving you an answer. This is a question to ponder for yourself. If you're still feeling the feeling you noticed during the exercise, pay attention to it as you read the next section.

Trading in the Now

Now take a look at the candlestick chart in Figure 17.1. This is a weekly chart, though the last bar represents only a single day. Can you see a low-risk trade? Can you see several low-risk trades?

First, there are five weekly candlesticks going up. The price is approaching an old high made about 20 weeks ago. Do you believe that that old high might provide some resistance? If it started to move in the opposite direction, where would you enter into the market? If you were wrong about what price might do, where do you believe you should place your stop? Can you see the potential for a 3:1 reward-to-risk trade in your favor? Perhaps even a 5:1 reward-to-risk ratio trade? If you were right about 50 percent of the time on such a trade, do you think you could make money?

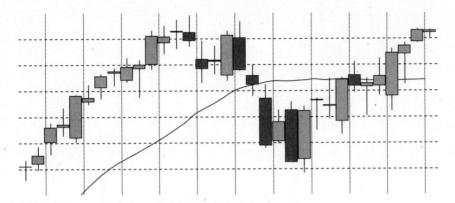

Figure 17.1   Weekly Candlestick Chart

Second, price is approaching a new high. Since it is at the same levels as the top of the old high candles, do you believe there is a chance that price might just move through those old highs? If it does, do you believe it might move to an even older high that was made five years earlier? Figure 17.2 is a monthly chart illustrating the earlier high.

If so, then the potential up move is at least as high as the up move made over the past 11 weeks. Do you believe that you could find a 3:1 reward-to-risk trade there? How about a 5:1, or even a 10:1? How would you know where to enter and where to place your stop to give you such a reward-to-risk ratio?

If you believe it, there is a potential nice move either long or short here. Do you think you could figure out a way to capture either one, no matter which way it moves, and make money?

Well, that's why I believe that trading is not about prediction, but about finding decent reward-to-risk trades. But, of course, that's my belief. Do you think you could just watch the markets and trade those moves and make money if you were in the state you got into during the last exercises? If you do, I've illustrated both the power of your beliefs and of your state of consciousness.

Now I'm not saying that you should just get into this state and trade, avoiding everything else I've suggested in this book. But what I am saying is that trading in this state, when you have a proven trading system, and then following all the other suggestions in this book will help you tremendously. Furthermore, you'll be able to see the markets for what they are. You'll know what's happening right now.

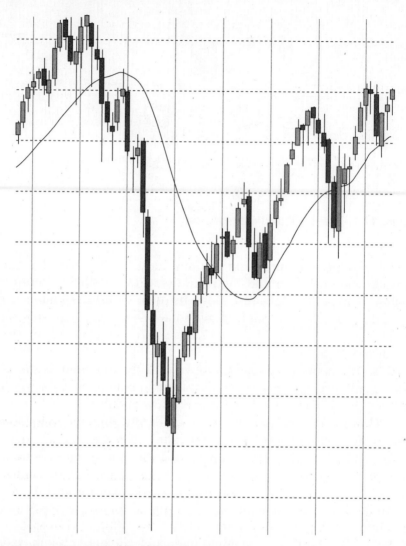

Figure 17.2 Monthly Candlestick Chart

Level IV Transformation

The final level of transformation (or is it just the beginning of a new journey of transformation?) occurs when "you"[2] seem to disappear and operate only in the now. When I started to write this book, we didn't have any permanently awakened traders, so there is no separate section for it. However, most people who shared their stories in the last section have had periods in which they've been in such a oneness state. You may have entered such a state after the meditation exercises you just completed.

You seem to disappear.

I've had many experiences in which laughter, accompanied by a feeling of joy, starts for no reason at all. Such oneness states, however, are not the same as permanent awakening, because "you" return. The internal peace goes, and the mind chatter returns. When the elation goes, you might even feel down for a while. And if you resist the down part, you might stay there for some time, because what you resist persists. But at some point, you experience another oneness state, only the joy is a little stronger, and the next down period, if it occurs, is a little less.

Right now several of our Supertrader Candidates and Graduates seem to be permanently awake and one has been confirmed by Oneness University. Perhaps a sequel to this book in a few years will include some Level IV transformations.

When a Level IV transformation happens, the following are true:

- Thoughts occur, but you do not identify with them at all.
- Seeing and listening occur, but there is no one there as the seer or the listener.

- Doing occurs, but it is automatic; there is no doer.
- The body is there, but you realize that it is not you. You are not your body.
- The mind is there, but you realize that it is not you. You are not your mind.
- Everything happens automatically.
- You understand that you have (or had) many personalities (what Libby Adams calls "little i's"), but none of them are you. In fact, you now understand that there is no person there at all.
- You are existence, consciousness, bliss.
- The whole world is your family.
- When I use the word "you" in these statements, it's misleading, because that "you" is only who you formerly thought you were. You no longer exist because you are one with everything.

If you want a perfect example of how an awakened being lives, read Byron Katie's *A Thousand Names for Joy*. If you want to experience it, keep practicing the exercises in the last section.

I am now a Oneness trainer, and we offer a Oneness Awakening course through the Van Tharp Institute. Through that course, people become Oneness Blessing givers—channels for the energy (from the divine) that accelerate transformation. Right now, I know of about 150 people who have permanently awakened through this process, although I'm sure there are many more. Oneness University claims there are now over 352,000 people in the world who have achieved it as of January 21, 2013, so they've already reached their goal for the end of the year. They also claim there are 103 million people experiencing awakened states.[3]

What's important about this level of transformation is that anyone who achieves it (although it's not so much an achievement as a realization) can trade effortlessly and make money easily if that's what they're moved to do. An example of this is given in the last chapter.

Questions on Raising Your Level of Consciousness

When I get into a topic like this, a lot of questions tend to come up, so I thought I'd address some of them in this section.

Why should I strive to raise my level of consciousness?

There is a one-to-one correlation between consciousness and happiness, according to David Hawkins. Your ability to function and get what you want increases with your level of consciousness (until you disappear). It is power versus force.

What would you recommend to measure my consciousness?

We have a free test at matrix.vantharp.com that you can take to measure your level of happiness and thus your level of consciousness.

Another way would be to look at Hawkins' chart in the Introduction to Section III (page 249) and look at the emotions associated with each level. How much time did you spend in each level over the last two months? If you average that out, you'll get some idea of your level of consciousness.

Raising my consciousness doesn't seem to have anything to do with trading. Can you give me some concrete examples of how raising consciousness has helped traders? I'm a numbers guy, so providing metrics showing "before raising consciousness" and "after raising consciousness" would tell me a story I could buy into.

Let me address this in several ways:

First, let's look at the emotions at each level of consciousness. If you're trading out of greed or fear, both ranked below 200, how do you think you will trade? Your performance would probably be dismal. Now imagine you're at acceptance (level 350), the level at which you accept whatever comes and just follow your system. How do you think you'd do? Obviously, you'd do much better at the level of acceptance.

Second, if you raise your consciousness and are generally happy all the time, how do you think you'd be as a trader? You'd probably do very well because you're already at the end state you'd expect from good trading.

Third, look at the example of the trader profiled in Chapter 16. She always trades from a high level of consciousness and only needs to trade several hours each day to make about 5R. How many traders do you know who consistently make 5R each day?

If my conscious level changes, will I be a different person?

If it moves up, you'll be happier, and your life will seem to work better.

I think I'm pretty smart. How can I jump in consciousness levels? I'd like to know the quick and easy road to enlightenment. Are there no shortcuts? Why am I not already there?

The "you" who is asking the question will never jump in consciousness. The "you" who is asking the question will never be enlightened. But your Higher Self is already there. The exercises you did earlier in this chapter are not a shortcut, but evidence of who you really are.

If God is as powerful as you say, why can't he just enlighten me or get me to instant trading success?

If you become one with your Inner Guidance, such things are possible, but a question like this is coming from someone who feels apart from God and is asking about a God "out there." Your first step is to connect with your Inner Guidance and develop a strong bond with it.

I've found with peak experiences that when the feeling has passed, there can be a dive into a very low state of consciousness because of a sense of loss. How can someone deal with this effectively?

There is nothing to deal with. Just fully experience what you're going through, and it will pass. Don't resist it. Just be aware and fully experience it. What you fully experience tends to disappear.

How do I know something is a major transformation?

First, something that has ruled your life, some of your old programming, will suddenly disappear. You'll know that because, for a while, you will feel much lighter and a lot different. After a while, though, this state will become the new norm for you.

Second, if the transformation is enough to raise your level of consciousness, your happiness should go up for seemingly no reason.

You tend to believe that when people complete five major transformations, they've completed the psychological section of the Super Trader program. Is that enough for everyone, though? If someone starts at a low level of consciousness and does five low-level transformations, is that enough to ensure continued growth?

A "low-level" transformation is not a major one. Notice the common elements among the major transformations in Section III.

When people have them, they start trusting their Inner Guidance. They find their purpose and finally clear some major issue, like fear or the need for control. Those are what I consider major transformations.

How do you know whether your transformations are lasting or just an idealistic part that is currently in charge and suppressing any conflicting parts?

It's actually quite obvious. Suddenly, one of the following occurs:

- You have an internal connection with your higher power.
- You have a mission and purpose in life.
- A major negative emotion stops coming up.
- Being right and being in control stop being issues.
- You're much happier than you were, for no apparent reason.

None of this means that more things won't come up, but those changes are pretty easy to spot.

What changes when you awaken?

The sense that you are something separate disappears. You stop judging and see the perfection in everything. You stop resisting what's happening out there. You become happy for no reason.

What's the difference between being in an awakened state and being awake?

Awakening begins when emotions disappear within 30 minutes of feeling them. When they last less than a minute, it's probably irreversible.

You can have periods when you are in bliss, peace, laughter—those are awakened states. When it's permanent, you don't return from those states. You are gone.

At some point, you are not there, and you notice that you are not your thoughts or feelings. Those ideas just flow through you.

What's the difference between being in an awakened state and being God realized? Who came up with the criteria?

I've already talked about being awakened. For God-realized criteria, read the steps to becoming God-realized in Chapter 10. I heard those criteria at Oneness University, and they seem to be echoed by awake people I've listened to recently. Most importantly, they fit my models and seem to be useful.

Do I feel different when I am in awakened states or awakened?

Several things will tend to happen: (1) you will immediately experience whatever comes up, and it will just move away; (2) your senses will be heightened; and (3) you will generally be happier.

How can one avoid the trap of identifying with the idea of being someone at a high level of consciousness and still work toward a goal of increasing one's level of consciousness? If one focuses on that idea, is it just another form of identification with form (in this case, a mental construct) and thus separation?

The key to all of this internal awareness is to notice what's going on inside you. Don't resist it, experience it fully, and it will pass. If you focus on a concept or idea, you are no longer in awareness. You tend to become your thoughts. That's fine; eventually, you'll move back to being aware.

18

Continuing the Journey

Van K. Tharp, PhD

 Before: No business handbook, no systems, not able to trade all market types, and every trade was a mistake.

 After: Has a business handbook as personal trading guide and at least three non-correlated systems to allow him to trade all market types. Can now trade mistake free.

I n the prior application chapters, we discussed two personal application areas: (1) learning Tharp Think concepts and (2) transforming yourself so that you can adopt those concepts. Now let's move on to areas three through five. I've included some checklists in this chapter that you'll hopefully find very useful.

Area Three: Develop a Personal Business Handbook for Trading/Investing

Developing a business plan to guide your trading is a lot of work, but it's one of the most important things you could possibly create. When you've done a sufficient amount of self-work, it's the next step.

We do a complete three-day workshop on developing such a plan called *Blueprint for Trading Success*. During that workshop, people go through more than 50 exercises in which they answer questions about themselves, their trading business, the markets, and their systems. They get about 15 minutes to answer each question, but some of the questions can take days or even weeks to answer adequately. I say this to convey how much work is involved in developing a business plan.

I've prepared a checklist for my Super Trader candidates and for people taking the *Blueprint* workshop that details what might be involved in developing such a plan. The checklist has 11 sections, including:

1. Your personal psychology
2. Your trading business, including all the numerous systems you might need to run a business other than trading systems
3. Worst-case contingency planning
4. Your entity structure
5. Your daily checklists
6. Big-picture planning
7. Your trading plan
8. Understanding your decision-making strategy
9. Key aspects of your first strategy and what market types it might fit
10. Key aspects of your second strategy and what market types it might fit
11. Key aspects of your third strategy and what market types it might fit

That overall checklist is given in Table 18.1. If your first thought is *Yes, but that's not enough information*, then you have a clue about some of your issues. Look at the limiting beliefs behind that statement and run them through the Belief Examination Paradigm.

You talk about a business plan and it looks very comprehensive, but I just want to trade. Why should I have all those details? Will I spend more time researching and filling out forms than trading?

Stopping one mistake could save you thousands of dollars. Avoiding one worst-case contingency could keep you playing the game. Need I say more?

Table 18.1   Checklist for Trading Business Handbook

Section 1: Personal Psychology	Check
Top 10 values	❏
Strengths and resources you bring to trading	❏
Your trading edges	❏
Your personality type and how it impacts you as a trader (take the Tharp Trader Test to find out)	❏
Major challenges for trading well (top five)	❏
Your plan to deal with each challenge when it arises	❏
Dream life	❏
Your whys, purpose, mission, feelings behind dream life	❏
Five-year goals	❏
Annual goals	❏
Monthly goals—next three months	❏
Implementation plan	❏
Financial Freedom Plan	❏
Health assessment/plan for improvement	❏
Exercise assessment/plan for improvement	❏
The aspects of your plan you are most resistant to	❏
Belief assessment for what you've put in Section 1. Anything not useful?	❏
Are you serious about continuing to work on yourself?	❏

Section 2: Your Trading Business	Check
Beliefs about your trading business	❏
Other systems	❏
• Cash flow and accounting	❏
• Data analysis	❏
◆ Collecting and using R-multiples	❏
• Other data needed including statistics	❏
• How will you collect and organize that data/statistics?	❏
• Collection of data for trading and dealing with errors in data	❏
• Research and development plan	❏
• Model for system design	❏
• Trading automation	❏
• Other business systems planned and needed?	❏
• Education plan	❏
• Plan for working on yourself and new issues that pop up?	❏
• Operations; running the business	❏

(continued)

Table 18.1   Checklist for Trading Business Handbook (*Continued*)

Section 3: Worst-Case Contingency Planning (in the eight major areas)	Check
1. Self and family	❏
2. Environment	❏
3. Broker	❏
4. Equipment	❏
5. Laws and regulatory disasters	❏
6. Market disasters	❏
7. System disasters	❏
8. Psychology issues	❏
Plans for rehearsal of what you will do in each contingency	❏

Section 4: Your Entity Structure	Check
• Why? New tax rules make it very hard to trade without an entity, so what sort of entity structure do you want for your business?	❏
• Works in your country? Why?	❏

Section 5: Your Daily Checklists	Check
• Tasks of trading	❏
• Daily procedures checklist for trading business	❏
• Anything else that's important	❏

Section 6: Big Picture Planning	Check
My beliefs about the big picture	❏
How I plan to keep track of the big picture	❏
• How will you know if you are wrong?	❏
How it will shape my trading	❏
• What kind of strategies?	❏
• Lucrative areas, markets to focus upon	❏

Section 7: Your Trading Plan	Check
Beliefs about the markets	❏
Beliefs about trading systems	❏
Beliefs about various types of systems	❏
• Trend following	❏

Table 18.1 *(Continued)*

Section 7: Your Trading Plan	Check
• Band trading	❑
• Chart pattern reading	❑
• Value trading	❑
• Sector rotation	❑
• Arbitrage	❑
• Option strategies	❑
Which of these strategies best fits you and why?	❑
What types of time frames fit you?	❑
For the above two questions, why?	❑
Financial freedom number	❑
Trading objectives	❑
• Position sizing strategy to meet objectives for each system under each market type	❑
• How will you know how to change your strategy?	❑

Section 8: Understanding Your Decision-Making Strategy	Check
• Success/failure differences	❑
• What is your decision-making strategy?	❑
• What is your convincer strategy?	❑
How will you decide when to use a system and when not to use it?	❑
How will you decide when a system is broken?	❑
When you have more entry signals than positions you can hold, how will you decide what positions to hold?	❑
What criteria does a system have to meet in order for you to be able to trade it, and are those criteria useful?	❑
How will you look at market type?	❑
What's your time frame for market type?	❑
What is your plan for eliminating mistakes?	❑
Assessment: Are you serious about trading, given what you've done with the first four sections?	❑

Section 9: Key Aspects of Your First Trading Strategy	Check
Beliefs about your trading strategy—why do you think it will work?	❑
Logically, how do you think it will perform in different market types?	❑
What edges does this system give you?	❑
Filters for entry	❑

(continued)

Table 18.1   Checklist for Trading Business Handbook (*Continued*)

Section 9: Key Aspects of Your First Trading Strategy	Check
Entry signal beliefs	❏
Initial stop beliefs	❏
Profit-taking exit beliefs	❏
Getting your R-multiple distribution	❏
Performance in the six market types, expectancy and SQN rating for each market type	❏
When will you trade the system, and when will you avoid trading it?	❏
How often does the system trade, and how often will you trade it?	❏
How much correlation is there between this system and the others?	❏
With this system, how well have you covered the six market types?	❏
What specific objectives do you have for this system?	❏
Given its R-multiple distribution, what position sizing strategy will you use for this system?	❏
Checklist for Trading System 1	❏

Section 10: Key Aspects of Your Second Trading Strategy	Check
Beliefs about your trading strategy—why do you think it will work?	❏
Logically, how do you think it will perform in different market types?	❏
What edges does this system give you?	❏
Filters for entry	❏
Entry signal beliefs	❏
Initial stop beliefs	❏
Profit-taking exit beliefs	❏
Getting your R-multiple distribution	❏
Performance in the six market types, expectancy and SQN rating for each market type	❏
When will you trade the system, and when will you avoid trading it?	❏
How much correlation is there between this system and the others?	❏
With this system, how well have you covered the six market types?	❏
What specific objectives do you have for this system?	❏
Given its R-multiple distribution, what position sizing strategy will you use for this system?	❏
Checklist for Trading System 2	❏

Table 18.1 *(Continued)*

Section 11: Key Aspects of Your Third Trading Strategy	Check
Beliefs about your trading strategy—why do you think it will work?	❑
Logically, how do you think it will perform in different market types	❑
What edges does this system give you?	❑
Filters for entry	❑
Entry signal beliefs	❑
Initial stop beliefs	❑
Profit-taking exit beliefs	❑
Getting your R-multiple distribution	❑
Performance in the six market types, expectancy and SQN rating for each market type	❑
When will you trade the system, and when will you avoid trading it?	❑
How much correlation is there between this system and the others?	❑
With this system, how well have you covered the six market types?	❑
What specific objectives do you have for this system?	❑
Given its R-multiple distribution, what position sizing strategy will you use for this system?	❑
Checklist for Trading System 3	❑

Area Four: Assessing Your Preparation for Trading

So, now you've completed the first three areas. But are you really ready to trade? Look at Table 18.2 and assess yourself. When you score above 130, you're probably ready to trade successfully. Notice how much work is involved.

To see where you are, use Table 18.3.

Table 18.2 Preparation and Commitment Checklist

Preparation + Commitment	Points
1. How well do I know who I really am?	❑
a. Are you aware of your strengths and weaknesses? Are you aware of what edges you bring to trading? Are you aware of your psychological issues and how they impact your trading? Can you list several hundred beliefs about yourself? Can you list several hundred beliefs that you have about the market? If you answer no to any or most of these questions, you probably have a lot of preparation work to do before you begin trading.	❑

(continued)

Table 18.2 Preparation and Commitment Checklist (*Continued*)

Preparation + Commitment	Points
Rate yourself from 0 to 10, with 10 being completely prepared and 0 being not prepared at all.	☐
b. When you have an obstacle in the way of a goal, do you do a dance with the obstacle and get emotional, or do you simply walk around it and head toward the goal?	☐
Able to deflect obstacles = 5 points, tendency to dance with obstacles = 0	☐

Big Picture	Points
2. Have I written down my thoughts about the big picture, and have I defined a process to monitor it? Yes = 5 points, No = 0	☐

Market Types	Points
3. Have I defined market types for myself, and do I follow a process that monitors the market type?	☐
Yes = 5 points, No = 0	☐

Systems That Fit Me	Points
4. Have I developed a trading system that fits me, my view of the big picture, and the current market type?	☐
Your system should have, at minimum, an entry, a worst-case exit that determines what a 1R loss is for you, one or more profit-taking exits, and perhaps a re-entry should you get stopped out when your idea is still working. Do you have at least one system that meets these criteria?	☐
Rate yourself on a 0 to 5 scale on how well you've done in developing at least one such system that fits you, the big picture, and one market type. Give yourself a 0 if you don't have such a system.	☐

Table 18.2 (*Continued*)

If you've been trading multiple systems already, answer questions 5–14.	Points

5. Do I understand that it's easy to develop a Holy Grail system for any one market type but impossible for one system to work well in all market types? Do I have at least one trading system for each of the following market types? ☐

Give yourself 1 point for each market type for which you have one system that only trades that market type, and 2 points for each market type for which you have 2 or more systems that only trade that market type. Maximum of 12 points for this question. ☐
   - a. Quiet up market ☐
   - b. Volatile up market ☐
   - c. Quiet sideways market ☐
   - d. Volatile sideways market ☐
   - e. Quiet down market ☐
   - f. Volatile down market ☐

6. Have I defined my objectives for each trading system? ☐
   Give yourself one point for each system for which you've defined your objectives.

7. Do I have a sufficient sample of trade results for each system? ☐
   - a. Do I know the expectancy of each system (mean R-value)? ☐
     Yes = 3 points, No = 0 ☐
   - b. Have I collected at least 100 R-multiples for each system? ☐
     100 R-multiples = 2 points; >50 = 1, <50 = 0 ☐

8. Do I have any idea of how each system will perform in the various kinds of markets to which I'm likely to be exposed over the next 10 to 20 years? ☐

Have I collected a sample of at least 30 trade R-multiples from each kind of markets in which I expect to trade this system? ☐

Give yourself two points for each market for which you've collected at least 30 R-multiples for each system. ☐
   - a. Quiet up market ☐
   - b. Volatile up market ☐
   - c. Quiet sideways market ☐
   - d. Volatile sideways market ☐
   - e. Quiet down market ☐
   - f. Volatile down market ☐

Trading Objectives

9. Have I given a lot of thought to and developed a set of strong trading objectives that fit me? These would include an earnings target and a point of ruin. Do I even have objectives? ☐
   Strong objectives = 10 points, No objectives = 0 ☐

(*continued*)

Table 18.2   Preparation and Commitment Checklist (*Continued*)

Position Sizing Strategy	Points
10. Do I have a position sizing strategy designed for each of my trading system's R-multiple distributions that helps me achieve my objectives? Yes = 20 points, No = 0	❑ ❑

Major Issues	Points
11. Have I identified major issues that could affect my trading, and am I doing everything possible to eliminate them? Each issue identified = 1 point, each issue solved = 1 point, 20 points max for this question.	❑ ❑

Issue 1:_____ Solved: Yes ____ No _____

Issue 2:_____ Solved: Yes ____ No _____

Issue 3:_____ Solved: Yes ____ No _____

Issue 4:_____ Solved: Yes ____ No _____

Issue 5:_____ Solved: Yes ____ No _____

Issue 6:_____ Solved: Yes ____ No _____

Issue 7:_____ Solved: Yes ____ No _____

Issue 8:_____ Solved: Yes ____ No _____

Issue 9:_____ Solved: Yes ____ No _____

Issue 10:_____ Solved: Yes ____ No _____

12. Do I perform the top tasks of trading regularly so that I can prevent and eliminate mistakes?

For each day of the last 20 on which you can honestly say you did all the tasks, give yourself 1 point; 20 points max

Mistakes	Points

13. Do I track mistakes, understand them, and help resolve them?
  Yes = 2 points for each question, No = 0
  a. Have I tracked my mistakes in terms of R-multiples?
  b. Do I understand the impact of mistakes on my trading?
  c. Do I understand what produces my trading mistakes?
  d. Do I spend enough time working on myself to minimize the impact of mistakes?
	❑
	❑
	❑
	❑
	❑
	❑

Table 18.2   *(Continued)*

Business Plan	Points
14. Have I prepared a business plan that incorporates all of this information to guide my trading journey?	☐
This plan is not the kind of business plan that people make when they want to raise money from other people. Instead, this is an attractive, enjoyable working document that will guide you as long as you are trading. It will probably never be complete because you'll constantly be working on it to improve your trading. Do you have such a document with each of the sections below?	☐
Yes + Complete = 2 points for each question, No = 0	
a. A list of beliefs about yourself.	☐
b. All of the information you listed in the first item about your strengths, weaknesses, psychological issues, etc.	☐ ☐
c. Your assessment of the big picture and the various events that will affect your trading.	☐
d. Your beliefs about the market.	☐
e. Three noncorrelated systems that tend to support your beliefs about the big picture.	☐
f. A worst-case contingency plan.	☐

Table 18.3   Score by Section

	Your Score	Max Possible Score
Preparation + Commitment—how well I understand myself and how I handle obstacles	☐	20
Big picture—definition and monitoring process	☐	5
Market types—definition and monitoring process	☐	5
System that fits me, big picture and market type	☐	5
At least one trading system per market type	☐	12
Objectives for each trading system	☐	6
100 R-multiples, plus the system expectancy	☐	5
System performance by market type and 30 R-multiples from each market type	☐	12
I use the system for the market type for which it was designed	☐	4
Strong trading objectives that are well thought out and that fit me	☐	10

(continued)

Table 18.3   Score by Section (*Continued*)

	Your Score	Max Possible Score
Position sizing strategy for each system	☐	20
My major issues are identified and fixed	☐	20
Regular practice of the top tasks of trading	☐	20
Mistakes	☐	8
Business plan to guide my trading journey	☐	12
Total Score	☐	164
Well-prepared to trade	☐	>130 points
Above average; continue doing your prep work	☐	115–130
Average; you still have a lot to do	☐	90–114
You are not prepared at all, so stop trading	☐	<90 points

Area Five: Understand Your Trading Mistakes

When profitable traders come to me for consulting, one of the first things I ask them to do is make sure they have written rules to guide every aspect of their trading. Everyone should have rules—even discretionary traders. After they write their rules, I review them to make sure they make sense and to determine the expectancy and SQN that those rules will produce under each market condition in which the system is to be traded. If they seem fine, I let them trade it, but only on the condition that they keep track of the R-multiple values of their mistakes, where a mistake means that they didn't follow their rules.

Similarly, when one of my Super Trader candidates begins to trade—even at a small position size—I ask her to keep track of the R-multiple values of her mistakes. Let's look at examples of what I mean.

Suppose you're risking 1 percent of a $100,000 account, or $1,000 per trade. Let's look at a series of 10 mistakes you might make.

1. You might take a trade because you hear a hot tip that wasn't part of your rules and lose $2,500. That's a 2.5R mistake.
2. Perhaps a trade is going in your favor but suddenly starts to move against you. Even though it hasn't hit your stop, you get out quickly and take a $4,000 profit. But then the trade starts to go back in your favor. In fact, you track it all the way until it reaches your initial target. Had you followed your rules, you would have made $12,000 instead of $4,000. Your mistake cost you $8,000, so it was an 8R mistake.

3. Suppose you take another trade on a hot tip and make $1,000. That's still a mistake, but you made $1,000 for +1R.

4. Suppose you execute poorly on a trade. Let's say you press buy instead of sell. You quickly realize your mistake and get out at a $70 loss. You then execute the trade correctly at a price $130 higher. That mistake basically cost you $200 in execution costs, or 0.2R.

5. Another trade comes along, and you get distracted at the end of the day. You don't check your numbers, and you don't raise your stop. Fairly early the next day, the trade goes down quickly. You get stopped out at the prior stop for a $1,500 gain. But you were supposed to have raised your stop by $300, so forgetting to do so was a $300 mistake, or a 0.3R mistake.

6. You take another trade, and it starts to go against you. It gets almost to your stop at $43, and you suddenly cancel it, thinking, "I don't want to take that loss, it's going up soon." But it doesn't go up. It goes all the way down to $27, where you get out at the end of the day. You've taken a $15 loss needlessly on 500 shares—a $7,500 loss you wouldn't have suffered if you'd followed your rules. That's a 7.5R loss.

7. Now you're upset at yourself and decide not to take the next trade. You don't have any rules that tell you to avoid a trade if you're upset. You just don't take the trade—one that would have been a 3R winner. Your mistake cost you 3R.

8. The next day, you decide that there's something wrong with your system because you've had so many losses. You miss two more trades—a 0.5R gain and a 2R loss. This time, your mistake actually causes a gain of 1.5R—but it's still a mistake. In fact, you could count it as two mistakes.

9. Now you hear about how everyone is making money in a particular stock, so you buy that stock the next morning, even though doing so isn't part of your rule set. However, you buy the stock and make 2R that day. Again, your mistake has led to a profit—this time, a 2R profit.

10. Your plan for that stock was to get out at the end of the day, but you're so happy with your 2R gain that you hang onto it over the weekend, even though doing so isn't part of your rule set. In fact, you don't even put a stop into the market—another rule violation. During the weekend, a news announcement comes up about corruption in the company. The stock gaps down for an 8R loss at the next day's open. Now you have an 8R loss, so the mistake cost you 10R.

Table 18.4   Cost of Mistakes

Mistake Number	Mistake Reason	Mistake Cost	
		Each	Cumulative
1.	Hot tip	−2.5R	Minus 2.5%
2.	Out too early	−8R	Minus 10.5R
3.	Hot tip	+1.0R	Minus 9.5R
4.	Execution error	−0.2R	Minus 9.7R
5.	Distraction	−0.3R	Minus 10.0R
6.	Don't take loss	−7.5R	Minus 17.5R
7.	Avoid winning trade	−3.0R	Minus 20.5R
8.	Miss two trades	+1.5R	Minus 19.0R
9.	Hot tip	+2.0R	Minus 17.0R
10.	Don't take planned exit	−10.0R	Minus 27.0R
	Total cost of mistakes		Minus 27R
	Average cost per mistake		2.7R/Mistake

Let's look at a summary of those 10 mistakes, shown in Table 18.4.

This table is quite typical of what I see. In this case, the mistakes each cost an average of 2.7R. I find that when I put most traders, even well-trained professionals, through this exercise, they're usually around 70 percent efficient or worse, meaning that they make three mistakes or more per 10 trades. Many of them make the same mistakes repeatedly—which is a good definition of self-sabotage.

For this reason, I generally have people go through psychological work before they start trading. When they've done that and *then* find themselves making mistakes, they usually know how to correct them quickly. If they haven't done the psychological work, mistake correction becomes very difficult. And perhaps this is enough to motivate you to do the Level II work in this book.

Most books that do interviews just give you the information contained in the interviews. I've done a lot more in this chapter because I've given you a step-by-step formula for success. It's the exact formula I put my Super Trader candidates through. Between the content of the other chapters and the steps in this chapter, you have everything you need. Now, you need to ask yourself: Are you willing to do the work necessary, or will you do a dance with the first obstacle you encounter?

Appendix:
Recommended Readings

There are certain core books that were recommended in many of the chapters. Those are listed first. Then books that were just mentioned in one or two chapters are given.

Core Readings

Anonymous. *A Course in Miracles,* 3rd ed., Helen Schucman, scribe. Mill Valley, CA: Foundation for Inner Peace, 2007.

Ardagh, Arjuna. *Awakening into Oneness.* Boulder, CO: Sounds True, 2007.

Dwoskin, Hale. *The Sedona Method: Your Key to Lasting Happiness, Success, Peace and Emotional Well-Being.* Sedona, AZ: Sedona Press, 2007.

Hawkins, David R. *Power vs. Force: The Hidden Determinants of Human Behavior.* Carlsbad, CA: Hay House, 1995.

Hill, Napoleon. *Think and Grow Rich.* New York: Fawcett Books, 1960.

Katie, Byron, and Stephen Mitchell. *A Thousand Names for Joy: Living in Harmony with the Way Things Are.* New York: Three Rivers Press, 2007.

Katie, Byron, and Stephen Mitchell. *Loving What Is: Four Questions That Can Change Your Life.* New York: Harmony Books, 2002.

Kinslow, Frank. *The Secret of Quantum Living.* Carlsbad, CA: Hay House, Inc., 2012.

Mother Meera. *Answers.* Ithaca, NY: Meeramma Publications, 1991.

Schwager, Jack D. *Market Wizards: Interviews with Top Traders.* New York: New York Institute of Finance, 1988.

Schwager, Jack D. *The New Market Wizards: Conversations with America's Top Traders.* New York: Collins Business, 1992.

Tharp, Van K. *Peak Performance Course for Traders and Investors,* 2nd ed. Cary, NC: International Institute of Trading Mastery (IITM), 2009.

Tharp, Van K. *Super Trader: Make Consistent Profits in Good and Bad Markets,* 2nd ed. New York: McGraw-Hill, 2007.

Tharp, Van K. *Trade Your Way to Financial Freedom,* 2nd ed. New York: McGraw-Hill, 2006.

Tharp, Van K. *Van Tharp's Definitive Guide to Position Sizing Strategies.* Cary, NC: International Institute of Trading Mastery, 2008.

Walsch, Neale Donald. *The Complete Conversations with God.* Charlottesville, VA: Hampton Roads Publishing, 2005.

Other Recommended Readings

Bateson, Gregory. *Steps to an Ecology of Mind.* New York: Ballantine Books, 1978.

Braden, Gregg. *The Isaiah Effect.* New York: Three Rivers Press, 2000.

Cameron, Julia. *The Artist's Way: A Spiritual Path to Higher Creativity.* London: Penguin, 1992.

Chopra, Deepak, Debbie Ford, and Marianne Williamson. *The Shadow Effect: Illuminating the Hidden Power of Your True Self.* New York: HarperCollins, 2010.

Coit, Lee. *Listening: How to Increase Awareness of Your Inner Guide.* Ventura, CA: Los Brisas Publishing, 1985.

Dilts, Robert. *Belief Systems, Health, and Longevity.* Pamphlet from a seminar given in Santa Cruz, CA: January 26–30, 1989. For more information, contact Dynamic Learning Publications.

Dyer, Wayne W. *Real Magic: Creating Miracles in Everyday Life.* New York: HarperCollins, 1992.

Franck, Frederick. *Zen of Seeing: Seeing/Drawing as Meditation.* New York: Vintage, 1973.

Frankl, Viktor E. *Man's Search for Meaning.* New York: Washington Square Press, 1959.

Gladwell, Malcolm. *The Tipping Point: How Little Things Can Make a Big Difference.* New York: Little, Brown & Co., 2000.

The Gospel of Ramakrishna, abridged ed. Translated into English by Swami Nikhilananda. New York: Ramakrishna-Vivekananda Center, 1970.

Hagstrom, Robert, Jr. *The Warren Buffett Way: Investment Strategies of the World's Greatest Investor,* 2nd ed. Hoboken, NJ: John Wiley & Sons, 2004.

Kinslow, Frank. *Eufeeling! The Art of Creating Inner Peace and Outer Prosperity.* Carlsbad, CA: Hay House, 2012.

Lipton, Bruce. *The Biology of Belief: Unleashing the Power of Consciousness, Matter and Miracles.* Carlsbad, CA: Hay House, 2008.

Losier, Michael J. *Law of Attraction.* New York: Wellness Central, 2003.

Lowenstein, Roger. *When Genius Failed: The Rise and Fall of Long-Term Capital Management.* New York: Random House, 2000.

Mooney, Stuart. *American Buddha.* Fairfield, IA: 1st World Publishing, 2007.

McMillan, Lawrence. *Options as a Strategic Investment,* 5th ed. New York: Prentice Hall, 2012.

Melchizedek, Drunvalo. *Serpent of Light: Beyond 2012—The Movement of the Earth's Kundalini and the Rise of the Female Light, 1949 to 2013.* San Francisco: Red Wheel/Weiser, 2007.

Palmer, Harry. *Living Deliberately: The Discovery and Development of Avatar.* Altamonte Springs, FL: Star's Edge International, 1994.

Price, John Randolph. *The Abundance Book.* Carlsbad, CA: Hay House, 1987.

Renard, Gary R. *The Disappearance of the Universe: Straight Talk about Illusions, Past Lives, Religion, Sex, Politics, and the Miracle of Forgiveness.* Carlsbad, CA: Hay House, 2002.

Schwager, Jack D. *Hedge Fund Market Wizards: How Winning Traders Win.* Hoboken, NJ: John Wiley & Sons, 2012.

Taylor, Jill Bolte. *My Stroke of Insight: A Brain Scientist's Personal Journey.* New York: Penguin, 2006.

Tharp, Van K., D. R. Barton, and Steve Sjuggerud. *Safe Strategies for Financial Freedom.* New York: McGraw-Hill, 2004.

Tharp, Van K., and Brian June. *Financial Freedom through Electronic Day Trading.* New York: McGraw-Hill, 2000.

Tolle, Eckhart. *A New Earth: Awakening to Your Life's Purpose.* New York: Penguin, 2005.

Tolle, Eckhart. *Practicing the Power of Now: Essential Teachings, Meditations, and Exercises from the Power of Now.* Novato, CA: New World Library, 1999.

Tolle, Eckhart. *The Power of Now: A Guide to Spiritual Enlightenment.* Novato, CA: New World Library, 1999.

Wattles, Wallace D. *The Science of Getting Rich.* Tucson: Iceni Books, 2002. Originally published in 1910.

Appendix:
Key Words Defined

1R-value   The initial risk taken in a given position, as defined by one's initial stop loss.

awakened state   Any time one's consciousness goes beyond 600 on the Hawkins scale. These would include, but are not limited to moments of bliss, rapture, peace, clarity, etc. It's a time when the ego seems to disappear. However, these are awakened states in that they are temporary.

awakening   When you permanently disappear and things seem to happen automatically. There is no seer, doer, listener, or thinker because things just happen. In addition, one is not attached to thoughts or emotions but just sees them as events that tend to flow through the mind.

awareness   Being aware of what happens inside. This includes being aware of thoughts, emotions, and the details or submodalities of those states. As you become aware, stop resisting, and just start experiencing, awakening begins.

belief   A filter through which you perceive reality.

belief examination paradigm   A set of questions to ask yourself about each belief, including (1) Who gave it to me? (2) What does it get me into? (3) What does it get me out of? (4) Is it useful? (5) Is it charged. The technique is used to evaluate the utility of your beliefs. And any nonuseful belief that is not charged can be easily replaced.

Bhakta Paradeena   Sanskrit for "the way of the devotee." It implies that your experience of God will conform to anything you'd like to be. You get to make it up, rather than accept someone else's version. And since you get to make it up, you can have the perfect relationship for you.

Big Money Game   Rules made up by larger corporations and their owners that tend to cause money to flow from you to them. For example, Big Money rules for winning the game might include having the most money (i.e., only one person can win), or having the most toys. Typically, you can afford any toy if the down payment is low enough. This idea draws you into financial slavery.

charged belief   A belief that brings up a strong negative emotion when you think about it. The charge tends to hold the belief in place even though it may not be a useful belief.

consciousness   Awareness of thoughts, beliefs, emotions, and personal programming.

expectancy   How much you can expect to make on average over many trades. Expectancy is best stated in terms of how much you can make per dollar you risk. Expectancy is the mean R of an R-multiple distribution generated by a trading system.

expectunity   A term that refers to expectancy multiplied by opportunity. For example, a trading system that has an expectancy of 0.6R and produces 100 trades per year will have an *expectunity* of 60R.

feeling release   Experiencing a feeling until it just disappears.

financial freedom   Occurs when your passive income (income that comes from your money working for you) is greater than your expenses. For example, if your monthly expenses total $4,000 and your money working for you brings in $4,300 per month, you are financially free.

game   Any interaction between two or more people in which someone wins and someone loses. The person who makes up the rules, especially those about how to win, tends to win.

God realization   Developing a bond and trust with your Inner Guidance such that you become one with that Inner Guidance.

Higher Self   Who you really are. That part of you that can live simultaneously your day-to-day world and experiences and knows the Truth. It becomes your source of guidance when you are willing to trust and listen.

Holy Grail System   A mythical trading system that perfectly follows the market and is always right, producing large gains and zero drawdowns. No such system exists, however, high SQN systems are possible for trading in one market type.

Impermanence Law (Anupassana)   Buddhist law that says that everything changes. There is birth, life, and death. There are gains and losses. Resistance to impermanence tends to be the basis for suffering.

Inner Guidance   Another word for Higher Self.

levels of consciousness   David Hawkins's term for the level of Truth in something. Human consciousness, according to Hawkins, forms a log scale from zero to 1,000. Anything below 200 is negative, and anything above 200 is positive. Each level tends to be associated with a particular mental state (i.e., fear, greed, acceptance).

level I transformation   (see Tharp Think) Adopting the ideas in Tharp Think so as to think differently about trading.

level II transformation   Transformation of beliefs, feelings, and parts so that you are much more likely to adopt Tharp Think ideas.

level III transformation   Raising your level of consciousness by sufficiently transforming yourself using Level II methods.

level IV transformation   When you become awake (i.e., your consciousness is permanently over 600 on Hawkins scale).

marble game   Trading simulation in which the R-multiple distribution of a trading system is represented by a bag of marbles with a different color representing each R value. Marbles are then randomly drawn from the bag and replaced to simulate trading.

market type   There are at least six market types: up, sideways, and down, under either quiet or volatile conditions. It is easy to develop a Holy Grail trading system for any one condition but insane to expect that same system to work well in all other market types.

Matrix   The idea that human beings are all programmed to respond automatically as in the movie, *The Matrix*. In real life, that programming is our beliefs and our experience tends to be illusory.

modeling   The process of determining how some form of peak performance (such as top trading) is accomplished and then passing on that training to others.

Mukthi Deeksha   This is a Oneness Blessing to start the process of awakening. The idea is that you need divine assistance to make changes to the brain for awakening to occur. People become Blessing Givers once they receive Mukthi Deeksha.

Neuro Linguistic Programming (NLP)   A form of psychological training developed by systems analyst Richard Bandler and linguist John Grinder. It forms the foundation for the science of modeling excellence in human behavior. However, what is usually taught in NLP seminars are the techniques that are developed from the modeling process. For example, we have modeled top trading, system development and position sizing strategies at the Van Tharp Institute. What we teach in our seminars is the process of doing those things, not the modeling process per se.

objective   What you want to accomplish in trading. Usually, this consists of some desired outcome or gain that must take place without some worst-case drawdown occurring. Part of a good objective is weighing the importance of both the drawdown and the goal being attained. There are probably as many possible outcomes as there are traders.

Oneness Blessing   A hands-on blessing from a Oneness Blessing giver in which divine energy flows through the blessing giver into the recipient. The divine energy makes changes to the brain to further the awakening process. The effect of any particular blessing depends on the intent of the recipient, the blessing giver, and the Divine.

part   One of your many internal selves. Parts were created by you with a positive intention in mind. They may represent (1) roles you play in life, (2) significant people in your life, or (3) feelings you don't want to feel.

parts negotiation   A conflict resolution technique in which two conflicting parts are brought into alignment through their positive intentions. Usually, the part that is perceived as the most negative needs to be given useful things to do to meet its positive intention.

parts party   Asking your parts to surface and talk to you about their intentions and the other parts that they may be in conflict with. A parts party exercise is given in Chapter 9.

passive income   Income that occurs because your money is working for you.

position sizing™ strategy   The most important of the six key elements of successful trading; it is the part of your system that really determines whether or not you'll meet your objectives. This element determines how large a position you will have throughout the course of a trade. In most cases, algorithms for determining position size that work are based on your current equity.

positive expectancy   The mean R-value for a distribution of R-multiples is a positive number. When this occurs, a system (or game) will make money over the long term if played at a low enough risk level to survive the worse-case drawdowns.

R-multiple   All profits and losses can be expressed as a multiple of the initial risk (R) taken. For example, a 10R multiple is a profit that is 10 times the initial risk. If your initial risk is $10, a $100 profit would be a 10R-multiple profit. When you do this, any system can be described by the **R-multiple distribution** it generates. That distribution will have a mean (expectancy) and standard deviation that characterize it.

reward-to-risk ratio   The average return on an account (on a yearly basis) divided by the maximum peak-to-trough drawdown. Any reward-to-risk ratio over 3 that is determined by this method is excellent. It also might refer to the size of the average winning trade divided by the size of the average losing trade. For individual trades the potential reward should be at least three times as big as the potential loss.

risk   The difference in price between the entry point in a position and the worst-case loss you're willing to take in that position. For example, if you buy a stock at $20 and decide to get out if it drops to $18, your risk is $2 per share. Note that this definition is much different from the typical academic definition of risk as the variability of the market in which you are investing. For individual trades the potential reward should be at least five times as big as the potential loss.

science of modeling   Using NLP techniques to determine the behaviors, beliefs, mental states, and mental strategies common to those who excel in a particular field. When you teach these models to others, they should be able to duplicate the results.

shadow self   Disowned parts of you that you project onto others. For example, you might hate bigots, which amounts to projecting your bigotry onto others. The outside world, in this way, can be a great clue to what is going on inside you.

standard deviation   The positive square root of the expected value of the square of the difference between some random variable and its mean. A measure of variability that has been expressed in a normalized form.

stop (stop loss, stop order)   An order you put with your broker that turns into a market order if the price hits the stop point. It's usually called a stop (or stop-loss order) because most traders use it to make sure they sell an open position before it gets away from them.

submodalities   The details involved in a particular modality. For example, a visual image might be associated (you see it out of your own eyes) or dissociated (you are in it); bright or dull; black-and-white or in color; still or a movie; framed or panoramic; to the right, left, or centered; etc. Usually, some submodality becomes an unconscious key trigger that runs your behavior. Judgments are unconsciously based upon submodality differences.

swing trading   Short-term trading designed to capture quick moves in the market.

system A set of rules for trading. A complete system will typically have (1) some setup conditions, (2) an entry signal, (3) a worst-case disaster stop loss to preserve capital, (4) a re-entry signal; (5) a profit-taking exit, and (6) a position sizing algorithm. However, many commercially available systems do not have all of these criteria. A trading system might also be described by the R-multiple distribution it generates.

System Quality Number Score or SQN Score A method of determining how easy it will be to meet your objectives through position sizing strategies with a particular trading system. The higher the SQN score, the easier it will be to meet your objectives through position sizing methods with that system. The method is proprietary and takes into account both the mean R and the standard deviation of R.

TEA (Thoughts, Emotions, Actions) Being aware of your thoughts, emotions, and actions is a key to gaining control within the Matrix.

Tharp Think A set of useful beliefs about trading that have accumulated through modeling successful traders. Dr. Tharp calls these principles Tharp Think because the Van Tharp Institute tends to be the only place that emphasizes all of them.

tick A tick is a minimum fluctuation in price of a tradable item.

trading Opening a position in the market, either long or short, with the expectation of either closing it out at a substantial profit or cutting losses short if the trade does not work out.

trailing stop A stop-loss order that moves with the prevailing trend of the market. This is typically used as a way of exiting profitable trades.

transformation Refers to changes in beliefs, emotions, programs, and consciousness. Three levels of transformation are described in this book.

Transformational Meditation (TfM) A conflict-resolution technique in which unhappy parts are brought to the Higher Self. They either accept the viewpoint of the Higher Self or are discarded. The technique was developed by Dr. Libby Adams at the Academy of Self-Knowledge.

Turtles A group of traders who were taught proprietary trading methods by Richard Dennis and Bill Eckhardt in the 1980s. Many of them became great traders as a result.

The Work® Byron Katie's method of becoming enlightened to one belief at a time through four questions and some turnarounds. All of her forms can be downloaded for free at www.thework.com.

Appendix:
Reference Notes

Preface

1. For a detailed study of the formation of the Federal Reserve, see G. Edward Griffin, *The Creature from Jekyll Island: A Second Look at the Federal Reserve,* 4th ed. (Westlake Village, CA: American Media, 2002).
2. Gandhi, for example, would go on a hunger strike. Normally, if an Indian prisoner went on a hunger strike, the British let him starve. But there was something about Gandhi (his consciousness) that would not enable the British to let him starve and would cause him to have a massive impact on the entire Indian population.

Chapter 1

1. See *The Definitive Guide to Position Sizing™ Strategies* (Cary, NC: Van Tharp Institute, 2009), www.vantharp.com.
2. It should be obvious to you, if you know much about trading, what sort of market type these systems were designed to function in.
3. Go to www.vantharp.com and download the free trading game. It's all done for you here.

Chapter 2

1. The turtles were a group of traders trained in futures trading by Richard Dennis. Many of them went on to have very successful trading careers.

Chapter 3

1. If you don't believe any of this, then, in your experience, you'll be right—which illustrates my point exactly.

Chapter 5

1. There are several examples in this book from different sources that suggest that most people who get paid a salary to trade have no idea what they're doing.

Chapter 7

1. R. Bandler and J. Grindler, *The Structure of Magic I* (Palo Alto, CA: Science and Behavior Books, 175), 10.
2. E. Hall, *The Dance of Life: The Other Dimension of Time* (Garden City, NY: Anchor Press, 1983), 28. An extraordinary discussion of the various cultural interpretations of time.
3. W.D. Gann, *How to Make Profits in Commodities* (Pomeroy, WA: Lambert-Gann, 1951).
4. Ken Long (see Chapter 4) likes to trade extreme moves, signified by five bars down. His reaction to the chart was, "I'd look for the start of an up move and then go long. If it keeps going down, I'd be out at a new low. If it keeps going up, I make money. And I'll probably be right about half the time."

    Well, the market went lower from there, but then it started to make a series of new monthly highs, and we had green bars. In fact, it was the start of a new bull market.
5. Harry Palmer, *ReSurfacing: Techniques for Exploring Consciousness* (Altamonte Springs, FL: Star's Edge International, 1997), 104.
6. Gregory Bateson, *Steps to an Ecology of Mind* (New York: Ballantine Books, 1978).
7. Robert Dilts, *Belief Systems, Health, and Longevity*. Pamphlet from a seminar given in Santa Cruz, CA: January 26–30, 1989. For more information, contact Dynamic Learning Publications.
8. See www.thework.com for more information.

Chapter 8

1. Similar methods include the Sedona Method (which actually included five different feeling release methods in one course); the Oneness method (which combines a spiritual component); the park bench method (which is used in this chapter); the "send it someplace method" (which we teach in the Peak Performance workshop), and even Stanislov Grof's Holistic Breathing techniques. I'm sure there are probably many more.

Chapter 10

1. *A Course in Miracles (ACIM)*, 3rd ed. T-Introduction, 1.2-3 (Temecula, CA: The Foundation for A Course in Miracles, 2007).
2. Lee Coit, *Listening: How to Increase Awareness of Your Inner Guide* (Santa Barbara, CA: Los Brisas Publishing, 1985).

3. *The Complete Conversations with God Books* 1–3. See Appendix: Recommended Readings for a complete reference.

4. Erik Hoffmann, "Brainmapping the Effects of Deeksha: A Case Study of Awakened Maneka Philipson." PDF available online at www.newbrain-newworld. com.

5. Mother Meera, *Answers* (Ithaca, NY, Meeramma Publications, 1991), 24.

6. Later, when I read the book on the four aspects of Divine Mother, I was surprised to see that Durga was not mentioned as one of them. Instead, they were Mahashakti, Mahalakshimi, Mahasarasvathi, and Mahakali. I think of Her as Mahashakti.

7. Remember that I was trained to be a research psychologist, and my training would suggest that, at this point, I had probably lost it with everything I was doing. Consequently, when I thought the retired engineer was strange, I was just projecting.

8. *The Gospel of Ramakrishna,* abridged ed., trans. Swami Nikhilananda (New York: Ramakrishna-Vivekananda Center, 1970).

9. There are a lot of people who call themselves God-fearing. By that they mean that they have a lot of respect and reverence for God. But to the human mind, fear means fear, and it really only means respect out of fear. Most of these people would deny that. But if that's you, at least think about how you might actually fear God and how that fear might limit your relationship with your personal God.

10. When I say this, I can't help but remember an episode of *South Park* in which God appears to the citizens in a form that no one would expect.

11. I could have listed this as a miracle, but you might not agree, so I didn't. However, I think the elephant blessing was part of Durga's message to me.

12. I did an exercise in which I wrote down every major memory I had over the past 65 years. Several things that I noticed from the exercise included (1) memories from one day ago are as cloudy as memories from 60 years ago; (2) negative memories are the ones that tend to stick; and (3) it's all distorted. Our memories are what we assume the past is and what we use to judge the future. But reality is only in the *now,* with no judgment. This exercise is now part of the Super Trader program.

13. *A Course in Miracles (ACIM),* 3rd ed., W-335 (Temecula, CA: The Foundation for A Course in Miracles, 2007).

Chapter 11

1. This is the author's opinion. The editor thinks that TfM is an excellent way to move toward Oneness and solve many issues, but is uncertain as to whether or not it actually removes charge. Charge removal usually requires some sort of feeling release as described in Chapter 8.

2. My work during the program has included Oneness Awakening workshops, A Course in Miracles, Byron Katie's "The Work," and many wonderful books by Eckhart Tolle, David Hawkins, Byron Katie, Gary Renard, and others.

3. David R. Hawkins, *Power vs. Force: The Hidden Determinants of Human Behavior* (Carlsbad, CA: Hay House, 1995), 285.

4. *A Course in Miracles (ACIM)*, 3rd ed., W-pI.62.1:4 (Temecula, CA: The Foundation for A Course in Miracles, 2007), 104. (Author's note: The course is not attributed to any authors and is said to have been channeled directly from Jesus Christ.)

5. *A Course in Miracles (ACIM)*, 3rd ed., W-pI.64.1:8 (Temecula, CA: The Foundation for A Course in Miracles, 2007), 110.

6. "Awake" means that the sense of "you," which actually comes from your little "i's," disappears or gets absorbed during the TfM process. Thus, at some point, all that's left is your Inner Guidance. Suddenly, your Inner Guidance is in charge, and everything happens automatically.

7. Editor's Note: This trader was making money before he joined the Super Trader program. He didn't want to do psychological work and only came for a systems workshop. Still, psychological/spiritual work was what he needed, and the Universe has a way of telling you that.

8. John Randolf Price, *The Abundance Book* (Carlsbad, CA: Hay House, 1987).

Chapter 12

1. *A Course in Miracles (ACIM)*, 3rd ed., T-7.VI.10.4-5 (Temecula, CA: The Foundation for A Course in Miracles, 2007).

Chapter 13

1. *A Course in Miracles (ACIM)*, 3rd ed., T-14.VI.1.4 (Temecula, CA: The Foundation for A Course in Miracles, 2007).

2. *A Course in Miracles (ACIM)*, 3rd ed., W-pI.47.1 (Temecula, CA: The Foundation for A Course in Miracles, 2007).

3. Napoleon Hill, *Think and Grow Rich* (republished in eBook format in 2007 by think-and-grow-rich-ebook.com. Originally published by The Ralston Society in 1937, now in the Public Domain).

4. *A Course in Miracles (ACIM)*, 3rd ed., W-pI.79.1:1 and W-pI.79.1:2 (Temecula, CA: The Foundation for A Course in Miracles, 2007).

5. David Mielach, "5 Business Tips from Albert Einstein." BusinessNewsDaily, April 18, 2012, www.businessnewsdaily.com/2381-albert-einstein-business-tips .html.

6. See Section 3 for further details about Oneness Awakening, Oneness Blessings, and Deeksha. See also www.onenessuniversity.org.

7. They didn't!

8. The Super Trader program basically consists of five parts: Tharp Think, psychological/self-work, business planning, system development, and mistakes analysis.

9. I imagine my Higher Power as a man with long hair sitting in the full lotus yoga position in front of the sun (hence, the picture of a sun in my right hand). Imagine your Higher Power any way that feels right to you. There are no hard and fast rules.

10. *A Course in Miracles (ACIM)*, 3rd ed., W-pI.49.1:2 (Temecula, CA: The Foundation for A Course in Miracles, 2007).

Chapter 14

1. I don't have an exact source for this statement. Based on my own observations, about 80 percent of IT projects fail to deliver against their initial plans of scope, cost, or time. I took a value of 50 percent because it's on the safe side.

2. There's a saying that goes, "It isn't the therapy that works; it's the therapist." I concur with that statement.

3. I was not sure who I was trying to talk to. In my belief system, the Inner Voice and God's Voice were closely linked and synchronized, so I didn't bother to differentiate. It was "that voice that would answer."

4. I still think that Elliott Waves are a very beautiful concept. I just haven't mastered them yet, and I decided that simpler approaches would be more effective in making me a profitable trader in a shorter time frame.

5. The German social security system for pensions works as a generation contract (i.e., the current working generation pays for the current retiree generation). I accept the general idea, but when I do the math, there will be about one working person for one retiree by the time I may want to retire. Bottom line: I do not expect to get anything out of the system.

6. For the non-German readers: Whenever I saw my grandmother or the friends of my grandmother, they would wear a piece of gold-coin jewelry about half the time. Once I knew the background, I understood that they were still living under the inflation impression on a daily basis more than 50 years after it happened. This had a lasting impact on my view of financial stability.

7. "*Metro, boulot, dodo*" is French and stands for the colloquial terms for "commute, work, and sleep." It is based on a poem from Pierre Béarn who critically looked at the monotonous rhythm of Parisians who just commute, work, and sleep—day in and day out.

8. I was immediately reminded of the famous deli scene in *When Harry Met Sally*, where Meg Ryan fakes the orgasm and another lady says to the waiter, "I'll have what she's having."

9. From Janis Joplin's famous "Mercedes Benz" song, (music: Janis Joplin; lyrics: Michael McClure and Bob Neuwirth). May you have blissful peace and all you want, wherever you are, Janis!

10. A lot of aids can be downloaded for free under www.thework.com.

11. As soon as I had some experience, I created a simple Excel template to make the analysis a little more efficient, and I could work through one person in about one hour.

12. The concept of protective distance gave me a new perspective on my attitude toward the proliferation of nuclear arms. If the bad person has a knife, about 10 meters will be enough. If he has a gun, a mile distance will be fine. But give him a nuclear bomb, and you have to move to another planet to create enough distance.

13. Actually, I currently have no conscious nonforgiveness toward any person. However, I am aware that this is just a point-in-time observation, and that deep down in my subconscious mind, there may be some anger left hidden in a dark corner. Consequently, I assume that 95 percent is not an

overstatement, and it still leaves some room for the ones I accidentally left behind.

14. For more information, go to www.onenessuniversity.org.

15. I also refer to it as the "pornography rule": You recognize it when you see it, even though it may be difficult to specify it from a purely technical standpoint.

16. As a mechanical engineer in a manufacturing environment, I've had the chance to see the failure patterns of machines in relation to their complexity. While highly complex machines will have a higher output, they often require meticulous maintenance, and they can deliver their edge only in a narrow band of outside parameters. In contrast, there are often simpler, less efficient machines that are virtually indestructible and easy to look after.

17. In my frame of reference, the consultant role means working for longer than four weeks for a single client at the client location. Work intensity would be between three to seven days per week (seven only in peak times). In contrast, the coach role would mean that the coach will only be at the client location for a day at a time, and the overall volume of delivered days would be much less.

18. See previous reference.

19. David Hawkins, *Power vs. Force*. See Appendix: Recommended Readings for a complete reference.

20. I reported under Transformation 5 that I used to spend about 25 percent of my time trying to overcome my negative internal chatter, but I only improved my productivity by 20 percent. This leaves a gap. I assume that my body used part of the old unproductive time for breaks. Some of this break time is still needed, but I spend it in a much better mood. (Baseline capacity = 100; net capacity = 100 × (100 percent − 25 percent) = 75; capacity after improvement: 75 × (100 percent + 20 percent) = 90. So, there is still some room for improvement!)

Chapter 15

1. Books I read that helped in my journey. For more specific references, see the Appendix: Recommended Readings section of this book.

The Disappearance of the Universe by Gary Renard

A Course in Miracles

Serpent of Light by Drunvalo Melchizedek

Awakening into Oneness by Arjuna Ardagh

The Biology of Belief: Unleashing the Power of Consciousness, Matter and Miracles by Bruce Lipton

Real Magic: Creating Miracles in Everyday Life by Wayne Dyer

The Science of Getting Rich by Wallace D. Wattles

Think and Grow Rich by Napoleon Hill

Law of Attraction by Michael Losier

Power vs. Force by David Hawkins

The Isaiah Effect by Gregg Braden

The Power of Now by Eckhart Tolle

Practicing the Power of Now by Eckhart Tolle

A New Earth by Eckhart Tolle

Man's Search for Meaning by Viktor Frankl

The Shadow Effect by Deepak Chopra, Debbie Ford, and Marianne Williamson

Loving What Is by Byron Katie and Stephen Mitchell

A Thousand Names for Joy by Byron Katie and Stephen Mitchell

Living Deliberately by Harry Palmer

2. Carol "Libby" Adams, founder of the Academy of Self-Knowledge.

3. This is a simplification of Libby's model for the sake of this discussion. She talks about the Big "I," or the conscious mind; the little "i," or the separated self; and THE SELF, or superconscious mind.

4. From *Real Magic: Creating Miracles in Everyday Life* by Wayne Dyer.

5. Eckhart Tolle mentioned this in *A New Earth: Awakening to Your Life's Purpose* as well as in the podcast series he did with Oprah Winfrey which is available free through itunes.

6. Eckhart Tolle's work also really made a difference in my life, and I regularly read his books.

7. The 12 Oneness teachings are:
   1. Mind is not mine.
   2. Thoughts are not mine.
   3. I, as a person, do not exist.
   4. This body is not my body.
   5. All things happen automatically.
   6. There is doing, but no doer.
   7. There is thinking, but no thinker.
   8. There is seeing, but no seer.
   9. There is listening, but no listener.
   10. I am love.
   11. The whole world is my family.
   12. I am existence, consciousness, and bliss.

8. This can be downloaded from www.thework.com for free.

9. I am referencing the consciousness scale proposed by David Hawkins in the book *Power vs. Force*. He goes into depth about how he tested for it, and how the scale of consciousness correlates with what type of feeling one gets. I consider the scale a useful tool for me to roughly gauge where I am at any moment.

10. C. G. Jung, *Psychology and Religion: West and East (The Collected Works of C. G. Jung,* vol. 11), Bollingen Series XX, 2nd ed., trans. R. F. C. Hull (Princeton, NJ: Princeton University Press, 1973), 75.

11. Eckhart Tolle calls anything that happens in your life, not your *life,* but your *life situation.*

12. *A Thousand Names for Joy,* Chapter 15, 43. See Appendix: Recommended Readings for the complete reference.

13. *A Course in Miracles,* T8.VIII.1.

Chapter 16

1. Tharp Think is my basic model for trading well and is the foundation for my book *Super Trader*. The Tharp Think model was presented in Section I of this book.
2. These techniques have been covered in Chapter 11 of this book.

Chapter 17

1. I'm teaching you to achieve a more effective state for trading. Frank Kinslow calls the feeling you get, a Eufeeling. For more information see his books, *The Secret of Quantum Living* and *Eufeeling! The Art of Creating Inner Peace and Outer Prosperity*. See Appendix: Recommended Readings for details.
2. That is your sense of self as a separate existence.
3. Since it's now estimated that the world population is 7.04 billion that means about 1.46 percent of the people in the world are experiencing awakened states and that 0.005 percent of the population is awake. But since one awake person can affect 100,000 people that's enough to transform the planet if they are correct in their estimate.

About the Author

For the past 30 years, Dr. Van K. Tharp has helped people overcome problems in areas of system development and trading psychology, and success-related issues such as self-sabotage. He is the founder and president of the Van Tharp Institute, dedicated to offering high-quality educational products and services for traders and investors around the globe.

While Van Tharp's expertise is in the area of finance, his mission is to touch people in a way that changes them for the better. In his books, courses, and workshops, he uses the financial metaphor to do so.

Tharp uses a combination of skills and education to fine-tune his strategies to coach, consult, and teach traders and investors. He received his PhD in psychology from the University of Oklahoma Health Science Center in 1975. He is a Master Practitioner of Neuro Linguistic Programming (NLP), a Master Time Line Therapist, a Modeler of NLP, and an Assistant Trainer of NLP. He has used his expertise in NLP to create the successful models of trading and investing upon which so much of his work is based.

Dr. Tharp is the author of numerous books, including *The Definitive Guide to Position Sizing™ Strategies, Super Trader, Trade Your Way to Financial Freedom*, the *New York Times* bestseller *Safe Strategies for Financial Freedom*, and *Financial Freedom through Electronic Day Trading*. In addition, Tharp is the only trading coach featured in Jack Schwager's best-selling book, *The Market Wizards: Interviews with Great Traders*.

Tharp has been featured in *Forbes, Barron's Market Week, Technical Analysis of Stocks and Commodities, Investor's Business Daily, Futures and Options World*, and *Trader's Journal*, just to name a few.

Dr. Tharp has collected over 5,000 successful trading profiles by studying and researching individual traders and investors, including many of the top traders and investors in the world. From these studies, he developed a model for successful trading and investing in which other people can adopt and learn. He has developed a five-volume *Peak Performance Home Study Course*, teaching the results of this 10-year study. He also developed the Investment Psychology Inventory Profile to help people better understand their strengths and challenges in relation to trading or investing.

Tharp's organization, The Van Tharp Institute, currently conducts 15 different trading-related workshops that are given in Cary, North Carolina, and periodically in various places around the world. These include both psychological and technical workshops. He also has a four- to six-year Super Trader program, and many of his students are featured in this book. Visit www.vantharp.com for more information on his institute.

A Personal Invitation
from Dr. Van K. Tharp

Get a Free Newsletter

I publish a free weekly e-mail newsletter with ideas on what I expect from the markets, trading tips, trader psychology, position sizing, a monthly update on the market conditions, plus many other ideas about how you can improve yourself as a trader. If you'd like that e-mail sent to you each week for free, simply go to www.vantharp.com and click subscribe.

Free Happiness Evaluation

If you'd like to know your level of consciousness, we have a test that you can take. It's the same test that was used by the people who wrote the chapters in Section III, and you can take it for free at matrix.vantharp.com, a subdomain specifically created for this book.

Play a Free Position Sizing Game

We believe that the best way to learn position sizing is to practice using it to meet your objectives. And to help you do so, we've developed a 10-level game. The first three levels are free, and you can download it at www.vantharp.com. Try it today!

Super Trader Lesson Five for Free

We are giving you one of the Super Trader lessons for free, and these are available only to Super Trader candidates at the Van Tharp Institute. This lesson will allow you to do a Life Review. Again, it's available for free at matrix.vantharp.com.

The Van Tharp Institute
(International Institute of Trading Mastery, Inc)
102-A Commonwealth Court
Cary, NC 27511
919-466-0043 phone
800-852-4486
919-466-0408 fax
or www.vantharp.com

Index